DICTIONARY OF
PERSONAL COMPUTING
AND THE
INTERNET

third edition

by S.M.H. Collin

PETER COLLIN PUBLISHING

Third edition published 2000

Second edition published 1998
First edition published in 1997

published by
Peter Collin Publishing Ltd
1 Cambridge Road, Teddington, Middlesex, TW11 8DT

© Copyright Simon Collin 1997, 1998, 2000

British Library Cataloguing in Publication data

A catalogue record for this book is available from the British Library

ISBN 1-901659-52-6

Text computer typeset by PCP
Printed and bound by WS Bookwell, Finland
Cover design by Gary Weston

Preface

The Internet is one of the most exciting and influential cultural developments most of us are likely to experience in our lifetime. But it is packed with complex terms, jargon and concepts.

Getting online has, since the first edition of this dictionary, become very easy - most new computers are sold pre-configured to help you get onto the Internet in just a few minutes. However, once you are online you will still find many of the concepts, and language, technical and packed with jargon. This dictionary helps explain the terms you'll come across when using your computer and the Internet.

New products and technologies appear all the time; I have updated this new edition of the dictionary to include the new developments in Windows, computing and the Internet.

In this dictionary I have tried to cover all the areas that include complex jargon and confusing terms: from the components that make up a PC, the way they work, to the software that they run. If you want to upgrade your PC, you will enter an equally complex area, with different types of memory, hard disks and network cards.

This dictionary also provides a thorough background to the complex Internet concepts and terms that are being developed - such as live video and audio transmission, new types of connection and access to the Internet via portable computers and mobile telephones.

To get the most from the Internet, you will need to look at the many different ways in which you can use it - including electronic mail, transferring files and the world wide web. Competent users can tackle the next stage and create their own web page - the technologies (such as JavaScript, ASP and XML) that you will encounter when developing a website are explained within the dictionary, and the appendix lists the main HTML commands used to format almost every web page.

This dictionary is aimed at any user who wants to understand the complex terms that are used to describe PCs and the Internet. I have included clear definitions for all the terms, and added notes and examples for many of the more important terms. If you are a student, new computer user or new to the Internet, you should find this dictionary useful.

Once you are connected to the Internet, you can use the websites listed at the back of this dictionary to help you get started. Or visit our website and see the full online version of this dictionary - we will be adding new terms to the online version as the new products and technologies are released. To view our website, connect to the Internet and type our website address into your web browser: **www.petercollin.com**.

Simon Collin

Finding Information

The entries in this dictionary are arranged in alphabetical order. Any terms that start with a number, such as '32-bit system' are listed as if the number has been spelt out - in this case under 'thirty two-bit system'.

Trademark Acknowledgements

All terms mentioned in this book that are known to be registered trademarks or trade names have been capitalised. Peter Collin Publishing is not associated with any product or vendor mentioned in this book and cannot guarantee the accuracy of this trademark or trade name information.

Aa

A: letter that is used in many operating systems, including DOS, Windows and OS/2 to denote the first disk drive on the system. Normally, a PC has two or three disk drives within its casing. The convention is to provide one floppy disk, called 'A:' and one hard disk called 'C:'. If you have a second floppy disk, this is called 'B:' and a CD-ROM drive is normally 'D:'. When talking about the different disk drives, you say 'Drive A' for the floppy drive, but normally write 'A:'. If you are using DOS, when your PC starts up it will normally show what's called the C-prompt (which looks like 'C:\' on your screen); this means you are currently looking at the hard disk. If you want to change to drive A to read data from a floppy disk, enter 'A:' and press return.
see also C:, FLOPPY DISK, HARD DISK

ACAP APPLICATION CONFIGURATION ACCESS PROTOCOL email system developed to work with the IMAP4 email protocol to provide useful secondary features such as managing an address book; originally termed IMSP (Interactive Mail Support Protocol)

accelerated graphics port
see AGP

acceleration
see MOUSE ACCELERATION

accelerator, accelerator key combination of keys that, when pressed together, carry out a function that would otherwise have to be selected from a menu using a mouse. For example, instead of selecting the File menu then the Save option, many programs let you use the accelerator keys Alt and S instead

accelerator card method of speeding up an old PC by replacing the existing processor with a special add-in card that has a newer, faster processor; although you replace the processor, you are still using the original (old and slow) memory and disks
see also UPGRADE

acceptable use policy
see AUP

access to use something, such as a shared resource on a network

access control list (ACL) security system in which a list that contains user names and passwords is used by an operating system to determine if a particular user is allowed to access or use a resource or feature of the computer or network

access counter
see COUNTER

access head part of a disk drive moves to the correct part of the disk's surface and reads information stored on the disk

access log File on your website server (created and setup by your ISP) that contains a record of every visitor to your website, when they visited and which pages they viewed - feed this into an access log analyser program and you'll get reports on your most popular pages and products. Essential to monitor response to your website and ad campaigns.

access provider
see ISP

access time time taken to find and retrieve a particular piece of data from memory or a hard disk. If you are adding more memory (RAM) to your PC, you have to make sure that your buy chips or SIMMs that are at least as fast as the existing ones. Memory chips have an access time or around 100nano-seconds. However, access time is normally used for hard disks as a way of giving some idea of the hard disk's performance. With hard disks, the average access time is often quoted and measured in milliseconds (ms), thousandths of a second; this is the time it typically takes for the drive to reach to a sector of the disk after the computer has requested that particular sector
see also SECTOR

account method of identifying a network or email user and storing the user's preferences and security settings; similar to a bank account, an electronic account has a password that only you know, together with an account name that identifies you. You account will also hold records of your rights to access parts of the network and will store any electronic mail that you receive

accounting software application for automating accounting and book-keeping

ACK ACKNOWLEDGE signal that is sent from a receiver to indicate that a transmitted message has been received and that it is ready to receive the next data transfer; for example, this signal is used between a computer's serial port and a modem to another to control the flow of information
see also FLOW CONTROL

ACL
see ACCESS CONTROL LIST

acoustic coupler   type of modem that does not plug into a standard telephone socket but uses rubber cups that fit around the mouth and ear-piece of a normal telephone handset. This converts data from the computer into sound that is then transmitted across the telephone network to another computer with a modem. Most modems plug directly into a telephone socket and provide better quality sound which means that they are more reliable when sending data. An acoustic coupler sends data more slowly than a modem plugged directly into the phone socket, but it is very useful if you are travelling and need to use public or hotel phone to send data.

ACPI   ADVANCED CONFIGURATION AND POWER INTERFACE specification that allows an operating system to control the power management in a computer and is used as part of the OnNow system
see also   ONNOW, POWER MANAGEMENT

Acrobat
see   ADOBE ACROBAT

acronym   abbreviation, formed from various letters, which makes up a word which can be pronounced. For example, the acronym RAM means Random Access Memory.

activate   to start or run a software program or module

Active Document   standard Windows application that is accessed from within a web browser and controlled by special commands in the web page

active matrix display   type of colour display used in laptop computers normally called TFT display; provides a clear, crisp display but is more expensive than a passive matrix display (often called STN)
see also   PASSSIVE MATRIX, TFT

Active Server Page (ASP)   web page created in real time by the web server; the system allows Microsoft's IIS web server product to run ActiveX scripts and components on the server to produce customised web pages that can be different for each visitor to the web site

active window   section of a screen that is currently being used. In Microsoft Windows, the active window is in front of any other windows and has its title bar (at the top of the window) coloured blue (windows which are displayed but are not active have a white title bar).

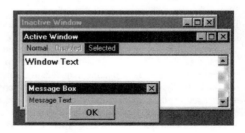

ActiveVRML
see VRML

ActiveX programming language and program definition used to create small applications designed to enhance the functionality of a web page; for example, if you want to add multimedia effects to your web page that you cannot support with basic HTML commands then you could develop an ActiveX program, called an applet, that is automatically downloaded by the user's browser and run on the user's computer
see also APPLET, JAVA, VBSCRIPT

adapter, adapter card card that plugs into an expansion bus in a PC and adds a new function to the computer, or allows it to communicate with another device. For example, a sound card is a type of adapter card that plugs into an expansion connector and allows sound to be played back or recorded.

adaptive compression data compression system that continuously monitors the data it is compressing and adjusts its own algorithm to provide the most efficient compression

ADB APPLE DESKTOP BUS communications port that was used in many older Apple Macintosh computers to link up to 16 input devices to the main computer - normally used to connect the keyboard and mouse

add-on, add-in device that connects to a computer, more properly called a peripheral. 'Add-in' is sometimes used to distinguish devices which fit inside the computer rather than plug into it. Some software packages are designed to allow 'add-on' or 'add-in' modules to be purchased that enhance the original program.

address (i) unique number that identifies a particular storage location in a computer's memory. Each location can store one byte of data (eight bits) and most PCs have 32Mb of main memory - 32 million separate addresses. Other parts of a computer system are often identified by numbers or addresses. For example, in a network, each PC typically has its own network or station address, a unique number that identifies it to other machines on the network; (ii) (on the Internet) unique series of numbers that identifies your web server or domain; for example, 152.222.33.2 might be the address of a web server, but it is normally written using characters, for example www.pcp.co.uk is the name address of the Peter Collin Publishing web server. When you want to access a page stored on a web server, you enter the name address in your web browser, this passes the name to a DNS computer that looks up this name and finds the correct numeric address and so can locate the web server; (iii) (in electronic mail) unique combination of a user's name and domain name that identifies you to other users; for example, if you want to send electronic mail to Peter Collin Publishing, you would use the unique address 'info@petercollin.com'. The part to the right

of the '@' symbol is made up of the domain, type of organisation and country, the part to the left of the '@' symbol identifies the individual user at the company or domain
see also DOMAIN, IP ADDRESS

address book list of network or Internet users and their electronic mail address, used with an electronic mail application to simplify sending mail to a user - you can select the user's name from the address book rather than enter their full email address

address bus set of electrical lines between the computer's processor and the storage devices. The bus normally has 24 or 32 separate lines to select any one of the millions of possible addresses; the addresses are selected by the processor. The number of lines in the address bus - also called its size or width - dictates how much memory can be accessed directly. An impractical example is a 2-wire (or 2-bit) address bus which can only access four memory locations, corresponding to off-off, off-on, on-off and on-on
see also BIT, DATA BUS

address mask pattern of bits used to filter out parts of an address from an address; normally used to read the network and subnet parts of an address within an Internet or IP address

address resolution converting an Internet address into the correct physical network address that will address the resource

address resolution protocol (ARP) standard that is used to find the physical network address of a device referred to by an Internet IP address

Adobe Type Manager (ATM) software standard that is used to describe the shape of fonts and how they can be re-sized to almost any size without changing the quality. This standard is used with Apple System and Microsoft Windows to display fonts that can be scaled to almost any point size, and printed on almost any printer. Adobe is a software company that developed products including Acrobat, ATM, and PostScript.

Adobe Acrobat software that converts documents and formatted pages into a file format that can be viewed on almost any computer platform or using a web browser on the Internet; for example, if you publish a newsletter, you could lay out the pages using a desktop publish system, print the pages for a paper version and convert the files to Acrobat format allowing you to distribute the same formatted pages on CD-ROM or over the Internet

ADPCM ADAPTIVE DIFFERENTIAL PULSE CODE MODULATION method of converting an analog sound or voice signal into a compressed digital signal

ADSL ASYMMETRIC DIGITAL SUBSCRIBER LINE high-speed transmission standard that uses the same copper telephone wires as a normal

telephone service, but is much faster than a standard modem or a digital system such as ISDN. As well as the speed, ADSL provides a user with an 'always on' connection to the Internet - there is no need to dial an access number and no delay. Typically, companies provide ADSL for a fixed monthly rental; data is usually transferred from the Internet to the user's computer at 2Mbps but transferred from the user's computer to the Internet at a slower rate of 256Kbps.
compare with DIAL-UP, ISDN

Advanced Research Projects Agency Network (ARPANET) original network of interconnected computers, linked by leased lines, that formed the first prototype for the current Internet; developed by the US Department of Defense (Defense Advanced Research Projects Agency)

agent software that will search the Internet for particular information; agents automate the work of using several search indexes

AGP ACCELERATED GRAPHICS PORT high-speed expansion slot developed by Intel to allow a high-performance graphics adapter card to be fitted to a PC. The port provides a dedicated route (called a bus) to transfer graphics data between the PC's main processor and its main memory; the port transfers information at up to 528Mbytes per second - so is much faster than the general-purpose PCI expansion bus (that transfers data at 132Mbytes per second). A computer fitted with AGP cuts the time taken to display complex three-dimensional images on the screen.

AI ARTIFICIAL INTELLIGENCE design and development of computer programs that attempt to imitate human intelligence and decision-making functions, providing basic reasoning and other human characteristics.

algorithm method or procedure that solves a particular problem or performs some desired task. Programmers write instructions to implement particular algorithms in their programs. The choice of algorithm affects performance, memory requirements and so forth. For example, some methods of sorting are very quick while others are slower but do not need as much memory or disk space to operate.

alias simple name for a user or group of users, interpreted by email software. Using an alias means you don't have to remember complicated mail addresses.

align to line up text so that either the left or right-hand margin is level. If text is left-aligned, all the characters line up on the left hand side, but do not on the right-hand side. If text is justified then the text lines up on both the left and right-hand edges.

Alpha processor chip developed by Digital Equipment Corp. that provides high-speed computing power; the Alpha chip is a 64-bit processor that uses RISC architecture and can run the Microsoft Windows NT operating system and applications

alt type of newsgroup on the Internet that contains discussions about alternative subjects; these are not official newsgroups and are not supported or monitored by any company, and any user can write just about anything that they want to say. Some of the larger online service providers do not allow their subscribers to view all of the alt newsgroups because they may contain offensive and pornographic material
see also NEWSGROUPS

Alt key key on a PC keyboard used to activate special functions in an application. The Alt key has become the standard method of activating a menu bar in any software running on a PC; for example, Alt-F normally displays the File menu of a program, Alt-X normally exits the program.

always on feature of high-speed broadband communications devices (such as cable modems and ADSL) that link your computer to the Internet - your computer appears to be permanently connected to the net and you do not need to dial up a special number.

America Online (AOL) largest online service provider in the world, with several million subscribers. The company provides custom software that allows a user to access the Internet and access to AOL's own databases of information that can only be accessed by its subscribers; AOL now owns CompuServe
see also COMPUSERVE, ISP, OSP

amplitude voltage level or size of a signal; for example, a loud sound has a high amplitude

analog *or* **(UK) analogue** signal whose value can vary continuously over time rather than taking a fixed values. For example, when someone speaks, the sound wave is an analogue signal; it varies smoothly as the person speaks. In contrast, a car's gear box is a digital device; a car can be in first, second, third or reverse but not in 'first-and-a-half'. PCs will only work with numbers so cannot directly deal with analog signals. To get around this, you need to fit an analogue-to-digital converters (A/D converters). For example, a sound card contains an Analog to digital converter to convert the sound signal from the microphone into numbers representing the volume.

analog monitor monitor that accepts analog video signals and so can display an almost infinite range of colours. Both VGA and S-VGA monitors are analog, whereas the older CGA and EGA monitors are digital and can only display a limited range of colours.

analog to digital conversion (ADC) electronic circuit that converts an analog signal (such as a sound signal from a microphone) into a numeric form. It does this by looking at the height of the analog signal thousands of times every second (a process called sampling) and storing the height as a stream of numbers.

AND operator (often used in searches) that matches text that contains both search words; for example, searching for 'cat AND dog' finds all entries that contain both the words 'cat' and 'dog'
compare with OR

animated GIF way of saving several small graphic images within one file so that they can be repeatedly displayed in sequence giving an impression of animation; often used to create animated buttons or other effects on a web page
see also GIF, TRANSPARENT GIF

animation software software that allows you to draw several separate frames, each slightly different, and then display them one after another in rapid succession to give the impression of movement. Each frame is called a cel and the objects that move are normally called actors.

announce a site to publicise a new or updated web site by registering the domain name with the main search engines; each search engine allows a person to add a new web site and enter a description and category; because there are now several hundred search engines, special software utilities are available to automatically register the web site with each engine

anonymous FTP method commonly used on the Internet that allows a user to connect to a remote computer using the FTP protocol and log in as a guest to download publicly accessible files; if you are using the FTP protocol to connect to a remote computer and you are asked for a login name and password, you can normally gain access to the remote computer's public areas by entering 'anonymous' as the login user name and your full email address as the password
see also FTP

ANSI AMERICAN NATIONAL STANDARDS INSTITUTE
American organisation that produces various formal standards for the computer industry. ANSI is best known to PC users for its screen control standard which is provided with DOS in the form of ANSI.SYS.

ANSI.SYS (software) device driver that is supplied with DOS and allows programs to use a series of special character sequences to change the colour and position of characters displayed on screen. ANSI.SYS also provides extra controls for the keyboard and is normally used within batch files to enhance the look of a program. If you want to experiment with ANSI.SYS, it must be loaded when the PC is started by adding a line such as
           DEVICE=\DOS\ANSI.SYS
to the CONFIG.SYS file on the disk used to start the PC. It is easy to spot if a program needs ANSI.SYS when ANSI.SYS is not loaded since the special character sequences will appear on the screen rather than being carried out,

leaving the screen display unreadable (no harm is done). These sequences show up as a left arrow, left square bracket and then a combination of letters and numbers. If ANSI.SYS is not required, it is best not to load it since it takes up memory. However, you may want to load it to customise your keyboard and screen. To do this, you need to send one or more ANSI sequences to the screen (some common ones are listed in the table). This can be done by creating a text file containing the relevant codes or using a program especially written for the purpose. It's also possible to use the PROMPT command. For example, the command

          PROMPT $e[33;42;m;$n$g

tells ANSI.SYS to display yellow text on a green display.
see also DEVICE DRIVER

answering machine   feature of a modem (that supports voice-mail) to automatically answer an incoming telephone call and record a voice message or present a caller with a choice of options to record a message
see also TELEPHONY, VOICE-MAIL

answer mode   operating mode of a modem when it is ready and waiting to receive a call from another modem; the waiting modem will answer the telephone and try and establish a connection with the originating modem
see also ORIGINATE

anti-aliasing   technique used to reduce the jagged edges that appear when circles or curves are displayed or printed out. The jagged edges are the steps in the pixels; anti-aliasing fills these gaps with a shade of the colour so that the eye blends these together to give the impression of a smooth curve.

anti-virus software   special software that detects and removes viruses from programs and documents. You should run an antivirus program on any file you download from the Internet or receive via email.
see also MACRO VIRUS, VIRUS

AOL
see AMERICA ONLINE

Apache HTTPD   the most popular web server software products, available as freeware, that allows you to setup a web server; the Apache software is very reliable and efficient, but it is not as friendly or simple to set up as other products
see also HTTP, WEB SERVER

API APPLICATION PROGRAMMING INTERFACE   set of standard and well documented functions that a programmer can use to control software or hardware.

APM ADVANCED POWER MANAGEMENT   specification that allows an operating system, such as Windows, to control the power management

features of a computer; this standard has been replaced by the ACPI standard in Windows 98 and Windows NT 5.0
see also ACPI

Apple Macintosh very popular range of personal computers developed by Apple. Originally, all Macintosh computers used the Motorola 68000 range of processors, but the latest Macintosh computers use the more powerful PowerPC processor. Although a Macintosh uses a different family and make of processor to IBM-compatible PCs, a Macintosh can run Windows software using special utilities or an add-in board. The Macintosh is operated using a mouse to control a graphical user interface in which a user points and clicks on objects. Compare this with the MS-DOS way in which a user types in commands
see also MOTOROLA

applet (i) (in Windows) term that is used to refer to small utilities within Microsoft Windows - it originally referred to the icons in the Control Panel window, but now means any utility that configures your system. An application, in contrast, is a full program that you might use everyday - like a word-processor program; (ii) (on the Internet) small applications designed to enhance the functionality of a web page; for example, if you want to add multimedia effects to your web page, you cannot carry out these functions with standard HTML commands, so you could write a small ActiveX program, called an applet, that is automatically downloaded by the user's browser and run on the user's computer
see also APPLET, JAVA, VBSCRIPT

application
see APPLICATION PROGRAM

application layer seventh and top layer within an ISO/OSI network that allows a user to request a network function (such as transfer files, send email or use a resource)
see also OSI

application program program that makes the computer do useful work, such as word processing or a spreadsheet. The five most popular application programs are word processing, accounting, database management, spreadsheet analysis and desktop publishing

application programming interface
see API

application service provider (ASP) specialist company that installs, configures and manages software on its own server and then allows any business to use the software via the Internet (or a private network); the user does not realise that the software is located on a distant server, and the business does not need to buy nor support the software, instead it normally just rents the software *see also* OUTSOURCING

application software
see APPLICATION PROGRAM

arbitrator software that is responsible for allocating resources to devices, often used to manage the way Plug and Play adapters use other resources in a computer

Archie system of servers on the Internet that catalogue the public files available on the Internet; you can use Archie to find a particular file and then download it using FTP; there are several ways of using Archie to find a file: you can send an electronic mail message to an Archie server, you can telnet to an Archie server and type in your request, or you can use special Archie software on your computer to carry out the request for you. There are many servers on the Internet that store the Archie index of files, in the UK you can try 'archie.doc.ic.ac.uk'. For example, to find files that contain spelling checkers, send an email to 'archie@archie.doc.ic.ac.uk' with a message that reads 'prog spell' and you will get a reply within a few minutes with a list of FTP sites that contain matching files. Alternatively, use a telnet program to connect to the 'archie.doc.ic.ac.uk' site and enter the 'prog spell' command manually
see also FTP

architecture general design of a processor, piece of software or computer system. Often used to refer to a type of compatible hardware - for example, Intel architecture means that the computer uses an Intel processor

archive (i) to move a file from your computer's hard disk onto another storage device stored away from the main computer. When you create a backup, you keep and use the original file on your PC; when you create an archive, you move files you want to keep, but don't use very often from your PC onto a disk or tape; (ii) collection of information or files that are available on a server and can be accessed by any user via the Internet
see also BACKUP, RESTORE

archive attribute one of the attributes stored with any file on a PC. The archive attribute is set to '1' whenever the file is changed and so acts as a reminder to the user or (more usually) to tell backup software that a file has changed since the last backup and so needs to be backed-up again. After copying each file, the back-up program then sets the archive attribute to zero so that the file won't be backed-up again unless it is subsequently changed.
see also ATTRIBUTE, PROPERTIES

archive site one computer on the Internet that provides a vast collection of public-domain files and programs (copied from other computers around the Internet) that a user can download; an archive site is a single, convenient site for any user

argument file name or options that are typed on the same line but after a command line command; for example, with the line 'DIR LETTER.DOC', the command is DIR and the argument is 'LETTER.DOC'.

arithmetic logic unit (ALU) part of a microprocessor that performs the simple commands such as addition, subtraction and multiplying that are the basic steps that form the basis of all instructions carried out by the processor

ARP ADDRESS RESOLUTION PROTOCOL standard that is used to find the physical network address of a device referred to by an Internet IP address

ARPANET ADVANCED RESEARCH PROJECTS AGENCY NETWORK
original network of interconnected computers, linked by leased lines, that formed the first prototype for the current Internet; developed by the US Department of Defense (Defense Advanced Research Projects Agency)

array list or table of data items. Each 'element' within the array is identified by a number that is its position in the array. For example, a program might use an array to hold different tax rates. Element 1 might hold the percentage for the first tax band, element 2 for the second tax band, and so on. Arrays are a central feature of programming and most programming systems, including those in database and spreadsheet packages, provide them.

arrow keys set of four keys on a keyboard that move the cursor or pointer around the screen; the four keys control movement up, down, left and right.

arrow pointer small arrow on-screen that you can move using the mouse. The pointer can change shape to show what's happening in your PC: it shows an egg-timer (if the computer is busy) or an I-beam (when you are typing in text).
see also POINTER

article one message in a newsgroup; if you want to say something that any other user can read, you would 'post' an article to the newsgroup
see also NEWSGROUP, POST

artificial intelligence (AI) computers that try and emulate human intelligence; for example, there are now computer programs that ask patients questions to try and establish a possible illness before the patient sees the doctor

ASCII AMERICAN STANDARD CODE FOR INFORMATION INTERCHANGE
numerical code used to represent characters. For example, A is assigned the value 65, B is 66. ASCII is used by almost all computers, software and communications systems, allowing different computers to exchange data.

ASCII is, unfortunately, not completely standard on all platforms. The first 128 characters are well defined and normally adhered to; these cover letters, numbers and simple controls such as delete and new line. However, the range of characters between 128 and the limit of ASCII, 255, are far from standard. The 128 character codes above 128 are called the extended character set and can hold graphics, foreign characters and symbols.

ASIC APPLICATION SPECIFIC INTEGRATED CIRCUIT
chip that has been specially designed and programmed for a particular function

ASP I) ACTIVE SERVER PAGE; II) APPLICATION SERVICE PROVIDER

aspect ratio ratio of the width to the height of a pixel shape or screen; for most PC displays, this ratio is 4:3 (for example, a screen resolution of 640x480)

assembly language, assembler programming language that uses mnemonics (instructions similar to English-like words) to represent machine code instructions that directly control the processor. An assembly language program is translated into its final numerical form by a program called an assembler. Assembly language programs are difficult to write and modify. Each instruction does one simple thing (such as move an item of data from memory into the processor) so many thousands of instructions are required to create a program that performs a useful job. In contrast, a language like C, Pascal or Basic is 'high-level'; particular instructions do more complete tasks, such as printing information or writing it to a file. To use such a language, each high-level instruction is translated by a compiler to a whole sequence of machine code instructions. However, assembly language is the most efficient way to program because it allows the programmer to specify exactly what needs to be done and how, resulting in the smallest and fastest programs. Few applications today are written in assembly language but it is still widely used for system-level software such as device drivers

assigned numbers document that contains a list of unique numbers that are each assigned to an Internet or network manufacturer's device, protocol or other resource; manufacturers apply for a unique ID number from the IANA organisation

asterisk (*) symbol used to indicate a wildcard in a selection process; if you want to search for all words beginning with 'comp' you could enter 'comp*' and the search will find 'computer', 'computing', 'compatible'; an asterisk translates to mean any number of any characters, unlike a question mark (?) which means any single character
see also WILDCARD

asymmetrical compression compression system that requires a lot of processing time and power to compress an image (or video sequence) but is very quick to decompress; this type of compression is normally used when creating video sequences for distribution

asynchronous communication between two devices or operation that does not require a clock signal to time the signals; each computer processes the information as it arrives; some communication links between two devices send data signals in time with the computer's clock signal (this is called synchronous), asynchronous communications happens when the devices and data is ready and is not regulated by a clock signal
compare with SYNCHRONOUS

asynchronous cache type of cache memory that provides the slowest performance and uses a type of SDRAM that is cheap but slow
see also CACHE, SDRAM

asynchronous transfer mode
see ATM

asynchronous transmission common method of transmission between computer and modem, in which each character transmitted is a self-contained unit with its own start and stop bits that indicate the start and finish of the data; the alternative is synchronous transmission in which both the sending and receiving computers use the same clock signal

AT PC standard originally developed by IBM that uses a 16-bit 80286 processor. The AT originally meant IBM's Advanced Technology personal computer, but is now used to describe any IBM PC compatible that uses a 16-bit or 32-bit processor (which includes the 80286, 80386 and 80486).

AT command set set of commands that are used to control a modem, developed by Hayes Corporation. For example, ATD123 means dial the number 123.
see also MODEM, HAYES MODEM

AT-bus expansion bus standard that was developed by IBM to allow adapter cards to be plugged into the computer. The AT-bus uses a long edge connector inside the computer to carry 16-bits of data and address information between the computer and the adapter card.

AT-keyboard standard keyboard layout for an IBM AT personal computer; the keyboard has 102 keys with a row of 12 function keys along the top, compare this with the older XT-keyboard which has only 10 function keys arranged to the left of the keyboard.

ATA AT ATTACHMENT hard disk drive technology in which the controller is part of the disk drive rather than being part of the main computer or located on the motherboard
see also IDE, SCSI

ATAPI ADVANCED TECHNOLOGY ATTACHMENT PACKET INTERFACE
type of standard drive interface that is based on the ATA drive controller and is used to connect a CD-ROM to a computer

ATM ASYNCHRONOUS TRANSFER MODE high speed data transmission system, often used to link two servers or to link an office to the Internet
see also ISDN, LEASED LINE

attachment file that is transferred together with an electronic mail message; the file can be any type of file such as a document, image, or spreadsheet. Microsoft Outlook and all popular Internet electronic mail software allow you to attach one or more files to an electronic message to provide a very convenient method of distributing information
see also ELECTRONIC MAIL, MIME

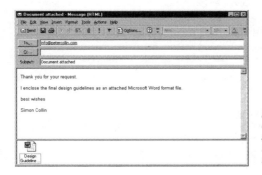

Sending a file as an email attachment, shown as an icon at the bottom of the message.

attention code the two characters 'AT' that are used to preface a command to a Hayes-compatible modem; for example, 'ATD123' tells the modem to dial the number '123'
see HAYES-COMPATIBLE

attribute (i) DOS stores a set of six attributes for every file. These settings can either be on or off and are recorded in the directory entry for the file that reflect some aspect of its status. For example, each file has a 'Read-only' attribute. If this is 'on' (also called 'set'), DOS will not allow the file to be altered, updated or deleted. If it is off (also called 'reset' or 'clear') then the file may be updated. The attributes read-only, archive, hidden and system may be altered by users using software such as the DOS ATTRIB command. The other two attributes, Volume and Directory, are used internally by DOS to identify volume label and sub-directory entries, as opposed to files, within a directory; (ii) Programming term for the colour intensity or style in which a character is displayed or printed.

audio sound; for a computer to produce sound, it needs a sound card that fits inside the computer together with speakers. The sound card converts digital information from the computer into analog sound signals that are then amplified and played through speakers
see also ANALOG

audio file file that contains digital sample data from a sound. In Windows, audio files normally have a WAV extension and are played back or recorded using the Sound Recorder utility in the Accessories group.

audio/video interleaved (AVI) standard, devised by Microsoft, that describes how video frames and simultaneous sound should be stored in a single file. In a PC, these files have an AVI extension and can be played back using the MediaPlayer utility in the Accessories group.

AUI ATTACHMENT UNIT INTERFACE connector used to connect a network cable to some types of Ethernet network card

AUP ACCEPTABLE USE POLICY set of rules that describe what a user can write or do on the Internet without offending other users; many ISPs publish their own set of AUP rules for their customers

authentication process that checks that a person or web site or email or digital signature is authentic and has been created by the authorised user; for example, public-key encryption provides a high level of authentication because only the person who created the key can encrypt the message, so you can be sure that it has been produced by this person; authentication is also used in secure web site (for example, in a web site that allows you to shop online or pay for goods by credit card) to prove to you that the web site is being run by the company that is advertised (and not by a fake company) - authentication of this type relies on a known company (called an authenticator) checking a digital signature produced by the web site against their records and then confirming to the user that this web site was created by the authentic publisher (this process all happens automatically when you visit a secure, authenticated web site and you only see a pop-up dialog box confirming that this is an authenticated site)
see also RSA, SECURE PAYMENTS, SSL

authenticator trust-worthy company that provides authentication for digital signatures on the Internet; this process is used by secure web sites (shopping or payment sites) to prove to a visitor that the web site has been created by the authorised publisher
see also AUTHENTICATION, RSA, SECURE PAYMENTS, SSL

authoring software (i) special application that allows you to create multimedia programs. Authoring software lets you design the pages of the multimedia book, and place video clips, images, text and sound on a page.

Almost all multimedia developers use some type of authoring software rather than a traditional programming language because it's a much faster and easier way to create multimedia programs; (ii) design software that allows you to create a web page - this is normally called web page design software

authoring   creating a multimedia title or designing a web page using HTML codes to format images and text

AUTOEXEC.BAT   one of two special text files that the user can create to control the startup process of a PC. AUTOEXEC.BAT is a batch file placed in the root directory of the disk used to start the PC (usually the hard disk if one is fitted or a floppy in drive A:). If this file is present, it is automatically executed once DOS is loaded (hence the name). The other startup file is CONFIG.SYS which contains special instructions rather than ordinary DOS commands that set up DOS initially. If your PC is already set up, you probably already have an AUTOEXEC.BAT file on your startup disk(s). You can check this with a command such as DIR C:\AUTOEXEC.BAT (hard disk) or DIR A:\AUTOEXEC.BAT (floppy system)
see also   CONFIG.SYS

automatic mailing list
see   LISTSERV

auto-reliable mode   modem mode in which the modem will try and establish a reliable connection with another modem using error correction

autosync   feature of a modem that allows it to transfer synchronous data signals to and from a computer that can only transfer asynchronous signals; if you want to connect your personal computer to a synchronous data source (such as a mainframe computer) you would need to install a special adapter card or use a modem that can convert the asynchronous data from your computer's serial port to synchronous data

avatar   (i) the graphical image that is used to represent a real person in a cyberspace or three-dimensional system, for example the image of a person in a three-dimensional adventure game; (ii) the name for the superuser account on a UNIX system
also known as   ROOT

AVI   AUDIO VIDEO INTERLEAVED
Windows file format used to store video clips and audio sections

Bb

BABT approval   official approval required before a new modem can be
sold and be connected to the UK telephone network; the approval does not
provide any quality assurance about the modem, but ensures that it is
manufactured in such a way that it does not damage the telephone network.
A green label is visible on modem equipment that has received BABT
approval

back door   unauthorised route into a computer system that by-passes the
main security or password protection scheme

back end   specialised processor (or server) that is designed to carry out
one task very efficiently - it is used to provide support to the main server on
a network
see also   FRONT END, SERVER

backbone   very fast communications link that connects major ISPs
together across the world. Large companies may also have a high-speed
backbone linking many network servers together.
see also   T1

background   (i) picture that is displayed behind the main windows and
icons on your desktop. In Windows you can define the colour and pattern of
the background (which is also called wallpaper), or you can display an
image; (ii) program that is running whilst you are working with another
application on the same computer or something that is happening (such as
printing a long document) whilst you are working with another application

background printing   method of sending information from your PC to
the printer whilst you are running some other application. For example,
Windows uses a utility called Print Manager to temporarily store any
document that you print; it then prints out the documents whilst you can
carry on working on another document. Without background printing (that's
also sometimes called spooling or print queuing), you would not be able to
use your word processor until it had finished printing out all the pages of
your document

backlit display   (in a laptop computer) very thin light-producing panel
that is behind the display and shines through, improving the contrast and
visibility of the characters and images on the display. Newer colour displays
use a different method of producing a very bright, clear image. A monitor
on your desk works like a television and uses an electron beam to illuminate

tiny dots of phosphor that coat the inside of the glass screen.

backup   second, safe copy of a file, letter or data. You should always do regular backups of your important work: it might seem very boring at the time, but it's far more boring to type all the information back in again! You normally backup your data onto a little cassette tape or, if you don't have too much, onto floppy disks. Windows includes a utility that will make backing up painless: just tell it which folder, directory or file you want to copy and whether you want to make a backup onto a floppy disk or tape and it does all the copying. Once you have made a backup, keep it well away from your main computer: if there's a fire then your PC and the backup will be destroyed. Ensure that you make a new backup of the latest versions of your data at least once a week. If you ever need to access the files you've backed up, you need to use another utility that will restore them; this copies them from the floppy disk or tape back to the correct folder or directory. *compare with*   RESTORE

backup agent   Windows 95 includes software utilities that will carry out an automatic backup of a set of files or folders for you at a regular time and date each week. Click on Start/Programs/Applications and you'll see the backup agent.

backwards compatible   new computer that will work with all the old adapter cards designed for earlier versions of the computer or a new piece of software that provides the same functions as the previous version and can read the files created in the previous version. For example, Windows 98 is backwards compatible with Windows 3.x since it can run the same programs. Microsoft Word 2000 is backwards compatible with Word 2, and provides the original functions (plus new ones) and can read documents written with Word 2.

bad sector   fault with a floppy disk or hard disk. Disks are divided up into tracks which contain many sectors; each sector can hold hundreds of bytes (often 256 or 512 bytes of data). If you have a bad sector, it means that the disk surface has been damaged at this point and that the disk drive cannot read the data that was stored there. Windows includes the Scandisk utility that will try and repair the problem
see also   SECTOR

balance   (in a stereo sound system) relative volume of the left and right speakers

bandwidth   measure of the amount of data that can be transferred over a link or circuit; for example, the bandwidth of an Ethernet network is normally 10Mbps, but this is normally only reached if a lot of users are transferring data over the network at the same time

bank   row or group of components that make up a single device; for example, if you increase the memory in your computer you might fit more memory chips to the existing bank (or collection) of memory chips

bank switching   (old) method of dividing a computer's main memory into section (called banks) that could be conveniently managed by the operating system software to get around the limitations of the early software
see also   VIRTUAL MEMORY

banner advertisement   image that carries an advertising slogan, logo or message and is displayed on a web page; a long, narrow strip is now the unofficial standard format for advertisements that appear on almost every commercial website on the net. Some banner ads are images, others include animation to attract the viewer's attention. If you click on a banner ad, you will usually jump to the advertiser's own site. If you would rather not see banner advertisements when you surf, you can install special software that blocks them. Websites normally charge advertisers according either to the number of times the banner ad is displayed (called the number of impressions) or the number of times that a user clicks on the ad (called the click-through rate).
see also   CLICK THROUGH, IMPRESSION

banner page   page that is printed out first with the time, date, name of the document and the name of the person who has printed it

bar chart   graph on which values are displayed as vertical or horizontal bars.

bar
see   TOOLBAR

base font   font and point size used by a wordprocessing package or DTP package if no style has been selected. This is normally a Times serif font that is displayed in 10point.

base hardware   minimum specifications for a PC that can run a particular software package. These are normally printed on the side of the software package. For example, if you want to run Windows 95/98 you will need a PC with at least 16Mb of RAM fitted, 100Mb of free hard disk space and a Pentium processor or better. Graphics programs often demand more sophisticated base hardware with more memory or a faster processor.

base memory *or* **conventional memory**   (in an IBM-compatible PC) the term that describes the first 640Kb of memory installed. Due to the historical design of early PC hardware and software, original versions of PC operating systems used the first 640Kb of memory in a different way to the rest of the memory that's installed. If your PC has 16Mb of RAM fitted, the first 640Kb is called the base or conventional memory, the next 384Kb is called the upper memory and the remaining 15Mb is called extended memory.
see also   EXTENDED MEMORY, UPPER MEMORY

baseband transmission medium that carries digital signals that are transmitted without modulation
compare with ADPCM, FM

BASIC BEGINNER'S ALL-PURPOSE SYMBOLIC INSTRUCTION CODE
programming language that uses instructions that sound like English words. MS-DOS comes with a copy of BASIC, called QBASIC, that lets you experiment with programming. Each line of the program is numbered and the lines contain program instructions that can calculate, open files, draw images, or print. Microsoft has a sophisticated version of Basic, called Visual Basic, that allows users to easily create Windows programs with little knowledge of programming

basic encoding rules (BER) standard method of encoding data that is stored in the ASN language; often used in libraries and other Internet data sites

bass low range of audible frequencies that make up a sound

BAT three letter file name extension that's given to batch program files that contain batch commands stored as text

batch file text file stored on disk that contains MS-DOS commands that you can type at the MS-DOS command prompt, together with some other special control commands. It's a convenient way of grouping together a series of commands that you need to run frequently. To run all the commands stored in the batch file, just type in the name of the batch file (without it's BAT extension) and each line will be run consecutively. When you first switch on your PC a batch file called AUTOEXEC.BAT is run automatically. This contains all the setup and configuration commands that define the environment and setup any special devices - like a CD-ROM drive or network. To see if you have any batch files on your hard disk, use the 'DIR *.BAT' command from the MS-DOS prompt or the File Manager/Explorer in Windows and look for the BAT file extension. To see what's inside a batch file, use the TYPE command in MS-DOS or open the batch file using a word processor or Notebook or WordPad.

battery meter (in a laptop computer) utility that tells you how much life or working time you have left in your batteries. In Windows 95, a tiny icon appears in the bottom right-hand corner of the screen and this shows you when you are about to run out of battery power and need to recharge.

baud *or* **baud rate** measure of the number of signal changes that occur in a signal every second. Modems and many other communications devices are sometimes described in terms of a baud rate. It's important to note that baud is not the same as the amount of data sent every second - see bits per second; with clever compression techniques, it's possible to send more data than there are signal changes.

bay space within a computer's case into which you can fit and secure a floppy disk drive or CD-ROM drive or hard disk drive. If you look at the front of your PC, you'll notice a floppy disk drive and, if you have one, a CD-ROM drive. If there's a blank plate below one of these drives then behind this is an empty bay into which you could fit another drive. To fit the drive into the bay you must open the case and connect the drive to the correct controller card.

BBS BULLETIN BOARD SYSTEM computer that supports remote users who connect via a modem link and can read and send messages and download files; bulletin board systems were very popular with hobby groups but were not interconnected. The Internet replaced most bulletin board systems as the standard way of exchanging information between groups of people

bcc
see BLIND CARBON COPY

benchmark program that measures the speed of the different components in your PC to get an overall impression of how fast and powerful your computer configuration is compared with another computer.

BER BASIC ENCODING RULES standard method of encoding data that is stored in the ASN language; often used in libraries and other Internet data sites

Berkley Software Distribution (BSD) popular version of the Unix operating system adapted and distributed by the University of California, Berkley that is very popular with Internet site managers and is used to run many Internet servers; normally written 'BSD4.1' referring to version 4.1 of the BSD Unix system

beta software early version of a software product that is still being tested and is not yet working properly, or still has a few bugs. Avoid using beta software for regular use, since it's not completely reliable. When all the bugs have been found and fixed, the software is then released.

Bézier curve geometric curve in which the overall shape is defined by two endpoints, called control handles. Bézier curves are a feature of many high-end design software packages since they allow the designer to draw complex, but smooth curves.

BGP BORDER GATEWAY PROTOCOL a protocol allows routers to share routing information to allow each router to calculate the most efficient path for information; this protocol is most often used between routers installed at Internet Service Providers (ISPs)

binary common name for base 2 arithmetic. In binary, the smallest unit is a bit (short for a binary digit) and this can have one of just two values: zero or one. Computers do all their calculations using binary arithmetic, since the two values are easy to represent electrically: zero volts for zero and (normally) five volts for a one. By comparison, in base ten (decimal) each digit can have one of ten (zero to nine) values.

binary file file that contains non-text information, such as a graphic image or a program file; if you want to send a binary file via electronic mail to another user, you need to send it as a MIME attachment, or encode it using uuencode
see MIME, UUENCODE

bind to connect or link one program file with another; normally used to link a configuration file to a driver (for example, to link a protocol with a network adapter driver)

BIND BERKELEY INTERNET NAME DOMAIN specialist software application that provides the functions of a Domain Name Server (DNS) for server computers running BSD UNIX

BinHex a method encoding binary data into ASCII characters; software programs and data files are stored as binary data (using all eight bits of information within one byte of storage space), wheras ASCII characters can be stored in just the first seven of the eight bits of storage space within one byte. Originally, email and many communication systems only supported the transfer of text (ASCII characters), so if you wanted to attach a data file to you email message, the data had to be encoded before it could be transferred; now, almost all email software and links between computers support full eight bit transfer so data does not have to be encoded
see also UUENCODE

BIOS BASIC INPUT/OUTPUT SYSTEM series of instructions that manage the basic functions within your computer. For example, the BIOS looks after how the keyboard works and makes sure that the right character code is sent when you press a key. It also manages the disk drives and the monitor. A software application, like a word processing program, carries out tasks by asking the BIOS to do the real work. It asks the BIOS if the user has typed any text; if they have, it asks the BIOS to display the character. You don't have to worry about the BIOS, and you are very unlikely to ever see it, since it's stored on a chip inside your computer. However, it's responsible for the real work and you'll see a message displaying the version number, date and company that developed the BIOS software routines appear when you switch on your PC.

bit BINARY DIGIT smallest unit in the binary or base two arithmetic system. A bit can have one of just two values: zero or one. Data is stored in a computer as a combination of bits; information is normally stored in groups of eight bits that are called a byte
see also BINARY

bit block transfer *or* **bitBLT** process of moving the contents of a section of memory from one location to another; usually used to update a screen image or during animation

bitFTP type of server that allows a user to retrieve a file using only an email link; the user sends an email to the bitFTP server, the email contains a series of FTP commands that ask it to fetch the file from a remote server, when it has done this, the bitFTP server sends an email back to the user as an email attachment or encoded mail message. If you want to retrieve a file, send a message that contains just 'help' to 'ftpmail@doc.ic.ac.uk' to find out how the system works

bitmap image that is made up of thousands of tiny dots (or pixels); the colour of each dot is controlled by the value stored in the bitmap file for that position. If you zoom in on a bitmap image you will see the dots grow larger and larger. Compare this with a vector image, in which the shapes are described mathematically and so they appear sharp however much you zoom in on the image. If you look at your Windows or Macintosh display, every icon is stored as a small bitmap image. You can create your own bitmap images by using the Paint utility in the Accessories folder. When you paint an image, you are colouring in the dots - to see what each dot looks like in close up, use the zoom function. Bitmap images are stored in files using the BMP, GIF, and TIFF formats.

bitmapped font type of font in which the shape of each character is defined by a pattern of dots in a matrix. Bitmapped fonts are quick and easy for a computer or printer to use, but they are of a fixed size: if you try and increase the size, you will see all the dots enlarged and the characters will appear very jagged. To solve this, outline fonts were developed: TrueType fonts or ATM fonts or PostScript fonts are used by Windows; these describe each character shape as a series of curves and mathematical equations. It means that you can change the size of the character and it will always have a smooth outline.
compare with OUTLINE FONT

BitNet network used to connect (mostly) academic sites and computers and allows transfer of electronic mail and listserver application; BitNet is similar to the Internet and is connected to allow the transfer of electronic mail to and from academic users to other users on the Internet

bits per second (bps)   way of describing the speed of a modem or serial link between two computers or a computer and a printer. It means how many single bits of data can be sent by the computer every second. If you are checking the specification of a modem, make sure that it is describing bits per second and not baud rate. For example, a fast modem that can support 36,600bits per second will probably use a slower baud rate because it includes some clever electronics. By compressing the data before it is sent, modems can easily send 50,000 bits every second. If you link two computers together with a serial cable you can transfer files between the two: it's great if you use a laptop and a desktop. Windows 95/98 includes the Direct-Cable Connection utility that lets you connect two computers via a serial or parallel port and transfer files between the two computers at high speeds: the maximum transfer speed over a serial port is normally 115,200bps
see also   BAUD, PARALLEL PORT, SERIAL PORT, USB

BIX   commercial online system founded by Byte magazine; contains a lot of technical and programming topics

biz   type of newsgroup that contains business discussions and opportunities; for example, 'biz.opportunities' contains messages from users that are offering ways of making money. Only the biz series of newsgroups are supposed to discuss commercial aspects, the rest of the newsgroups are for technical or academic discussion
compare with   ALT

blind carbon copy (bcc)   feature of many electronic mail programs that allows a user to send one message to several users at a time (carbon copy) but does not display this list to the recipients

blink   way a cursor flashes on and off to show you where you are positioned on the screen or in a document.

BLOB   BINARY LARGE OBJECT   field in a database that can contain a large quantity of unstructured binary data - normally an image or sound file

block   section of text that you have marked before moving, deleting or editing it. If you use a Windows wordprocessing program, you can mark a block of text by moving to cursor to the start and clicking and holding down the left-hand mouse button then, with the button held down, move to the end of the section of text. You'll see the block highlighted in reverse. Once you have selected the block, let go of the mouse button; you can now delete the block or change its fonts or size, or move it using cut and paste from the Edit menu.

Bluetooth   a short-range radio communications system that is designed to provide a simple way for computer, Internet and input devices to communicate; for example, a palm-top computer could transfer information to a mobile phone using a Bluetooth link. The technology was developed by a group of computer and telecoms companies that included Ericsson, IBM, Intel, Nokia and Toshiba

BMP three letter file name extension that's given to files that store bitmap image data. If you use the Paint utility in Windows, you can save or open BMP files created in other paint programs; you can also insert BMP files into some wordprocessing packages to enhance your letters or reports.
see also GIF, JPEG, TIFF

body *or* **body text** (i) main text of a document or book. If you use a Windows wordprocessing package that lets you define styles, there is probably a default style for the body text that is used if no other is specified; (ii) main part of an electronic mail message
compare with HEADER, ATTACHMENT

bomb (software or computer system) to fail or not work correctly

book multimedia title. The name comes from the fact that most multimedia titles are arranged as a series of different pages which together form a book.

bookmark code used by a multimedia title or wordprocessor or web browser that allows the user to move straight back to this point at a later date. The software keeps a list of all the bookmarks you have inserted together with the relevant page number

Boolean mathematical functions that refer to binary logical operations that are define the way in which a computer works. If you search for text in a multimedia encyclopaedia or on the Internet, you will probably use the Boolean operators: AND, OR, XOR, NOT. For example, searching for 'cat AND dog' will find any entry that contains the word 'cat' and the word 'dog'. In binary (base two) arithmetic, Boolean operators work in a similar way: 1 AND 1 is equal to 1; 1 AND 0 is equal to 0; 1 OR 1 is equal to 1; 1 OR 0 is equal to 1.

Boolean search search that uses the AND and OR functions

boot *or* **boot up** process that is carried out when a computer is switched on. A sequence of instructions stored with the BIOS (in a ROM chip) are executed and these instruct the computer to load the main operating system from a boot disk. A PC checks the floppy disk drive and the then the hard drive for a valid boot disk that contains the operating system.

boot disk disk that contains the operating system that is loaded when a PC is switched on. The boot up instructions tell the hardware to read in the operating system software. Normally, the boot disk is your main hard disk. However, you can use a floppy disk as a boot disk, if it is formatted as a system or boot disk (using the Format /S command).

bootable storage device that holds the commands to boot up a computer and load the operating system; your main hard disk is a bootable device and your computer will normally boot up from this disk unless you insert a floppy disk into drive A: (in which case the computer looks on drive A: for the operating system)

boot sector part of a disk that contains instructions that are read by the computer when it is first switched on or reset; the instructions tell the computer how to load the operating system from the disk

BOOTP BOOTSTRAP PROTOCOL an Internet protocol that is used by a diskless workstation to find out its IP address, then load its operating system from a central server; this protocol allows a workstation to start up and load all its software over the network; a normal workstation would load its operating system software stored on an internal floppy or hard disk drive

border thin line around a window or box or button or image. If you are using a DTP application, the border style command will change the look of the lines around a box or image. For example, you could change the border to show a double line or a dashed line border style.

bot utility program that helps a user or other application carry out a particular task - for example a search bot will help a user search the Internet by submitting the query to several engines at once; a link bot will check that all the hyperlinks on a web site are correct

bounding box rectangle that determines the shape and position of an image that's been placed in a document or on screen. In graphics applications there is normally a special tool that allows you to select an area of an image to operate on: this area is shown as a dashed or flashing bounding box and can be stretched by moving the mouse.

bounce electronic mail that is returned to the sender because the address is incorrect or the user is not known at the mail server

bpp BITS PER PIXEL number of bits of data used to store the colour information of each pixel; a display that can display 16 different colours uses four bits per pixel

bps BITS PER SECOND measure of data communications speed. Often confused with baud, which refers to the number of transitions made per second and which equals bps only at low speeds, such as 300 bps.

break to stop or interrupt a program; on a PC there are two ways to stop or interrupt a program, either by pressing the Esc key (in the top left-hand corner) which normally interrupts a process such as a search and replace in a wordprocessor; if this does not work, pressing Ctrl-C will also sometimes work or pressing Ctrl-Break will also sometimes interrupt a program that is not working correctly

bridge interconnection device that can connect LANs at the data link level so allowing similar LANs using different transmission methods, for example Ethernet or Token Ring to talk. Bridges are able to read and filter the data packets and frames employed by the protocol and use the addresses to decide whether or not to pass a packet.

Briefcase utility (in Windows) a special utility that allows you to keep files stored on a laptop and a desktop PC up to date. In order to use the briefcase utility you will need a serial cable to connect the two computers and you will have to install the option from the Windows/Control Panel/Install Programs option.

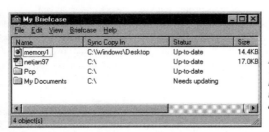

Briefcase - a Windows utility to help manage file transfers between a desktop and laptop.

broadband transmission channel or medium that can carry a wide range of frequencies and so can carry many different modulated signals at the same time

broadband communication device new communication channel and device that lets a computer connect to the Internet at a very high speed, often several thousand times faster than a standard modem connected to a telephone line. The three most popular broadband communication devices are ISDN, cable modems and ADSL (part of the wider DSL standard). Each country has different prevalent standards and pricing models. For example, ISDN provides a digital link that can transfer data at the rate of 64Kbps; it dials an access number and provides a link when required. ADSL, in contrast, provides a direct connection that appears to be 'always on' using a network adapter to link the computer to the Internet provider. ADSL normally supports a transfer speed of up to 2Mbps.
compare with DIAL UP, MODEM

broadcast special packet of information that is received by all network adapters on a LAN or by all servers on a WAN or Internet

brouter device that combines the functions of a bridge and router in connecting two networks. A brouter will route data packets if the protocol is known and bridge them if the protocol is unknown.

browser   software program that is used to navigate through web pages
stored on the Internet; a browser program asks the Internet server (called the
HTTP server) to send it a page of information, this page is stored in the
HTML layout language that is decoded by the browser and displayed on
screen. The browser displays any hotspots and hyperlinks and will jump to
the correct page if you click on the hyperlink.
see also   HTML, NETSCAPE, INTERNET EXPLORER

browsing   to move through a multimedia title or through a list of files or
through sites on the Internet in no particular order. You control which page
you move to next and what you view.

brush   tool in a paint program that lets you draw a line on the screen. You
can normally change the colour of the paint on the brush, together with the
width of the brush. In the Paint program in Windows, the colour used and
the width of the brush are defined in the bottom left-hand corner. If you
draw a line it will appear as if it has been painted with the brush: in the
colour and width of the brush.

BSD
see   BERKLEY SOFTWARE DISTRIBUTION

bubble-help   single line that appears on screen to describe what you are
pointing at: if you're not sure what a button does, move the pointer over it
and wait a second or two and a little 'bubble' with a one-line description
will pop-up (not all software has bubble help)

buffer   area of memory that is used for temporary storage of information
before it's needed. If you type very fast, the wordprocessor software might
not be able to display the characters as quickly as you type them in, so the
keystrokes are stored in a keyboard buffer. Similarly, if you print a
document before you have switched the printer on, the data is stored in a
print buffer until the printer has been switched on and ready to print.
see also   DOUBLE BUFFERING, FRAME BUFFER

bug   error in a computer program that means it does not work properly.
See also   BETA.

built-in   feature that is already included in a computer. For example, most
PCs have a hard disk and a floppy disk drive built-in as standard.

bullet   symbol (often a filled circle or square) printed or displayed in front
of a line of text and used to draw attention to the text. If you are creating a
presentation, you can indicate and highlight the important points of the
meeting by placing a bullet symbol in front of each point. If you are using a
Windows wordprocessor, you can add a bullet by changing the font to
Symbol or Wingdings and choosing one of the many bullet characters - to
see all the characters in a font, use the Character Map utility in Windows

and cut-and-paste the character into your document.

bulletin board (BBS)   computer that you can call up and connect to via a modem and a telephone line. Bulletin boards normally have lots of free software that you can download onto your computer, together with forums where you can discuss topics with other users. Most BBSes have electronic mail facilities that allow users to send messages to other users. More sophisticated BBS systems have links to other BBS computers or even the Internet, so that you can send and receive messages to any user on other systems

bundle   special deal available when buying a computer system or software package that includes extras that would normally cost more to buy separately

bureau   company that specializes in printing out high-quality images or typesetting text prepared using a desktop publishing program. A bureau normally has a typesetting machine that can produce very high quality text or black and white images onto film or photographic paper ready for a professional printer. Bureaux can also scan in colour photographs or slides at a very high resolution.

burst mode   method of transmitting data in a computer in which a particular device in the computer (such as the memory controller, graphics adapter or disk controller) will take control of the main data bus and transmit a lot of data to another device all in one go rather than waiting for the central processor to allow it to transmit data in several short sessions

bus   set of wires or cables that connect the main parts of the computer together. For example, the data bus is normally made up of 16 or 32 wires that carry the data around the computer, from the processor to the memory or hard disk controller. In practice, the wires are actually thin copper lines on the motherboard inside your computer. There are usually three main buses within a computer: the address bus, which carries the memory location for the data that's travelling at the same time on the data bus. The third is the control bus, and this carries a whole set of control and timing signals to make sure that all the components are working together.

bus clock   speed at which data is transferred along the main bus in a computer; this is not always the same speed as the processor speed
see also WAIT STATE

bus clock speed   frequency of the clock that governs the main bus in a computer, which is not necessarily the same frequency as the clock speed of the main central processor

bus master   device in your PC that is able to control the bus. Normally, this would be the processor, but in high-performance computers, the video adapter or disk controller can take over control of the bus to allow it to

exchange data very rapidly with the main memory. In short, it's a way of
moving data to and from main memory without troubling the processor. If
your PC has a bus master graphics card it can transfer data and draw images
on screen faster than a normal graphics card.
see also LOCAL BUS

bus topology way of designing a network in which all the connections
are linked as branches to one central main cable. This is the usual topology
for networks based on an Ethernet transmission system, wheras Token Ring
uses a ring topology. Bus networks are easy to implement, but one break in
the wire brings the whole network down. Star topology networks (such as
10Base-T) avoid this problem using one central connection point - the hub -
with lots of short wires to each node

bus unit (within a microprocessor) the place where instructions flow
between the main memory and the processor

button square shape that's displayed on the screen. When you move the
pointer over the button and click on the mouse button, something will
happen. For example, when you want to leave Windows it displays a small
box with the message 'are you sure you want to leave' and two buttons
labeled 'OK' and 'Cancel'. If you move the pointer over the OK button and
click on the mouse button, you'll quit Windows. Similarly, in Windows 95
there's always a Start button displayed in the bottom left-hand corner of the
screen: move over this and click and you'll see a menu of options. Just to
confuse the issue, there are all sorts of buttons, but radio buttons and
push-buttons are the most common. A radio button lets you choose only one
from a number of possible options (unlike a check-box), whilst a
push-button starts some action. In many multimedia applications, or in a
web page on the Internet, you'll see images that are used as buttons, or areas
of the screen that start an action if you click on them. These are normally
called hot-spots to differentiate between this special type of button and a
normal visible button
see also HOT SPOT, RADIO BUTTON

button bar line of tiny buttons along the top of the screen - just below
the menu bar - in many applications such as Microsoft Word, Works and
Excel. Each button on the bar contains a picture (called an icon) that helps
describe the function of the button. If you're not sure what the picture
means then move the pointer over the button and wait for a few seconds
without clicking: in many applications you should see a description of the
button pop up beside it.

byte group of eight bits (eight binary digits) which is the usual form in
which data is manipulated within a computer. One byte can hold numbers
between zero and 255. For example, each different character in the alphabet
has a special code that describes it (see ASCII code). This code is stored

within one byte, and so your computer can identify 256 different characters.
see also   BINARY, BIT, WORD

bytecode   form of Java instructions that can be executed in a Java Virtual
Machine; when a programmer develops a program written in Java, the Java
compiler converts the instructions in a bytecode form that can then be run
on any computer that supports the Virtual Machine software
see also   JAVA, VIRTUAL MACHINE

Cc

C programming language that is used by experienced programmers to create applications; C is more complex than BASIC but produces applications that run much faster and more efficiently

C++ programming language that is used by experienced programmers to create applications. C++ is derived from the C programming language and is often considered better for Windows programming since it allows programmers to create object-oriented applications that are better suited to the way Windows works

C: drive letter that is used in many operating systems, including DOS, Windows and OS/2 to denote the main hard disk drive on the system. Normally, a PC has two or three disk drives within its casing. The convention is to provide one floppy disk, called 'A:' and one hard disk called 'C:'. If you have a second floppy disk, this is called 'B:' and a CD-ROM drive is normally 'D:'. When talking about the different disk drives, you say 'Drive A' for the floppy drive, but normally write 'A:'. If you are using DOS, when your PC starts up it will normally show what's called the C-prompt (which looks like 'C:\' on your screen); this means you are currently looking at the hard disk. If you want to change to drive A to read data from a floppy disk, enter 'A:' and press return.
see also FLOPPY DISK, HARD DISK

cable collection of wires
see also DIRECT CABLE, NULL MODEM CABLE, PRINTER CABLE, RIBBON CABLE

cable modem device that links a computer to the Internet via an existing cable television line; this system provides very high speed access to the Internet (up to 2Mbps) sharing the coaxial cable that is used to distribute cable television signals. This system is fast becoming popular in the USA, which has an existing infrastructure for cable television, but in many other countries the ADSL high-speed system is being used over existing telephone cable

cache (electronic memory components that provide a) section of very high-speed memory that is used to temporarily store data before it is used by the computer's processor. A cache can dramatically speed up the effective rate at which data is read from a hard disk drive: the computer reads more data than is requested and stores the excess in the cache ready to be accessed with the next request to read data. The memory used for the cache

can be up to 100,000 times faster than a hard disk drive
see also L2-CACHE

CAD COMPUTER AIDED-DESIGN
software application that allows designers and architects to draw precise
blueprints on screen, then model them in three dimensions to see how the
design will appear in real life before it is manufactured.

caddy
see CD CADDY

Calculator software utility that's supplied with Windows and works just
like a normal calculator. To start the Calculator, double-click on the icon in
the Accessories group of Windows 3.1 or choose
Start/Programs/Accessories in Windows 95.

Calendar simple calendar and diary that was supplied with Windows 3.1.
This has been replaced by the more sophisticated Schedule+ in Windows
3.11 and by Outlook in Windows 95/98.

calibrate to adjust a monitor or joystick so that is is responding correctly
and accurately to the signals or movements. For example, this ensures that
the monitor is displaying a true representation of the colour that will be
printed.

callback security system that's used to reduce the risk of any
unauthorised user connecting to your computer if you have installed dial-in
networking (part of Windows 95). Callback works in a simple but effective
way: you use your communications software and modem to dial the remote
computer and enter your name and password. The remote computer then
hangs up the telephone line and calls you back on a preset telephone
number.

call discrimination feature of a modem that allows it to check if an
incoming telephone call is from a fax machine, another computer with a
modem or from a person; this feature is useful if you have one telephone
line and are using your modem to receive fax transmissions and spoken
messages

Cancel button that is normally displayed beside an OK button to give you
a chance to stop the action you were about to carry out

Caps Lock key key on a PC keyboard (on the left-hand side) that
switches the letters typed between lowercase and uppercase; this key works
as a toggle - press once to switch to uppercase, press again to switch to
lowercase

caption descriptive text that appears at the top of a window, in white text
on a blue background: for example, in Windows 95, double-click on the
MyComputer icon and you will see a small window pop up; the top of the

window has the caption: My Computer in white characters on a blue background. If you click anywhere outside this window, the blue background to the caption turns grey, to show that the window is no longer active
see ACTIVE WINDOW

capture (a printer port) way of redirecting data intended for a printer port over a network to a shared printer; when several PCs are connected together to form a workgroup or network, one computer will be connected to a shared printer. To use this shared printer, you have to tell Windows that you want anything that is normally sent to the printer port on your computer redirected over the network to the shared printer: this can be setup using the Printer icon in the Control Panel group.

capture (a screen) to store the image that is currently displayed on the screen in a file. In Windows, you can save the current screen as a graphics image by pressing the PrintScreen key on the keyboard; this graphics image can then be pasted into a document or paint program (start the Windows Paint program and choose the Edit/Paste menu command to paste the image of the screen).

carbon copy (cc) feature of electronic mail software that allows you to send a copy of a message to another user
see also BLIND CARBON COPY

card (i) electronic components mounted on a board that plugs into an expansion bus in a PC and adds a new function to the computer, or allows it to communicate with another device. For example, a sound card is a type of adapter card that plugs into an expansion connector and allows sound to be played back or recorded; (ii) a single page within a multimedia book

CardBus high-speed (up to 33MHz) version of the original PCMCIA PC Card standard that also allows 32-bits of data to be transferred in one operation compared to the 16-bit capability of the original PC Card standard

caret (^) (i) symbol that is normally used in manuals to represent the Ctrl key, for example ^C means hold down the Ctrl key and press the C key at the same time; (ii) means 'raise to a power of', for example 2^4 means 2 raised to the power of 4.

carriage return (CR) historically, this is a printer command that moves the print head to the start of a line; now refers to a code or keypress that breaks a line and starts a new line
see RETURN KEY

carrier (signal) continuous, steady sound tone that is used by a modem to send data along a telephone wire. The modem changes the frequency of the carrier (the tone) to represent different characters. If you have a modem and connect to an on-line service you can tell when your modem has recognised the distant modem when the carrier detect (CD) light lights up on the front of your modem.

CAS COMMUNICATING APPLICATIONS SPECIFICATION
standard developed by Intel and DCA to allow communication software to control a fax modems

cascading windows way of arranging lots of windows on screen so that they overlap, with only the title bar and caption of each window showing. This is a much neater and more efficient way of displaying lots of windows on the screen at the same time. The alternative is to tile the windows: each is displayed beside the next with no overlap. Another alternative is to minimise each window into an icon (or, in Windows 95, onto the status bar along the bottom of the screen).

case-sensitive software that can detect the difference between lower-case and upper-case characters; for example, if you have a case-sensitive password then 'Fred' will not be the same as 'fred'. Youire more likely to find this as a feature of search and replace functions in a wordprocessor.

cast each individual part of a multimedia presentation or animation: the members of a cast can be individual images, sound clips or text.

CBT COMPUTER BASED TRAINING
software designed to help teach a student a subject (such as a language or school subject) or help train people how to use something (such as a new type of software or device)

cc
see CARBON COPY

CCD CHARGE-COUPLED DEVICE
tiny electronic component that has an array of thousands of light-sensitive cells on its surface; a CCD component is used in video cameras, electronic cameras and some scanners to detect a picture and turn it into electronic signals that can be processed by a computer.

CCITT COMITÉ CONSULTATIF INTERNATIONALE DE TÉLÉGRAPHIE ET TÉLÉPHONIE
international organisation (part of the United Nations) that sets international telecommunications standards, now called the ITU.
The CCITT defined many of the standards used to dial up a computer and access the Internet, including the V-series used for telecommunication links (for example, when using a modem)

V.21	(old) full duplex communications at 300baud (in the USA, the Bell 103 standard was used instead)
V.22	half-duplex communication at 1,200bps (in the USA, the Bell 212A standard was more commonly used)

V.22bis full-duplex modem communication transferring data at up to
2,400bps
V.29 half-duplex modem communication transferring data at up to
9,600bps (this standard is generally used by fax modems)
V.32 full-duplex modem communication standard that can transfer data
at up to 9,600bps but can also automatically adjust its speed
based on the quality of the telephone line - to avoid errors
V.32bis similar to the V.32 protocol, but able to transfer data at rates up to
14,400 bps.
V.34 full-duplex modem communication standard that can transfer data
at up to 28,800 bps. Like V.32, the V.34 standard allows the
modem to automatically adjust its speed based on the quality of
the telephone line to avoid errors.
V.42 error-detection system that can be used to reduce errors due to
poor telephone line quality (see also MNP standard)
V.42bis data compression system that increases the data transfer rate up to
34,000 bps.
V.90 full-duplex modem data communication at up to 56,600 bps.

CD COMPACT DISC
small plastic disc that is used to store masses of data: up to 650Mb of data.
The data is stored in the form of tiny holes etched into the surface of the
disc; a CD drive spins the disc and uses a laser beam to read the holes in the
surface. A CD can store any type of computer data from images to text to
music. However, it can only be read by a user - you cannot save data onto a
CD. A CD normally refers to a normal music disc which can be played in
your HiFi or in your PC's CD player (just plug in a pair of headphones and
use the MediaPlayer utility to start playing). In the computer world, the
same type of plastic disc is used to store files and data and is called a
CD-ROM (Read Only Memory).

CD caddy flat plastic container that is used to hold a compact disc. The
caddy is inserted into a CD-ROM drive: some CD-ROM drives use a caddy
to hold the disc, others use a motorised tray onto which the 'bare' compact
disc is place. A compact disc is inserted with the printed side facing up

CD-audio or CD-DA COMPACT DISC-DIGITAL AUDIO
standard that defines how music can be stored as a series of numbers (digital
form) on a compact disc.

CD-I COMPACT DISC-INTERACTIVE
set of enhancements to the normal CD-ROM standard, developed by
Philips, and aimed for home use. The system uses its own special hardware
console with speakers, joystick and a connection to a television screen to
display the images. The special feature of CD-I is that it allows you to
interact with what you see on the television screen and choose options or
respond to questions or a game.

CD-ROM XA enhanced method of storing data onto a CD-ROM disc that lets the computer read sound from the disc at the same time as images or text. If you want to play a CD-ROM XA disc on your computer, you will need to make sure that the CD-ROM drive is XA compliant; a CD-ROM XA drive can read a PhotoCD disc

CD-ROM
see CD

CD-ROM drive mechanical device that spins a compact disc and reads data stored on the surface of the disc using a tiny laser beam; the speed of a drive is given as a multiple of a basic drive. For example, a double-speed drive spins the disc at twice the standard speed; current drives work at 24 times (written 24x) the standard speed

cel single frame in an animation sequence; computer animations are normally made up of lots of images that are each slightly different. When the sequence of images is displayed one after the other, the action appears to move

Cello web browser application
see also BROWSER, NETSCAPE, MICROSOFT IE

centre text option in every wordprocessing package that lets you place the line or paragraph of text in the centre of the page. Move the cursor to the line of text then click the centre text format button or choose Format/Paragraph/Alignment/Centre menu option (in Microsoft Word).

Centronics port standard that defines the way in which a parallel printer port on a PC operates
see also PARALLEL PORT

CERN research laboratory in Switzerland where the world wide web was originally invented

certificate a unique set of numbers that has been generated by a trusted company (such as VeriSign or Thawte) - but only once they are satisfied that the company is legitimate and authentic. The company can now use this certificate to provide authentication (that it is who it claims to be) and set up a secure website to accept payments online.

certificate authority a specialist trusted organization that issues digital certificates that are then used to setup digital signatures and secure websites; if you want to get a personal digitial signature or setup a secure website (using the SSL standard) you need to apply to a certificate authority for a digital certificate - you will need to provide comprehensive proof of your (or your company's) identity
see also DIGITAL CERTIFICATE, DIGITAL SIGNATURE, SECURE WEBSITE, SSL

CGA COLOR GRAPHICS ADAPTER

very early graphics adapter standard developed by IBM; you will hardly
ever see this now except listed as an option in the setup program for your
computer - CGA provides few colours at a low resolution and was replaced
by EGA then VGA then SVGA

CGI COMMON GATEWAY INTERFACE

standard that defines how a WWW page can call special scripts stored on an
Internet server to carry out functions that enhance a web page; for example,
if a web page provides a search function, the search function will be a
special program that is called by the web page using CG' commands
see also PERL

CGM COMPUTER GRAPHICS METAFILE

standard graphics file format
see also GIF, JPEG

channel (i) (in graphics) one layer of an image that can be worked on
separately or which can be used to create special effects; (ii) (in MIDI
music) a method of identifying each individual instrument in a MIDI
orchestra: there are 16 channel numbers and an instrument can be assigned
to each; (iii) (on the Internet) method of transmitting information and news
to users over the Internet; there are many sources of information channels
that you can subscribe to (normally without charge) and receive the news on
your web browser
see also PUSH

character letter or number that is displayed or printed. The shape of each
character is determined by the typeface and font that is used: each font
includes 256 different characters normally with a to z and A to Z together
with foreign characters, symbols and punctuation marks.

character generator electronic chip that stores the patterns of pixels
that form a character

Character Map utility that is provided with Windows to allow you
access the full range of 256 characters that make up every font rather than
the limited range that you can access from the keyboard. The extra
characters include foreign characters and symbols.

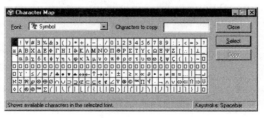

character mode *or* **text mode** operating mode of a computer or display screen that will only display pre-defined characters and will not allow graphic images to be displayed; Windows operates in a graphics mode, MS-DOS normally operates in a text mode

chassis metal frame that is the basis for the computer system on your desk; the chassis normally has a number of devices attached to it including the motherboard, the power supply unit and the disk drives

chat to send and receive messages, in real time, with other users on the Internet; to chat to other users, you will need special software
see also INTERNET RELAY CHAT

chat room area of a website where visitors can exchange messages with other visitors; if a visitor types in a message, special software displays the name of the visitor and their message to all the other visitors, allowing them to 'talk' and exchange messages, in real time

Cheapernet slang term for Thin-wire Ethernet - because it is cheaper than Thick-Wire Ethernet.

checkbox method of allowing a user to choose an option from a selection of possible options (in a program or a web page). The checkbox is a small box displayed; if you want to select the option, move the pointer onto the checkbox and click once, the box will now have a cross displayed inside it; if you do not want the option, click a second time and the box will be empty. The main feature of a checkbox is that you can choose several options at the same time. A radio buttons only allows you to choose one option at a time.
see also RADIO BUTTON

checksum number calculated from data that is used to make sure that the data is correct and valid; this is a simple process, for example if you are using a barcode scanner to read the barcode on the back of this book, the last digit is actually calculated from the other digits in the sequence and is used to make sure that the scanner reads the code correctly

child (window) small window that is displayed inside a main window - often used to display options, for example if you want to change a font or check the spelling of a document then the options are all displayed in a child window.

chip small electronic device that is at the heart of every computer and electronic gadget. A chip is a small thin piece of silicon crystal onto which is etched a tiny circuit with hundreds of thousands of components. These components will carry out simple mathematical operations such as adding and subtracting numbers (in a processor chip) or storing numbers (in a memory chip). If ever you open your PC (with the mains power unplugged) you will see a mass of small black boxes with tens of metal legs on each side: these are the chips.

cipher text text that has been encrypted; before it is encrypted, it is called plain text
see also ENCRYPTION

chroma colour of a part of an image or pixel, defined by its he, saturation and luminance

CIDR CLASSLESS INTER-DOMAIN ROUTING a system of organising IP addresses that is more compact and efficient; the older system used three classes of IP address (A, B and C) that could each represent hundreds or thousands of individual addresses; the new system adds a slash and a new IP Prefix number that represents a number of individual addresses. For example, the old system used an IP address such as '194.124.0.0' wheras the new scheme would replace this with '194.124.0.0/12'; the IP Prefix number 12 represents 4,096 unique addresses and the lower the number the more addresses are represented

circuit board fibre glass sheet onto which electronic components are mounted and connected together to form a computer or other electronic device. If you open up your computer, you will see one large circuit board, normally at the bottom of the computer's box, called the motherboard

circuit switching method of describing a type of communication system in which a path from sender to receiver is created when required rather than using a permanent, fixed line; the normal telephone system is an example of a circuit switching network

CISC COMPLEX INSTRUCTION SET COMPUTER
design of a processor chip that contains a wide collection of instructions that makes it easier to program in assembly language, but its speed is generally slower than a RISC processor that is designed to execute just a few instructions

class (i) (in Java and other object-oriented programming languages) self-contained defined program or module or routine that can be run or called from another routine; (ii) (in a computer) method of grouping similar types of hardware resource so that they can be managed and used with a particular type of device driver

Class 1, Class 2 standards that define how a to control a fax modem using software; the standard uses extensions to the Hayes AT command set used for data modems. Class 2 expects the modem to carry out more work in managing fax communications; Class 1 units can often be upgraded through software. Only modems advertised as 'Class 2.0' follow the true Class 2 standard.

clear to send (CTS) signal used in an RS-232C serial port to control the flow of data to another device (such as a modem); when the modem is ready to receive data, it sends a signal on the CTS pin of the RS-232C connector to the computer's serial port to tell it to send more data
see also HANDSHAKE, FLOW CONTROL, REQUEST TO SEND

click to press down once and release a key (on the keyboard) or one of the buttons on a mouse; normally used also to mean the action of moving the arrow pointer over an icon or menu or option and pressing once on a mouse button. Windows uses a click on the left-hand mouse button to select an icon and a click on the right-hand button to display a menu of options that apply to the icon (such as its name and properties). Wordprocessing applications often use different clicks to mean different things: move the pointer over a paragraph of text and click once with the left-hand button: the cursor is position where you clicked. Click twice and the word is highlighted, click three times and the paragraph is highlighted. If you want to open a document or icon (such as My Computer) or start an application then you need to double-click on the icon. A double-click is two rapid clicks on the left-hand mouse button; if nothing happens, try again making the clicks as short and fast as possible. One neat feature of Windows is click and drag (also called drag and drop). This lets you move an icon around the screen or move text in a word processor. First, move the pointer over the icon and press down on the left hand mouse button. Keep the button pressed down and move the mouse and you will find the icon moves with the pointer

click-and-mortar an online shop version of a real shop, for example the bookshop Barnes & Noble has a chain of real bookshops and an online shop at www.bn.com; compare this with Amazon.com that has an online shop but does not have real physical bookshops

click through action of someone clicking on a banner advertisement and jumping to the advertiser's website.

click through rate (CTR) a method of charging an advertiser for the display of a banner advertisement on a website. Each time a visitor clicks on a displayed ad (that links to the advertiser's main site), the advertiser is charged a fee. A click through rate of just a few percent is common and most advertisers have to pay per thousand impressions of their banner ad, sometimes written CTM (click through, per thousand).

client computer that is connected to a network or the Internet, or a computer that is using the resources of another computer; if you are connected to the Internet, your computer is the client and runs client software (such as a web browser)

client-server computing system consisting of networked 'clients' which request information and a central 'server' which stores data and manages shared information and resources. Client-server software tries to reduce the amount of data traffic flowing over the wires between clients and server. It does this by processing data at the server as well as simply retrieving it. For example, a client PC with a simple front-end application asks the server to find all contacts in South London: the server searches through the database and returns the correct matches. The alternative is for the client to request the entire database to be sent which it then searches itself. The difference means that only the question and answer travels across the network rather than the entire database, which means that there is less traffic on the network

client-side   often used to refer to a program or script that runs on a user's computer rather than on the web server; for example, there are two ways of carrying out functions such as image maps and forms: either your computer stores the image and does the processing (called client-side) or the server computer does the work (called server-side); client-side is one way of implementing image maps
see also   IMAGEMAPS

clip-art   library of pre-drawn images, drawings or photographs that you can use in your presentations, reports or desktop publishing documents. Normally, there are no copyright fees if you use the images for non-commercial use. You will find that most presentation programs come with hundreds of pre-drawn images, borders and icons in a clip-art library

Clipboard   (in Windows) area of memory that is used for temporary storage of data; for example, if you select some text in a wordprocessor then cut it (using the Edit/Cut menu option), the text is actually temporarily stored in the Clipboard. If you choose the Edit/Paste menu option you can copy the text back from the Clipboard to the document. In Windows, the Clipboard can store any type of data: from text to sound, images, data and drawings. It is a very useful way of moving data from one program to another: for example, to copy your signature you have drawn in Paint to the bottom of a letter written in Microsoft Word, first choose Edit/Copy in Paint, switch to Word move to the bottom of the letter and choose Edit/Paste - your signature will appear. To see what is currently stored in the Clipboard, you can start a utility called Clipboard Viewer in the Accessories group in Windows. Almost all Windows applications use Ctrl-C to copy to the Clipboard, Ctrl-V to paste from the Clipboard and Ctrl-X to delete without copying

Clipper chip   electronics component (an integrated circuit, or chip) that was designed under the instructions of the US Government to provide a data encryption feature for computers, Internet traffic, telephones, and television programmes; in the original scheme the US Government held the master key to the chip and so could decrypt and read any encrypted messages - this angered many groups concerned with freedom of speech and the US

Government has since re-designed the original scheme and suggested an alternatives

clipping to view part of an image or to select an area of an image that is smaller than the original; if you are using the Paint program that is supplied with Windows you can use the area select tool to clip an image to keep the section of the image you want. The area select tool is the top right hand corner of the tools: select this and then move the cross-hair cursor to the top left hand corner of the area you want to click then, with the left-hand mouse button pressed down, drag the area you want to clip.

clock (i) tiny crystal in your computer that sends out a regular signal hundreds of thousands of times every second; it is used by all the electronic components to keep in time with each other so that data is not lost when it is transferred. The central processing unit normally carries out one instruction every clock pulse, so the faster the clock the more instructions it carries out. The speed of a processor (and so the clock) is measured in megahertz (MHz) which represent one million pulses every second: a processor that runs at 50mhz uses a clock that sends 50 million signals every second; (ii) Windows includes a utility called Clock that displays the current time in a window or as an icon: to start the utility, double-click on the Clock icon in the Accessories group. Windows 95 displays the time in the bottom right-hand corner of the screen. To see the date, move the pointer over the time and wait a couple of seconds: the data will pop up

clock doubler special chip that works beside the central processing unit to double the number of clock pulses and so effectively double the speed of the central processor.

clock speed frequency at which a clock runs in a computer or other electronic device. Clock speed of a processor is normally measured in millions of cycles per second (MHz).

close menu option (normally under the File menu) menu option that will shut the document that is currently open, but will not exit the application. If you have not saved the document, the application will warn you before it closes the document and give you the chance to save any changes.

cluster smallest element that DOS (the operating system software that controls your PC) can read from or write to a disk.

CLUT COLOUR LOOK-UP TABLE table of numbers used in Windows and graphics programs to store the range of colours used in an image *see also* PALETTE

CLV CONSTANT LINEAR VELOCITY physical format used in creating a spiral track on a CD-ROM so that the data is always delivered at the same rate, regardless of the position of the access head

CMOS COMPLEMENTARY METAL-OXIDE SEMICONDUCTOR
method of designing and manufacturing a range of electronic components; it
produces components that are fast and consume little power, but are more
expensive and cannot store as much information as other types of
semiconductor

CMYK CYAN MAGENTA YELLOW BLACK method of describing any
colour by the percentages of these four colours; normally used in high-end
graphics and desktop publishing programs.

co-axial cable (coax) special cable that is used to connect computers
linked in a network. Co-axial cable looks like television aerial cable and is
made from a central core of copper surrounded by plastic with a mesh of
copper and a plastic outer covering.
compare with TWISTED PAIR

codec CODER-DECODER electronic device that compresses video
and sound signals before they are transmitted over a telephone modem
connection or over the Internet; the signals are decompressed at the
receiving end. To achieve good-quality live video transmission over the
Internet, you need to use a high-speed codec that can compress the data and
transmit it to the receiver

codepages definition of the character that is produced by each key on
the keyboard: the layout is different for different countries: the UK and the
USA use the QWERTY standard (defined by the top line of characters on
the keyboard), whilst France uses AZERTY and other countries incorporate
accents and special characters. In order to use your computer when typing in
a different language you need to change the keyboard layout and the font
that is used for the characters - both are defined by the codepage. You can
change the properties of the keyboard by opening the Keyboard icon in the
Control Panel.

cold boot to switch off a computer completely and then switch it back on
again
compare with WARM BOOT

collate to print multiple copies of a document in correct order: if you
want three copies of a document then, instead of the usual method of
printing three copies of page one, three copies of page two and so on, the
wordprocessing software is clever enough to print all the pages in order and
repeat this three times.

collision two signals that interfere with each other over a network,
normally causing an error

co-location an Internet server computer that is located at a specialist site
designed to support and maintain servers on behalf of their customers. If
you want to set up a website, you might start by renting web space from

your ISP or web hosting provider; if your website grows in popularity or requires complex or secure e-commerce facilities, you might find it effective to rent or purchase a server computer dedicated to serving your website - you could locate this server computer anywhere (for example, in your office), but you would need to install a high-speed link to the Internet and maintain the computer and its software; a more cost-effective solution is co-location: moving the server to a specialist site, often provided by an ISP, who takes on the job of supporting the high-speed link and the computer

colour *or* **(US) color** any colour displayed on a monitor is made up of three tiny dots behind the front of the glass screen. The colours from these three dots combine to create millions of different colours and shades that you can see. Although the monitor is capable of displaying millions of different colours, it is also dependent on the graphics adapter which has to control the electronics in the monitor.

colour bits number of bits that define the colour displayed at each pixel location. One colour bit allows the pixel to display two colours, two colour bits can display four colours, eight colour bits can display 256 colours, 16 colour bits can display 65,536 different colours and 24 colour bits can display 16 million colours. Full colour or true-colour displays that can show photographic-quality images usually use 24 colour bits. There is a tradef off: the more colour bits you use for each pixel, the more memory this uses up. The number of colour bits that is used depends on the capabilities of the graphics adapter fitted in your computer; this has a limited amount of memory installed and can allocate this either to higher resolution display with more pixels or a display with more colours. A display with 24 colour bits will take three times as much memory as one with eight colour bits.

colour depth number of different colours that can be displayed by any single pixel in a display - determined by the number of colour bits in each pixel.

colour palette selection of colours that are currently being used in an image. Even though a pixel might have only eight colours bits, and so can display 256 different colours, you can choose these 256 colours from a range of millions of different colours: your choice of colours is the colour palette.

colour printer device that can produce printed colour output on paper or film. The most common and cheapest colour printers are ink-jet printers. These use four coloured inks which are squirted in tiny dots onto the paper; by combining different coloured dots together, a wide range of different colours can be printed. Thermal-wax printers are the most accurate and the most expensive colour printers available. They use a tiny heating element to blend together four colour waxes that cool when they hit the surface of the paper.

com suffix on a domain name that means that the Internet domain name is a company and (usually) based in the USA; for example, 'microsoft.com'; other common suffixes include 'co.uk' for UK-based companies, 'edu' for educational organisation and 'net' for ISPs
see also DOMAIN

COM type of file that contains a program; COM program files are always less than 64Kb in size, wheras EXE program files can be almost any size. To view a list of program files that are stored on your hard disk, move to DOS (if you are in Windows, start an MS-DOS session) and enter 'DIR *.COM'; to run a COM program, enter the program name without the COM extension and press Return. For example, to run EDIT.COM type 'EDIT' and press Return
see also EXE, PROGRAM

COM port *or* **COM device** *or* **COM1** name used in PCs to represent the first serial port on the computer. If you plug an external modem into the first serial port, you are connecting it to COM1. There are normally two serial ports (COM1 and COM2) in a PC, although it can support four. Some PCs have a mouse plugged into the first serial port and the modem plugged into the second port. If you have connected a modem to a serial port on your PC you will need to configure your communications software so that it knows to which port your modem is connected by selecting the correct COM port.

COM COMPONENT OBJECT MODEL set of rules that define the way in which objects within the Windows OLE system interact with other documents, objects and applications

command instruction that tells the computer or a program to do something. For example, if you type in the command 'DIR' at the DOS prompt this tells the operating system of the computer to display a list of the files stored on the disk. The command to shut down the computer when using Windows 95 involves clicking on the Start button and selecting the Shutdown menu option

COMMAND.COM program file that contains the command line interpreter for MS-DOS. Do not delete this program file if you see it on your hard disk or your computer will not respond to your commands
see COMMAND INTERPRETER

command interpreter operating system software that runs on a computer and recognises commands entered by a user that control the actions of the computer. For example, in older computers the command interpreter was usually Microsoft's MS-DOS and translated typed commands into actions; in new computers the command interpreter is Windows 95 which translates mouse movements and menu selections into computer actions

command line   method of describing software that is controlled by typing in words. If you are used to Windows, where you point and click to make things happen, and think that this sounds strange remember DOS. DOS is command-line driven: to list the files that are stored, type in DIR, to change directory type in CD. To view DOS, double-click on the MS-DOS icon in the Accessories group of Windows 3.1 or select Start/Programs/MS-DOS Prompt within Windows 95/98

command mode   operating mode of a modem in which the user (or communications software) can send instructions to the modem that it will then try and execute; the standard method of switching a modem to command mode is to type or send it the three characters '+++' the modem will reply with an 'OK' message and is ready to execute configuration or other commands
see also AT COMMAND SET, HAYES COMPATIBLE

command prompt   symbol that tells you that the software is ready to receive the next command. In DOS, this is normally the 'C:\' symbol; to make this rather more friendly it is usual to include the path so that the command prompt might read 'C:\WINDOWS\ to indicate that you are looking at the C: drive and are in the \WINDOWS subdirectory. Since the command prompt is not very friendly and you have to remember dozens of special command words, it is hardly surprising that Windows was developed!

commerce
see E-COMMERCE, SECURE WEB SITE, SHOPPING

commerce server   specialist web software that supports the main functions of an online shop including managing the shopping cart and dealing with the credit card payment processing

common gateway interface
see CGI

communications port   connector and electronics that form a serial port in a computer; normally referred to as COM1, COM2, etc for the first and second serial ports in a PC
see also COM1

communications software   software that allows you to connect to a remote computer using a modem to send and receive information. The software will dial the telephone number and displays information that is received as well as sending any text that you type in on your keyboard. Some on-line services use their own specially-written communications software that can only be used with this service. More complex communications software packages let you send and receive faxes and send and receive files.

comp   type of newsgroup that provides discussion about computers and computer programming
see also   ALT, BIZ, NEWSGROUPS

compact disc
see   CD

compatible   one version of hardware or software that will work with another type or version of hardware or software. For example, IBM designed the first PC but there are now hundreds of manufacturers that produce compatible computers that work in exactly the same way.

compiler   software used by programmers that converts a file of program instructions written in a programming language into a form that can be understood by the central processing unit. The final form is normally stored as an EXE or COM program file that contains machine code instructions to control the processor. If you want to create software you first write the program (either by typing in instructions or designing a flow-chart), this is passed to the compiler program that produces the finished application that you can then run.

compliant   device that conforms to a particular set of standards. For example, if you want to read PhotoCD compact discs in your computer you must be sure that the CD-ROM drive is PhotoCD or CD-ROM XA compliant.

component   small, add-in program that provides a specialised function and is used to enhance a web browser or other application
see also   ACTIVEX, JAVA, PLUG-IN, VBX

Component Object Model (COM)   set of rules that define the way in which objects within the Windows OLE system interact with other documents, objects and applications

composite monitor   colour monitor that receives the colour display signals from a graphics display adapter combined into one signal which must then be electronically separated inside the monitor into the red, green and blue colour signals
compare with   RGB

composite video   video signal that is supplied as several separate signals including the colour, brightness and synchronisation signals

compound document   one document that contains data that was created by other applications; for example, if you have a wordprocessor, you can insert images from a paint program or sound clips - the result is a compound document.

compression   to reduce the size of a file by encoding the data. For example, if the file contains five letter 'A's next to each other, which take up five bytes of space, the compression software could encode this to 5A which takes two byes of space. The compression software uses all sorts of encoding tricks to code the way data is stored to reduce the space it takes *see also* DATA COMPRESSION, PKZIP

CompuServe on-line service that provides access to the Internet and also supplies its own databases, information sources and discussion forums that can only be accessed by subscribers dialing in to the main computer with a modem. CompuServe is based in the USA and contains reference databases, such as stock exchange prices and weather maps, but it also has thousands of individual forums

The CompuServe online service provides its own forums and information services as well as access to the public Internet.

computer electronic device that can carry out mathematical functions *see* PERSONAL COMPUTER

computer names (in Windows 95) series of words that identify a computer on a network; each computer that is connected to a network is given an identifying name, if you are linked to an office network, you will see an icon on your Desktop called Network Neighborhood. Double-click on this and it will display a list of the other computers on the network, and their computer name

CON special name used in PCs to represent the console which is the monitor and keyboard; this name is rarely used

concatenate to join two or more items or files together one after another

concurrent two or more tasks running simultaneously on a computer; in practice this means that you can run more than one program at a time, for example to type a letter in a word processor and also checking the stock market figures from the Internet and recalculate your company's profit margin in a spreadsheet. In an multiprocessor computer there are several processor chips, each of which can run one program. Most PCs use one single processor and achieve a similar result using Windows or OS/2 software: the operating system software switches very rapidly between each program. For example, if you are running three programs the operating system would divide the processor's time into tiny slices and give each a slice. This way, although the processor is servicing three programs, it is fast enough to look as if they are all running concurrently

condition   state of a particular electronic device or option; for example a check box condition can be either checked or blank. Also refers to the amount of electrical charge in a battery

CONFIG.SYS   One of two special text files that the user can create to configure the initial environment of the PC and load special device drivers. CONFIG.SYS is a file stored in the root directory of the disk used to start the PC (usually the hard disk if one is fitted or a floppy in drive A:). If this file is present, then the special commands stored in it are automatically executed when DOS starts up.
see also   AUTOEXEC.BAT

configuration   way in which a particular computer or software application has been set up and customised

configure   to set the function of software or hardware to your particular settings. You can configure Windows so that it displays a different colour background, or so that it uses a larger font that is easier to read. If you install a new software application there are two main steps: the first is the installation, which simply creates a new folder and copies the files onto your hard disk from the floppy disk or CD-ROM. Once the program is installed, you can configure it to work the way you want. For example, if you are adding Microsoft Word, you install it and then configure the way it looks and works. The Tools/Customize option lets you change the icons and menus that are displayed, whilst the Tools/Configure option lets you change the initial settings for the software. To change the way Windows looks, use the Control Panel. In Windows 95 and later, select Start/Settings option to view a set of icons that lets you define the basic look and feel of Windows: from the speed and sensitivity of the mouse to the language used and the type of printer that is connected to your PC; If you are using Windows 3.1x, open the Main group and double-click on the Control Panel icon; Windows configuration information is stored in INI files (for Windows 3.x) and in the Registry (for Windows 95 and later)
see also   PLUG AND PLAY, REGISTRY

configuration file   file that contains data that describes how a particular software program or device has been configured; for example, the main Windows configuration file is stored in a file called the Registry; older versions of Windows used a separate configuration file (ending in the .INI file name extension) for each application

congestion problem that occurs when the bandwidth of a link cannot carry the amount of data traffic; on the Internet, this normally occurs when too many users connect, each user can still access information, but the response is very slow

connection general term for a link that has been established between two devices on a network or between two modems; the link allows data transfer and could provide data compression and error correction

connection-oriented data transfer that occurs according to a series of fixed, pre-defined steps that will create a known and reliable path between the two devices; for example, TCP/IP is a connection-oriented protocol that uses a known modem or network adapter to contact another known computer and establish a link via TCP/IP commands

connectionless data transfer that occurs between two devices that do not have a fixed or permanent link and so can take different routes between the two devices
see also CIRCUIT SWITCHING

console (CON) keyboard and monitor in a computer system

consumables extra materials that you need to buy to keep a printer or computer working properly; these could be a steady supply of blank floppy disks for the PC, and paper and ink or toner for the printer. These extras can easily cost as much as the basic equipment over the course of several years. When choosing a printer, look to see how much the consumables for this particular model will cost. If you are choosing a laser printer you will need to replace the toner cartridge (which contains dry, powdered ink) after a few thousand pages. An ink-jet printer will require new ink cartridges that will last for several few hundred pages
see also TONER

content general term that refers to information or text provided by a publisher that is useful to or of interest to a user

content provider company that supplies information (text, news stories, images, video, software) for a publication in a website or other medium

content-rich web site that contains a lot of useful information

contention two electronic devices that are trying to send information over a network at the same time; one device has to stop to allow the other to transmit

context-sensitive help type of help that displays information about the particular function that you are trying to use. For example, if you are using the search and replace function and press the F1 key (this is almost always the Help key), the software should display advice on using the search and replace function. If the software does not have context-sensitive help it would just display a general manual and you would then have to look for the section on search and replace.

continuous tone   image that uses all possible values of grey or colours, such as a photograph
see also   GREY-SCALE, LINE ART

contrast   difference between the light and dark areas in an image

control key (Ctrl)   key on the keyboard (in the bottom right and left corners of the main character pad) that is used for special functions. The control key is used with another key: press and hold down the control key and then press a second key and you will activate a special function. The keys and the functions all depend on the way the software was written: in many Windows-based applications there is a set of standard control key functions: Ctrl-S will save the current document, Ctrl-N will create a new document, Ctrl-P will print the document. You will often find that the control key is most useful in a wordprocessor when editing text: Ctrl-X will cut selected text which you can then paste back with Ctrl-V. In older wordprocessors, there was a standard developed by WordStar which used Ctrl-Y to delete a line, and Ctrl-T to move the cursor forward by one word. When using a Windows wordprocessor, because they use different functions! To move around any Windows application, Ctrl-right-arrow will move the cursor one word to the right, Ctrl-left-arrow will move it one word to the left; Ctrl-up-arrow will move the start of the paragraph, Ctrl-down-arrow will move to the end of the paragraph. Ctrl-Home will move to the start of the document and Ctrl-End to the end of the document.
compare with   ALT KEY

Control Panel   collection of icons that let you configure the basic functions of Windows and your PC. In Windows 3.1x, open the Main group and double-click on the Control Panel icon. In Windows 95, click on the Start/Settings button option. Within the Control Panel there are icons to define the fonts that are installed on your computer, the colour of the background to Windows, the type of printer that is installed, how a network works and a mass of other options.

control unit   part of a microprocessor that is responsible for the entire operation within the processor - including moving instructions and data around the processor in the correct order

controller   device that works as a middle-man, allowing a computer to use another device; for example, you need to fit a controller to support a CD-ROM drive

conventional memory   memory between zero and 640Kb. This area of memory is used to store programs when they are being run, together with device drivers and data. It is the main area of memory that is fitted in all

PCs. However, because it is not really enough for the big software applications that are used today (such as Windows), most PCs are fitted with more memory - also called RAM. A standard PC would be fitted with 16 or 32Mb: the first 640Kb is still called the conventional memory, the next 384Kb is called upper memory and the remaining 31Mb is called extended memory

convergence (i) the combination of two or more different technologies producing a new technology (for example, fax machines are the product of convergence of telephone, scanning and printing technologies); (ii) (in a colour monitor) the accuracy with which the picture beam strikes the three colour dots that form each colour pixel
see also PICTURE BEAM, PIXEL

cookie tiny file that is stored on your computer when you connect to a remote Internet site using a browser; the cookie is used by the remote site to store information about your options which can then be read when you next visit the site. Cookies are normally totally harmless and sometimes necessary for some sites, typically shopping sites, to work at all. If you would prefer not to accept cookies, you can prevent them being stored on your hard disk using the options within your web browser program.

cookie file file that contains the cookie data supplied by the remote Internet site; cookie files are normally stored in the same directory as your Internet browser program

coprocessor electronic device that works as a secondary processor to support the computer's main processor; a coprocessor normally carries out a range of more specialist instructions, such as mathematical functions or image operations
see also NUMERIC COPROCESSOR

copy to make a second, identical version of a file or section of text. If you copy a file, you make a second, identical file (use the COPY command). If you want to copy a section of text, highlight it then choose Edit/Copy, move to the place you want to add the copied text and choose Edit/Paste.

CORBA COMMON OBJECT REQUEST BROKER ARCHITECTURE
specification developed by the Object Management Group that defines how objects can interact and how an application can access an object; similar in function to Microsoft's COM standard

counter small program that counts the number of visitors to a web site and displays the current count on the web page; many web sites use this feature to give an indication of the popularity of the web site - the program can be written in PERL or provided as a add-in feature (such as the counter Bot in Microsoft Frontpage)
see also ACCESS LOG, BOT, PERL

Courier   one of the fonts that is included with Windows and is also on almost every printer: it looks like a typewriter font and is a fixed width (also called monospace) font - each character is the same width, which makes it good for tables and charts.

CPA   COST PER ACTION   the cost of displaying a banner advertisement once on a website, normally called an impression.
see also   BANNER ADVERTISEMENT

CPU or processor   CENTRAL PROCESSING UNIT   electronic component that provides all the functions that control your computer and run software programs; a processor contains millions of tiny electronic components that have been designed to carry out basic arithmetic and control functions. A CPU can add or subtract two numbers, move numbers from one memory location to another or control an external device. Each of the actions of a CPU is controlled by an instruction - these are the machine code instructions that are used to create software programs. The specification of a CPU is defined in several ways: its speed (for example, 200MHz) roughly defines the number of instructions that it can process each second - 200 million in this case. The power of a CPU is also defined in its data handling capabilities: a 32-bit CPU can add, subtract or manipulate numbers that are 32-bits wide. A 16-bit processor can only handle 16-bit numbers, so would take twice as long to deal with a big number. Lastly, there are two main families of CPU. The Intel-developed range of CPUs includes the 80386, 80486 and Pentium. These are used in PCs and are backwards compatible. Other manufacturers, such as AMD, are licensed to manufacture these CPUs and they work in exactly the same way. The second main family is the 68000 and PowerPC range from Motorola. These are used in Apple computers and are not directly compatible with the Intel range, although the PowerPC can run modified PC operating system software. A new range of processor, the Alpha range has been developed by Digital Equipment Corp. provides 64-bit data handling and can run Microsoft Windows NT
see also   COPROCESSOR, INTEL, MOTOROLA

CPU clock   clock inside a processor device that generates a regular signal millions of times every second to control operations and data transfer within the processor

CPU clock speed   frequency of the CPU clock that controls the operations within the processor; the clock speed is normally measured in megahertz (MHz) - millions of signals per second. For example, current PCs have processor components that work at a clock speed of over 400MHz

CR   CARRIAGE RETURN   code that (in a printer) moves the printhead to the left margin and (on a monitor) normally moves the cursor to the left margin and down one line. To enter a typed command you follow the

command by pressing the carriage return key - also called the Enter key - which is on the right-hand side of the keyboard
compare with LINE FEED

crash event that occurs when a computer goes wrong and stops working. A crash can be caused by all sorts of problems with the software, but is normally because the computer has got itself into a terminal muddle or that the software you are using has still got bugs in it. When a PC crashes, the only way to get out of this is to switch off or reset (using the reset button or by pressing Ctrl-Alt-Del at the same time). Unfortunately, you will lose any new work keyed in since you last saved your work, so make sure that you save your work regularly.

CRC CYCLIC REDUNDANCY CHECK error detection check used in modem communications and many file transfer protocols that looks at one bit in every n bits and compares this with the original to see if an error has occurred in the last n bits

crop (in a paint or image editing program) to select and use a particular area of a picture. Paint programs all have a crop tool, which lets you stretch a border around the area you want to keep, you can then cut and paste this into a new picture. In some DTP software programs, you can adjust the size of a window that displays a small part of an image

crosshair (in a drawing or paint program) shape of the cursor which looks like a cross. It is used when drawing lines or positioning an object.

cryptography study of the mathematical methods of encrypting information so that it cannot be read without a special secret key
see also CIPHER TEXT, DECRYPTION, ENCRYPTION, PLAIN TEXT

CSLIP version of the SLIP protocol that compresses data before it is transmitted, resulting in greater data transfer rate
see also SLIP

CTI COMPUTER-TELEPHONY-INTEGRATION software and hardware that links a computer to a telephone line and allows the computer to manage and distribute telephone and fax calls, operate as an answering machine, telephone exchange and voice-mail system

CTM CLICK THROUGH PER THOUSAND method of charging an advertiser for the display of a banner advertisement, where the price covers one thousand visitors clicking on the advertisement (and jumping to the advertiser's website)
see also CLICK THROUGH

CTR
see CLICK THROUGH RATE

Ctrl
see CONTROL KEY

cursor   flashing shape on the screen that shows you where the next character you type in will appear. When entering text, the cursor is normally a flashing vertical bar.
see also POINTER

cut and paste   to select a section of text or an image or other data, cut it from the original document (it is actually temporarily stored on the Clipboard) and then paste it at a new position or into a new document. To cut data, highlight the text or image and choose the Edit/Cut menu option. Move to the new position and choose the Edit/Paste menu option.
see also CLIPBOARD

cXML   COMMERCE XML   feature of the XML web page markup language that provides a standard way of producing pages about products for sale on an online shop; the new features allow designers to include information about the product being displayed and how it can be purchased by the viewer
see also DTD, E-COMMERCE, XML

cybercafé   company that provides a shop with terminals connected to the Internet as well as coffee and pastries; you can rent a terminal to try out the Internet, and have a cup of coffee

cyberspace   world in which computers and people interact, normally via the Internet; first coined by novelist William Gibson and now used to refer to the Internet, its users and culture

cybersquatting   act in which someone registers a website address, normally a trademark or brand name, then tries to sell the name to the rightful owner; although not yet illegal in most countries, court cases almost always find in favour of the company trying to recover its name. For example, if you registered the domain name 'windows.com' then tried to sell this back to Microsoft Corp. you would be guilty of cybersquatting

cyclic redundancy check (CRC)   error detection check used in modem communications and many file transfer protocols that looks at one bit in every n bits and compares this with the original to see if an error has occurred in the last n bits

Dd

DAC DIGITAL TO ANALOG CONVERTER electronic device (that is normally part of a sound card) that converts numbers into sounds or other analog signals.
compare with ADC

daemon utility program that runs on a Unix server in the background and carries out a function; often used to route network traffic, process requests, organise files, search for information or download data; for example, the main function of a web server is to process HTTP requests - this is carried out by the HTTP-daemon; daemon is often abbreviated to 'd' at the end of a protocol or function (for example, HTTPD, gated, routed)

daisy-chain to link several computers or other devices together in a daisy-chain fashion: the first is linked to the second, second to the third and so on. This is the system that is used in Ethernet networks and to link several disk drives to one computer - normally using a SCSI controller card.
see also NETWORK, SCSI

DAO DATA ACCESS OBJECTS programming interface provided with many of Microsoft's database applications that allow the developer to access Jet or ODBC compatible data sources
see also JET, ODBC

dark fibre fibre-optic cable that is not yet being used

DAT DIGITAL AUDIO TAPE small tape cassette that uses 4mm wide magnetic tape to record music or computer data in digital form. If you use a DAT for music, it provides the same quality as a compact disc. DATs are most used to provide a backup of computer data since each tape can store over 1.3Gb of data.

data collection of numbers, characters or symbols which are used by a computer. Once a computer has finished processing data, it presents this as information, which can be understood by a user.

data bus collection of 32 tiny copper parallel tracks within a computer that carry the electrical signals that make up the individual bits of data from the CPU to the memory and any adapter cards.

data carrier detect (DCD) signal (part of an RS-232C connection) that indicates that a connected modem is receiving a carrier signal from a remote modem and can or has established a communications link

data compression techniques used to reduce the amount of data storage required to hold information; data compression is very important in modems, allowing more information to be transferred in a shorter period of time, and when storing data on a disk drive. Some methods of data compression analyse the data and look for repeating patterns in the data: for example, if the data is '1110011111' this could be reduced to three-ones, two-zeros and five-ones (3, 2, 5) which might take less space
see also JPEG, MNP, PKZIP, V42BIS

data dictionary file that contains the definitions and properties of the elements that make up a database; the properties include any links to other fields or databases, data relationships, functions, records, structures, etc

data encryption techniques used to convert information into a form that cannot be read without the correct key; for example, if you want to send your credit card details to a shop on the Internet, you should ensure that you encrypt the data so that only you and the shop can read the credit card details
see also ENCRYPTION, PGP

data encryption standard (DES) system of encrypting data developed by the US government and used in many security products and software. There are different levels of security available with the DES system that are determined by the size of the key used; companies working in the USA can use very secure 50-bit or greater key sizes, but exported products have to use a less secure 40-bit key size

data rate speed of transfer of data between two devices (such as between two modems) normally specified as the number bits transferred per second
see also BAUD, BPS

data set ready (DSR) signal that is part of an RS-232C serial connection that indicates that a connected modem is linked to a telephone line and is ready to dial

data terminal equipment (DTE) electronic device at the start or end of a communications link; for example, a modem is a DTE

data terminal ready (DTR) signal that is part of an RS-232C serial connection that indicates that a connected modem is ready to transmit data

database software that lets you enter information into one big, structured file so that it can then be searched. For example, a database could contain all your contact names and addresses or your customer details or your record collection. Each separate entry is called a record and each individual part of a record is called a field. For example, if you have a database of names and addresses, my details would be stored on one record, with my first name in one field and surname in another.
see also RELATIONAL DATABASE

datagram   packet of data and a header that are sent over a network; the header specifies the destination of the data

date-time   current time and date stored on your computer; each PC has a tiny battery inside it that allows one area of memory to store the current time and date. If you need to change the time or date, use the Control Panel feature of Windows

daughterboard   type of expansion card that plugs into the main motherboard in the computer and adds extra functionality

daylight saving time   scheme that defines the changes in time over the course of a year; in the UK this means moving the clocks forward or backward by one hour each season. Windows will automatically detect if the system time and date needs to be adjusted and warn you

DCE rates   number of bits of information that a modem can transmit per second over a telephone line (such as 36,600 bps); this is not the same as the DTE rate which measures how fast a modem can exchange data with another PC and takes into account data compression

DCOM   DISTRIBUTED COMPONENT OBJECT MODEL enhanced version of the COM specification that allows applications to access objects over a network or over the Internet

DCT   DISCRETE COSINE TRANSFER   algorithm used in many image and video compression systems

DDE   DYNAMIC DATA EXCHANGE   (in Windows) system that allows two programs to exchange data. The two programs must both be running and one asks the operating system (Windows) to create a link to the second program. Most Windows applications support DDE; it is invisible to the user, but it does let you swap data between applications very easily - for example, you can use it within a wordprocessor to ask a spreadsheet to carry out a calculation.
see also   OLE

debugger   software tool used by programmers to help find and remove errors (bugs) from new software under development

decay   shape of a sound signal as it fades away. The shape of the signal as it starts is called the attack, the main sound is called the sustain and then the decay is its shape as it fades. If you have a sound card and sound editing software, you can define the decay of a sound to create your own sounds.

decimal   number system used for base 10 with the numbers 0...9. This is the number system we use every day, but it is not used by computers - they have to convert all numbers into binary, base 2
see also   BINARY

decode unit   part of a microprocessor that translates a complex instruction into a simple form that the arithmetic and logic unit (ALU) part of the processor can understand and process

decryption mathematical process using a secret key of converting encrypted cipher text back to its original plain text form that can be read

dedicated computer or printer that is only used for one particular job. If you have a network, you might find that you do a lot of printing or need to store lots of files, in which case it would make sense to set aside one computer as a dedicated PC that looks after printing - it would not be used by any user, except for printing over a network. A dedicated terminal, for example, would be used to enter one type of data - maybe stock control or to type letters, it would not be used for anything else.

default options that are used if no others are specified. For example, if you run a wordprocessor and start typing a letter, it will use the default font and typeface and the default paper size and margins. You can always change these default settings later.

deferred printing delaying printing a document until a later time. This is particularly useful if you have a very long file to print - and you want to print it out overnight so that you do not hog the printer all day. To defer printing you will need a special utility or be connected to a network to set a new time for printing.

definition ability of a display or printer to show fine detail.
see also RESOLUTION, PIXEL

defragmentation effect that is caused when a file is saved to disk, the operating system does not necessarily save it over a continuous area of the disk. If the disk is full, it might have to split the file up and save it in several little chunks in different places. This does not matter to the software or to the user, but it does mean that it takes longer to retrieve the file. Windows includes the Disk Defragmenter utility (Start/Programs/Accessories/System Tools) that will reorganise your hard disk so that all the files are stored in continuous areas of disk and can reduce the time taken to access files

delete to select text or other data and remove it from a file; to remove a file from your disk. If you delete a section of text, you can immediately undelete (using the Edit/Undelete) function. If you delete a file from your disk, you can sometimes undelete it depending on your PCis setup. If you are running Windows, there is a Recycle Bin that stores files that have deleted for a period of time - double click on the bin icon to see your file. In Windows 3.1x you can sometimes undelete a file by using the UNDELETE command from the DOS prompt.
see also RECYLE BIN, UNDELETE

delimiter special character or code that marks the end of a section of data, such as each field in a database record. The most common delimiter in databases is the comma and Return code. Commas are used to mark the end of each field and the end of each record is marked with a Return character.

demo trial version of a software application that shows you the main features, but has been crippled in some way - sometimes you cannot save the work, or it will only work for a few weeks.
see also SHAREWARE

density (i) darkness of a printed image. If the ink or toner is running out in your printer, you will notice that the images it prints are not are dark as usual: areas of solid black are grey or streaked. You can sometimes adjust the density with a dial on the printer, otherwise you will need to replace the ink or toner cartridge; (ii) the amount of data that can be stored on a floppy disk; a single-density 3.5-inch disk can store 720Kb of data, a double-density disk can store 1.44Mb of data.

depth cuing reducing the colour and intensity of an object within a three-dimensional image to provide the illusion of distance within an image

DES DATA ENCRYPTION STANDARD system of encrypting data developed by the US government and used in many security products and software

Desktop (in Windows 95 and later) refers to icons you can see on the screen when Windows starts up. The icons, status bar, Start button, Recycle Bin are all sitting on the Desktop. On your Desktop you can place folders, or shortcuts to files or programs; Windows also includes icons for a waste-bin, network access, email software and access to your disk-based files via the MyComputer icon. The Desktop contains all these icons and objects, together with a background pattern and any windows or applications that might be open.

desktop background pattern or image that is displayed by Windows as a backdrop (it is often called the wallpaper); your icons and program windows appear on top of the desktop background. To change the pattern or colour of your background or to display an image, open the Control Panel and select the Display which will let you change all the background options.

Desktop icons icons that are displayed on the Desktop. There are two icons that are always on your Windows 95 Desktop - My Computer and Recycle Bin. If you are connected to a network, you might also see an Inbox icon which lets you send and receive mail messages. Any other icons are called shortcuts and provide a link to a program or to a document. You can create a shortcut to any file by highlighting the file (in Explorer) and clicking on the right-mouse button - you will see a menu option that says 'create shortcut'. For example, if you create a shortcut to a document file called 'letter to boss', this will appear on

your Desktop; if you double-click on this icon Windows will start your
wordprocessor and automatically load the document.

desktop publishing (DTP)   design, layout and printing of documents,
books and magazines using special desktop publishing software. DTP
software allows you define the size and shape of a page, position blocks of
text and pictures and manipulate the text to change its size, colour, typeface,
leading and alignment.

Desktop taskbar   status bar that is normally displayed along the bottom
of the screen in Windows 95. At the far left is a button marked Start, at the
far right is a status display with the current time. If you click on the Start
button, you will see a list of the main activities: start a program, change the
settings for your computer, get help or, lastly, shut down the PC in an
orderly manner. If you have several windows or programs running, you will
see that each has an entry button on the desktop taskbar. If you want to
switch to another window or program, just move to the taskbar and click on
the button you want. The taskbar can be moved to the top or side of the
screen: move the pointer over the taskbar (but not over a button) and click
and drag the bar to a new position.

desktop video   combination of special software and extra hardware that
allows a user to edit video on a PC. The hardware connects the PC to a
video recorder or camera and captures the video frames; the software can
then be used to cut individual frames, re-arrange the sequence of frames and
add special effects or titles.

destination object   (in a drag and drop operation in Windows) when
you drag and drop an icon in Windows, you drag it onto a destination
object. For example, if you want to delete an icon, drag it onto the Recycle
Bin icon - this is a type of destination object. If you want to start your
wordprocessor program and automatically load an existing document, drag
the document file onto the wordprocessor program icon - the program icon
is another type of destination object.

device   electronic circuit that carries out some function; for example, a
printer is a device, so is a serial port, so is a sound card.

device dependent   software program that will only work on a certain
type of computer or with a certain type of device

device driver
see DRIVER

device manager   software (normally part of the operating system) that
lets you change the settings or configure a device such as a printer or

monitor; in Windows 95 and later, right-click on the My Computer icon on the Desktop and click on the Device Manager page tab - you can now see and manage all the devices connected to your computer

DHCP DYNAMIC HOST CONFIGURATION PROTOCOL
TCP/IP protocols that is used to assign an Internet address to nodes (workstations or servers) in a network; a special server running DHCP software manages the process of assigning addresses - a client computer can then ask this server for the address of another node on the network

dial to use a computer to make a telephone call, usually by using a modem (although a telephony device can do the same). From your PC you can send instructions to your modem - which is connected via a serial port to the PC. To dial the access number of an on-line service or to dial your friends and colleagues. To use your PC as a telephone book, you will need software that can instruct the modem to dial a number

dial modifier extra commands sent to a Hayes-compatible modem that instruct the modem to use a particular system when dialing a telephone number; for example, the command 'ATDT123' tells the modem to use tone-dialing to dial the number '123'
see also AT COMMAND SET

dial-up access a connection to the Internet that is not permanent; you need a modem (or ISDN adapter) and dial a telephone number to connect to the Internet (similar to making a normaly telephone call); when you want to connect to the Internet, your modem dials the access number and links you to the net. Most ISPs provide dial-up access for users; if you use the Internet a lot or you are a business and want to connect a network to the Internet, you can set up a permanent link to the Internet such as a leased line or ADSL line.

dial-up connection connection that uses a standard telephone line or ISDN link to connect your computer to an ISP or another computer; for example, if your main computer is at the office, but you decide to work from home, you can dial-up the office computer and access all the files stored on it or even log onto the office network and send messages - just as if you were there. To do this you need two modems, one on each PC, and the dial-up software that is supplied with Windows 95 (install the dial-up networking option of Windows to use this feature).

Dial-up Networking the part of the Windows operating system that supports and manages a dial-up link to a remote computer, for example, if you want to connect to the Internet via your ISP using a modem, the process of dialing and connecting to the ISP's remote computer is managed by the Windows Dial-up Networking software

Dialer (or Phone Dialer) utility that is provided free with Windows 95 (it is stored in the Accessories folder) - to use it you need to have a modem connected to your PC. Dialer will dial telephone numbers for you, saving you the bother; when the person answers the phone, you pick up the handset and talk as normal

dialog small window that is displayed in Windows in response to an action or to prompt the user for an answer; a dialog box is normally used to display a message (which could be a warning) from the program to the user. At the bottom of the dialog box are buttons: OK and Cancel are the two standard buttons, but there could be others depending on the message that is displayed. A simple dialog box might report back after a search and replace and just say 'replaced 23 items' with an OK button.

DIB DEVICE INDEPENDENT BITMAP standard file format used to store image information
see also GIF, JPEG

digital refers to numbers and signals that represent a number rather than a continuously variable signal. For example, a gear box is a digital device since a car can be in first, second, third or reverse but not in 'first-and-a-half'. Compare this with analog, which refers to a signal whose value can vary continuously over time rather than taking a fixed values. For example, when someone speaks, the sound wave is an analog signal; it varies smoothly as the person speaks. PCs will only work with numbers so cannot directly deal with analog signals. To get around this, you need to fit an analog-to-digital convertors (A/D convertors). For example, a sound card contains an analog to digital converter to convert the sound signal from the microphone into numbers representing the volume. If a computer wants to create a sound, it must use a digital to analog convertor (D/A convertor) to change numbers into variations in volume.
see also BINARY, DAC

digital camera device that looks like a normal camera but stores an image in digital form on a small, removable disk that can then be read by a PC

digital cash method of paying for goods over the Internet; there are several payment systems that use different models including a new bank account for each customer and an electronic purse that carries electronic tokens paid for by a customer

digital certificate
see CERTIFICATE.

Digital Equipment Corporation computer company that produces a range of high-performance workstations, mini computers and developed the new Alpha processor that offers high-performance 64-bit data handling and can run Windows NT and standard Windows applications

digital monitor monitor that can only show a fixed number of colours or shades of grey. The monitor accepts a digital signal from the computer and converts it internally into an analog signal. For example, early MDA, CGA and EGA monitors are digital monitors that can show just a few dozen colours.

compare with   ANALOG MONITOR

digital signal processing (DSP)   electronic device that carries out mathematical calculations on digital signals which have been converted from an original analog signal such as a voice, sound or video signal. These devices are normally used to create special effects in multimedia or sound cards or to enhance video or audio signals.

digital signature   method used by the sender of a message or publisher of a web site to produce a unique series of numbers that can then be checked to prove that they are the real sender (for example, if you receive a message from John Smith, you can check his digital signature to make quite sure that the message was from John Smith and not from someone else pretending to be John Smith)

see also   AUTHENTICATION

digital subscriber line (DSL)   system of transmitting data at high speed over standard telephone wire (normally referred to as POTS or standard copper wire); one of the most popular DSL implementation is the ADSL (asymetric digital subscriber line) scheme that provides a permanent, high-speed connection to the Internet over standard telephone lines

see also   ADSL, POTS

digital to analog convertor (DAC)   electronic device (normally part of a sound card) that converts numbers stored on a computer into sound

digital versatile disk
see   DVD

digital video interactive (DVI)   set of standards that define how video and sound are compressed and stored onto a disk and then de-compressed and displayed in real-time.

digital wallet   feature of new web browsers that makes it simpler and more secure to buy goods from online shops; the digital wallet contains a unique personal digital signature and allows the user to pay for your goods in many different ways, including credit card or digital cash

digitize   to convert an analog signal (such as speech, sound or light) into a numeric form which can be processed by a computer. For example, if you digitize speech you use an analog-to-digital converter to convert the sound into a series of numbers that can be stored on disk and then played back. If you digitize an image, you use a camera to convert the reflected light into an array of dots, each one a number that represents the brightness at that point.

DIMM   DUAL INLINE MEMORY MODULE   method of supplying

high-performance RAM memory chips arranged on two sides of a tiny
expansion card that can be inserted into a slot on a computer's motherboard
to upgrade the main memory; DIMM cards are similar to a SIMM card but
have more electrical pins (168 pins) and provide faster performance by
allowing 64-bit data transfers. Many high-performance PCs provide both
SIMM and DIMM sockets on the motherboard to allow a user to expand the
main memory
see also RAM, SIMM, SYNCHRONOUS DRAM

DIP switch DUAL INLINE PACKAGE SWITCH small bank of
switches that are used to configure a device

DIR DOS command that displays a list of the files stored in the current
directory.

direct cable connection utility supplied with Windows 95 that allows
you to link two computers together using a serial cable plugged into each
serial port. The two computers can exchange files or share printers. The
utility is particularly useful if you have a desktop PC and a laptop and you
want to copy files from one to the other.
see also BRIEFCASE

directory method of organising files on a disk; a directory can contain
files or other sub-directories. To imagine how a directory is related to a hard
disk, think of the hard disk as a filing cabinet: each draw is a directory. If
you open a directory, you will see lots of folders (these are sub-directories).
Look in a folder and you will see documents or files. In Windows 95,
Microsoft changed the name from 'directory' to 'folder'
see also FOLDER

directory services system that stores the full network address of every
device (and user) on a network and is used as a central telephone-directory
by all applications and users on the network to locate other users and
resources; directory services are essential when managing large distributed
networks and intranets and allow any person on any part of the network to
find the address, locate and use any resource anywhere else on the network

directory synchronisation way of ensuring that the files stored in
similar directories on two computers contain the same, up-to-date
information; normally used as a way of moving electronic mail from one
server to another

directory website a website that contains a list of other websites,
normally organised into sections and often with a search feature. Yahoo!
(www.yahoo.com) is one of the best-known directories and lists over half a
million websites.
see also SEARCH ENGINE

disc
see CD

discussion group (i) feature of a website that lets visitors discuss a particular subject; any visitor can write and post a message that is displayed to any other visitors, who can then add their comments in reply to the message; (ii) see NEWSGROUP

disk flat, circular piece of plastic that is coated with a substance that is capable of being magnetised and so store information. A hard disk consists of several rigid plastic discs arranged in parallel; a floppy disk has one thin, flexible plastic disc. The discs are spun by a motor at high speed and data is written to or read from the surface of the disc by a magnetic head (much like the one in your cassette recorder) that moves across the surface of the disc. Note, in computing you normally write 'disk' when referring to the storage device, or 'disc' when referring to a CD-ROM
see also FLOPPY DISK, HARD DISK, REMOVABLE DISK

disk cache high speed section of memory that is used to temporarily store frequently used data that has been read from the disk; the computer checks the cache to see if the data is there before it accesses the (much slower) disk and by using special controller software, this system can dramatically improve apparent disk performance

disk compression method of increasing the apparent capacity of a disk to store data. The trick is carried out by a special piece of software that compresses the data as it is being saved to disk and then decompresses the data when it is read back

disk controller electronic circuit that converts the requests for data issued by the computer into instructions that control the disk drive. In many PCs, the disk controller is built into the main circuit board of the computer (the motherboard) and will control the floppy disk and hard disk. If you want to add a CD-ROM drive, you will probably need to buy a special disk controller called a SCSI controller just for the CD-ROM drive.

disk crash error that could corrupt the data stored on your hard disk; this type of error occurs rarely and is most likely to happen if you knock your computer sharply. During normal operation, the discs inside the hard disk drive are spun by a motor, an access head is used to read and write data onto the disc's surface actually has two tiny wings and 'flies' just above the surface of the disk. If you knock the PC, the magnetic head could wobble and touch the surface of the disc. If this happens, it will damage the surface of the disc and you could lose some data

disk drive mechanical device that spins a floppy or hard disk and moves the access arm over the surface of the disk to read or write data

disk operating system (DOS) software that controls the basic

operations of the computer and the way in which data is stored on disk
see also OPERATING SYSTEM

disk partition
see PARTITION

disk tools set of software programs that help you monitor the
performance of your disk, maintain it and ensure that it is storing data
efficiently and is in tip-top condition. If you look in the
Start/Programs/Accessories folder of Windows 95, you will see the disk
tools that are provided: disk defragmentor will gather up data that is spread
all over the surface of your disk and store it neatly. Scandisk will look at
every part of the disk and check it for faults and, if it finds any, will try and
fix them. You should run both of these tools around once a month to prevent
any problems.
see also DEFRAGMENTATION

diskette
see FLOPPY DISK

display monitor that shows images or text

display adapter device that controls what you see on a monitor. The
display adapter takes instructions from the PC and converts these into
electrical signals that define the colour, images and character shapes you see
on your screen. If you have a graphics display adapter, such as an SVGA
adapter, fitted in your PC then this will manage all the high-resolution
graphics and colour and characters that you see on the monitor.

dissolve special effect that is used in presentation graphics software or
multimedia to fade out one image and the next fades in - it can also be used
with sound segments in the same way.

distributed database collection of separate data files stored on
different computers on a network that appear to a user to be one big file

distributed network network in which each node can operate as a
server storing files or working as a print server
see also PEER-TO-PEER NETWORK

distributed processing technique to enable processors or computers
to share tasks amongst themselves most effectively. Each processor
completes allocated sub-tasks independently and the results are then
re-combined.

dither (i) to smooth out any jagged edges of a curve (for example, in a
drawing or on a character) by placing shaded pixels between the pixels that
make up the curve. Some graphics programs will do this automatically and
some high-resolution laser printers will do this to improve the quality of the
print; (ii) to create a new colour by displaying a pattern of coloured pixels

that appears, to the eye, as a new colour: the eye blends the tiny pixels together and is fooled into thinking that this is a new colour. For example, a pattern of black and white pixels equally spaced would appear as grey; increase the number of black pixels and the grey darkens.

DLL DYNAMIC LINK LIBRARY file that contains part of a program stored on disk; the application loads the program code from the file when it needs it. This method ensures that program code is only loaded from disk when it is required. Large applications, such as a complex wordprocessor, might use several DLLs: one to carry out the spell-check, one to manage printing a letter and third for formatting the text. DLL files have a DLL three-letter extension and so are easy to spot using the Windows Explorer. Windows itself uses DLLs to carry out tasks that are only occasionally required - Windows stores its DLL files in the System sub-directory.

DMA DIRECT MEMORY ACCESS high-speed method of accessing the contents of memory chips in your computer; normally, if one device in your computer, such as a video card, wants to read information from the main memory it has to ask the central processor chip which then accesses the memory location and passes the information back to the video card. When using DMA, the video card temporarily takes over control of the computer from the central processor and directly retrieves the information from the memory. In the first case, the processor has to stop what it is doing and service the request from the video card. In the second case, the processor can carry out its calculations without interruption. To support DMA, you need a PC that is designed with a central bus (the electronic connections that link all the components together) that can support an intelligent video card (also called a bus-master)
see also BUS MASTER

DNS
see DOMAIN NAME SERVER, DOMAIN NAME SYSTEM

dock to connect a laptop computer to a special docking station on a desk to give it the same resources as a normal desktop

docking station or docking unit special base unit that allows a laptop computer to be inserted into it and provide the same resources as a normal desktop - such as mains power, a network adapter, connection to a full-size monitor, and extra expansion ports

DOM DOCUMENT OBJECT MODEL scheme that describes how the different parts of a web page (the text, images, and hyperlinks) are represented; each item is an object and has a set of attributes that defines how it is displayed and managed by a web browser; dynamic HTML (DHTML) uses DOM to change how a web page is displayed by a user's web browser - currently, the Microsoft and Netscape web browsers currently use different DOM specifications

domain (i) (in Windows) group of users, computers or servers on a network; (ii) (on the Internet) name for a server or organisation on the Internet

domain name unique name that identifies the location of an Internet server or computer on the Internet. For example, 'petercollin.com' is the domain name for the Peter Collin Publishing website; the domain name is in a convenient text format but refers to a physical address that locates the computer that stores the web site for the domain name; this physical address is called the IP address and is in the format '194.33.322.22' - the domain name system (DNS) is used to translate the domain name into its correct IP address. The domain name is made up of two or three parts, separated by a 'dot'. For example, 'pcp.co.uk' has the company name 'pcp' followed by the domain type 'co' (for company) and lastly the country of origin 'uk' (for the United Kingdom). Other domain types include 'com' for a company (originally those based in the USA, but now worldwide), 'edu' for an educational establishment, 'net' for a network or Internet supplier, 'gov' for a US government domain and 'mil' for a military site. With the exception of the USA, all other countries generally use the longer format for domain names with the last two characters referring to the country of origin such as 'au' for Australia, 'cn' for China, 'uk' for the UK, 'de' for Germany.

domain name registration before you can use a domain name, you must check that it is available and then fill in an application form with your country's local registration office (your ISP will also be able to help); domain name management is centered in the USA at the InterNIC organisation - you can also register a domain name directly with the InterNIC using its online order form (www.internic.net); once the domain name has been approved, it will be assigned a unique IP address that will be used by your ISP to modify the DNS to allow your web site to be located by other users
see also DNS, IP ADDRESS

domain name server (DNS) computer on the Internet that stores part or all of the domain name system database

domain name system (DNS) A method of converting the domain name to the IP (Internet protocol) address (a series of numbers) that's actually used to locate the computer. The list of names and addresses are stored on a domain-name server (also called DNS). For example, if you type in the domain name 'www.microsoft.com' in your web browser, this is passed to a DNS that translates the name to a set of numbers that points to the Microsoft server. With the correct IP address (a number in the format '123.33.322.22'), the browser can locate and make a connection to the server where the domain name home page is located. This system is also used to locate the recipient when you send an electronic mail message.
see also DISTRIBUTED DATABASE, IP

dongle special device that plugs into a port on your computer and allows a protected software application to run; dongles are used to prevent software piracy - even though the software can be copied, it cannot work without the special dongle device which is difficult to copy and manufacture

DOS DISK OPERATING SYSTEM common operating system in use before Windows 95. DOS manages how files are stored on the disk; it keeps track of where the files are stored, how big they are and when they were created. It also provides time and date functions, together with the ability to start other software programs. DOS is controlled through a command-line interface, which means that you have to type in words to get it to do something. For example, if you want to see the files stored on a disk, type 'DIR' (short for directory). DOS is flexible and quick but is difficult for beginners to use because it is not in the least bit friendly. Microsoft Windows changed this by getting rid of the command-line interface and providing a graphical user interface in which you control actions by pointing and clicking with a mouse - there is no need to learn or type in command words.
see COMMAND LINE, MS-DOS

DOS prompt indicator that shows that DOS is ready to accept a command typed in at the keyboard; the prompt usually shows the disk drive letter and current directory, for example 'C:\'. You can change the prompt using the PROMPT command
see COMMAND LINE, PROMPT

dot full stop or (US) period, used to separate the parts of an Internet domain name (between the company name, type of site and country) and normally spoken when reading an Internet addresses; for example 'pcp.co.uk' is spoken as 'pcp dot co dot uk'

dot-matrix type of printer that prints characters and numbers using a matrix of tiny dots of ink; impact dot-matrix printers use tiny metal pins that press against an inked ribbon to print the dots, while ink-jet printers fire tiny dots of ink onto the paper

dotted-decimal-notation method of writing a domain name, email address or other IP network address using a decimal point (the full stop) to separate the numeric parts of the address, for example 'www.petercollin.com' is the domain name that can be written in dotted-decimal-notation as '133.223.33.22'

dots per inch (dpi) number of individual dots that a printer can print on an inch of paper. The greater the number of dots, the smaller each must be and therefore the printer is capable of producing sharper and clearer text and graphics. A laser printer can normally print 300 dots per inch both vertically and horizontally. Some bubble-jet printers can manager 360 dots per inch horizontally, but only 200 vertically. High-resolution laser printers use a variety of techniques to increase the apparent number of dots per inch. For the best quality printed output, pick a laser printer with a resolution of 600 dots per inch. Some laser printers use tiny dots in between the main dots to smooth edges and jagged curves, giving even crisper print-outs.

dot pitch spacing between two adjacent pixels displayed on a monitor

double buffering to use two separate buffers (regions of memory) that contain the next two consecutive images within a computer animation - this provides a smoother transition between frames in the animation, making it appear smoother to the viewer. If a single buffer is used, the computer needs to retrieve the subsequent frame from the hard disk. Since it takes longer to retrieve data from a hard disk than from electronic memory, there is a slight delay which can, in complex animations, lead to a jerky playback.

double-click to click twice in rapid succession on a mouse button. If you double-click on an application icon, Windows will try and run the application. If you double-click on a file, Windows will try and start the application that was used to create the file. A double-click has to be done fast enough for Windows to realise what you are doing! To practice, use the utilities that come with your mouse. As a tip, rest your hand on the mouse with your finger resting gently on the left-hand button. Do two short presses in quick succession. If you try and hold the mouse too tightly or press down too far, you will not be able to double-click fast enough. If you move the pointer over an icon and do a single click, the icon will be selected and you can change the icon's name or properties. Lastly, a double-click normally only refers to the left-hand mouse button, since the right-hand button is used to control the properties of an object.
see also DRAG-AND-DROP

double-density disk diskette that can store twice as much data as a single-density diskette

double-speed drive refers to a CD-ROM drive that spins the disc at twice the speed of a normal drive. The advantage of this is that the data can be read from the disc twice as fast (since the disc is travelling past the read-head at twice the speed) and so you will notice that the response of multimedia titles is quicker and programs load faster; current PCs use CD-ROM drives with a 24-times speed

DoubleSpace software program that is part of MS-DOS 6 and is used to provide disk compression.
see DISK COMPRESSION

down computer that is not currently working, either because it is switched off or due to a fault

download to copy a file from a remote computer onto your local computer; normally this means copying a file from a remote server over a

modem link or Internet connection or via a cable link from a laptop
compare with UPLOAD

downsize change in way a company uses computers so that tasks that
were previously carried out by a mainframe or minicomputer are now
carried out by cheaper networked PCs

downward compatibility
see BACKWARDS COMPATIBLE

dpi
see DOTS PER INCH

draft quality printed output that is formatted and readable, but might not
have all the illustrations in place or uses ragged typeface which are both
faster to print

drag and drop feature of Windows (and other graphical operating
systems including Apple System 7, IBM OS/2 and Unix/X) in which you
can move a highlighted icon or piece of text. For example, if you want to
delete a file from the Windows 95 Desktop, you move the pointer to the
file's icon, click once to highlight the icon and then press and hold down the
left-hand mouse button. You have now 'picked up' the icon and can move it
around the Desktop. With the mouse button still pressed down, move it to
on top of the Recycle Bin icon - the Recycle Bin icon will change colour to
indicate that it has recognised that you want to use it. Now release the
mouse button and you will have deleted the file using drag and drop. In
other applications, for example Word for Windows or other wordprocessors,
you can highlight a section of text in a letter and then click and hold down
the left-hand mouse button to move the section of text to another place in
the document - or to another document

DRAM DYNAMIC RANDOM ACCESS MEMORY electronic memory
component that will retain information for as long as it has electrical power
supplied; DRAM is used for the main memory of almost all computers
compare with STATIC RAM

drive mechanical unit that holds a disk - which could be a floppy disk,
CD-ROM or a hard disk - and responds to the instructions of a controller
card. The drive will have a motor that spins the disk and an access head that
can be positioned over the disk. The access head can, in the case of a floppy
or hard disk, write or read data from the surface of the disk. In the case of a
CD-ROM, the access head uses a tiny laser to read the holes etched in the
surface of the disc.

drive array multiple hard disk drives linked together with an intelligent
controller that uses the drives to store multiple copies of the data on each
drive for reliability or parts of each data on each drive for speed
see also RAID

drive letters Windows and DOS use a system of letters to identify the different drives that are fitted to the PC. A PC can have up to 26 drives fitted - one for each letter of the alphabet. Each drive is normally given a drive letter, for example the hard disk is normally drive 'C'. This is usually written as 'C:'. The standard configuration is: drive A: is a floppy disk drive, drive B: a second floppy disk drive, C: is the hard disk drive and D:is a CD-ROM drive. If you are connected to an office network, you might have other drive letters that actually map to a disk drive on someone else's PC. Lastly, if you have a very big hard disk drive, it might have been partitioned when you bought the PC. This means that the drive has been split up into manageable sections, called partitions. For example, if you have a hard disk drive with a 4Gb capacity, you might find it more useful to split it up into two sections each 2Gb in size. In this case, the first would be referred to as drive C: and the second as drive D:. If you added a CD-ROM drive to this PC, it would now be called drive E:.

driver a special piece of software that sits between Windows and a peripheral and translates the instructions from Windows into a form that the peripheral can understand. In DOS, before Windows 95 arrived, all drivers were loaded when the PC was first switched on from within the CONFIG.SYS file. Now, a lot of drivers are built into Windows, although some will still have to be loaded from the CONFIG.SYS file - which is why your screen flashes between text and graphics mode when you first switch on your PC and it loads Windows 95.
see also CONFIG.SYS

drop-down menu a list of options that is displayed beneath a menu bar when you select a particular menu option. For example, if you select the File menu from any Windows application, a list of further options is displayed beneath the word 'File' - this is a drop-down menu

DSL
see DIGITAL SUBSCRIBER LINE

DSP DIGITAL SIGNAL PROCESSOR electronic device that carries out mathematical calculations on digital signals which have been converted from an original analog signal such as a voice, sound or video signal. These devices are normally used to create special effects in multimedia or sound cards or to enhance video or audio signals.

DSTP DATA SPACE TRANSFER PROTOCOL scheme used to store and retrieve web-based data using the XML page markup system

DTE DATA TERMINAL EQUIPMENT electronic device at the start or end of a communications link; for example, a modem is a DTE

DTE rates measure of how fast a device (normally refers to a modem) can exchange data with another PC taking into account data compression and coding systems; the DTE rate is normally much higher than the DCE rate

DTMF DUAL TONE MULTI-FREQUENCY system of dialling a telephone number using individual tones (sounds) for each number

DTP DESKTOP PUBLISHING using special software to layout text and images on screen, apply text formatting and special fonts before printing out the finished page on a high-resolution laser printer which could then be used as artwork for a commercial printer to print a book, brochure or newsletter

dual-scan display colour LCD screen that updates the image on screen in two passes; dual-scan displays are cheaper than TFT displays, but are not as bright nor provide as crisp an image
see also LCD, TFT DISPLAY

duplexing technique to increase the fault tolerance of networks. In a duplexed disk system, there are two identical controllers and disk drives. Data is written to both via a separate controller. If one goes wrong, the second device is switched in under software control with no effect to the user. This is a more fault-tolerant system than disk mirroring.

DVD DIGITAL VERSATILE DISK highly efficient and flexible way of storing data on a CD-ROM disc, offering up over twenty times the storage capacity of a standard CD-ROM - a standard CD-ROM can store 650Mb of data, a DVD can store between 4.7Gb and 15.9Gb of data. This increased capacity provides vast data capacity and a DVD can carry a full-length feature film. Most new computers now include CD-ROM drives that can read DVD discs as well as standard CD-ROMs; because of their popularity for storing films, stand-alone DVD players are available that plug into a television set and provide similar playback features of a video machine.

DVD+RW type of rewritable DVD disc that allows a user to store data on the disc; DVD discs offer much greater storage capacity than a standard compact disc in a similar-sized disc; this standard was developed by Hewlett-Packard, Philips and Sony and has a capacity of 3GB per side

DVD-RAM type of rewritable DVD disc that allows a user to store data on the disc; this standard was developed by the DVD Consortium and competes with the DVD-RW standard - it provides storage capacity of 2.6GB per side

DVD-ROM type of compact disc, a flat disc, that can store up to 17GB of data; the data is stored in the surface of the disc, which is then coated with a transparent plastic layer to protect the data. DVD discs are read using a device that shines a laser beam onto the spinning disc; DVD disc players are backward-compatible older CD formats and can read CD-ROM or DVD-ROM discs. DVD-ROMs can be used to store computer data, software programs, images or video

DVD-video standard that defines how full-length films can be compressed and stored on a DVD disc and played back on a dedicated player attached to a television set or viewed on a computer fitted with a DVD drive

DX suffix after an Intel processor model number that signifies that the processor has a floating-point arithmetic unit, a 32-bit data path and a built-in cache; for example 80486DX has these features, the 80486SX does not

dynamic data exchange (DDE) in Windows, a method for two programs to exchange data. The two programs must both be running and one asks the operating system (Windows) to create a link to the second program. Most major Windows applications support DDE; it is invisible to the user, but it does let you swap data between applications very easily - for example, you can use it within a wordprocessor to ask a spreadsheet to carry out a calculation.
see also   OLE, DLL

dynamic link library
see   DLL

dynamic RAM
see   DRAM

Ee

EBCDIC EXTENDED BINARY CODED DECIMAL INTERCHANGE CODE
numerical system used mainly on IBM computers in which each number represents a different character or symbol, similar to the ASCII system

ebook
see ELECTRONIC BOOK

echo reflection of a wave along a telephone line or other transmission line that causes interference and errors in the data being transmitted

e-commerce ELECTRONIC COMMERCE general term that refers to the process of buying and selling products on the Internet

ECP EXTENDED CAPABILITIES PORT high-speed parallel port that transfers data between a PC and a peripheral, normally allowing two-way communications so that the peripheral (such as a printer) can send status information back to the computer

edge (in a signal) the fraction of a second when a signal changes from high to low or from low to high

edge connector electrical connector along the edge of an expansion card; normally arranged as a row of thin metal strips leading to the edge of the card, an edge connector can be inserted into an expansion bus of a computer to allow electrical signals to be transferred to and from the expansion card

edge-triggered (something) that is started by a change in a signal; for example, in your computer there are many devices that are activated by an edge-triggered interrupt - this means that they are activated by the change in an interrupt signal, either when it changes from high to low or from low to high
see also INTERRUPT

EDO memory EXTENDED DATA OUTPUT MEMORY latest development in memory components that can provide better performance by temporarily storing the last piece of data that was saved to memory in a cache ready to be read back from memory; this means that the processor can read more data from the memory component within one clock cycle, so improves the amount of data that can be transferred

edu suffix at the end of an Internet domain name that indicates that the

organisation is an educational institute rather than a commercial company
see also DOMAIN NAME

EEMS ENHANCED EXTENDED MEMORY SPECIFICATION
improved version of the EMS specification that now forms part of EMS 4.0
see also EMS

EEPROM ELECTRICALLY ERASABLE PROGRAMMABLE
READ-ONLY MEMORY
memory chip that can store data without requiring power (like a
conventional ROM chip) but its contents can be erased by a special signal
applied to one of its connections
see also EPROM, RAM, ROM

EGA an old popular standard for colour graphics that is now hardly ever
used. It could display images at the highest resolution of 640x350 pixels and
was superseded by VGA.

EIDE EXTENDED INTEGRATED DRIVE ELECTRONICS
enhanced IDE specification that improves the performance and data transfer
rates to and from a hard disk drive
see also IDE

eight-bit system (8-bit) processor and computer hardware that works
with eight bits of data at a time; the first PC used an 8-bit processor, but
current Pentium processors can manipulate much larger quantities of data -
32-bits at a time - to provide better performance and functionality
see also THIRTY-TWO BIT

EISA ELECTRONICS INDUSTRY STANDARDS ASSOCIATION
group of computer manufacturers that together defined an expansion bus for
the PC. The expansion bus is called an EISA bus and is a rival to the MCA
bus that was developed by IBM. Both types of bus allow expansion cards to
take control of the computer and so improve the speed at which data is
transferred between the expansion card and the computer. Most PCs have an
ISA expansion bus which allows 16 bits of data to be transferred, the EISA
and MCA buses allow 32-bits of data to be transferred. The advantage of
EISA over MCA is that you can still use the older ISA expansion cards in
an EISA slot, wheras an MCA expansion slot will only work with special
MCA cards.

electronic book *or* **ebook** electronic version of a book; the text and
any pictures are stored in a file format that can then be displayed using
special software on a PC or laptop screen or on a dedicated portable (or
hand-held) device that consists of a screen and buttons to move from one
page to the next
see also ADOBE ACROBAT, MICROSOFT READER

electronic commerce
see E-COMMERCE

electronic mail or email way of sending and receiving messages between users on a network or over the Internet; messages can be simple text or can include attached files (such as a document or database); some electronic mail systems allow enhanced text (called rich text) messages with bold, italics and other formatting features. If you are connected to a local area network, you will need to use email software that works on a local area network such as cc:Mail or Microsoft Mail. Network email software normally uses one of the three main standards (MAPI, VIM or MHS) to send and receive messages over the local network. If you are connected to the Internet you will need to use Internet email software. Many web browsers (including Microsoft's IE and Netscape Navigator) include Internet email features in their applications, or you can use a dedicated program such as Qualcomm's Eudora. Internet email software communicates with a mail server (normally located at your Internet provider) and sends and receives mail messages using one of the three main Internet mail standards (POP3, SMTP, IMAP)
see also ATTACHMENT, IMAP, MAPI, MIME, MHS, POP3, SMTP

email
see ELECTRONIC MAIL

email-enabled application software application (such as a wordprocessor or spreadsheet) that includes a direct link to an email application to allow a user to send the current document as an email. In Microsoft applications, there is a Send option under the File menu that allows a user to send the document using the Microsoft Exchange email software

embedding feature of Windows that lets you include a document, picture or sound into another document using the OLE standard. For example, if you type a letter in WordPad and then want to add your signature, start the Paint program, draw your signature and drag the image into the WordPad document. Embedding really means that you can include any compatible data object (such as the Paint file) in any other document
see also OLE

EMS (expanded memory system) system in a PC that defines the section of memory that lies above the 640Kb mark. Below the 640Kb mark the memory is called conventional memory and any program can use this. If you add more memory to your computer, you are actually adding expanded memory (since your PC will already have a basic 640Kb of memory fitted). If your PC has 32Mb of memory fitted, the first 640Kb is conventional memory, the remainder is EMS

emulate to imitate something else. For example, a special piece of software running on an Apple Macintosh can emulate Microsoft Windows and allow you to run PC programs on a Macintosh

enabled function or menu item that is available to be used. If an option on a menu appears in grey text rather than black, this indicates that these are not enabled and that you cannot use the option. For example, if you are using a wordprocessor and have not selected an area of text, the copy and cut commands under the Edit menu are displayed in grey and cannot be used. If you now select an area of text, look at the Edit menu again and you will see these options now appear in black and have been enabled.

encode to convert data from one form to another, for example to compress data

encryption to convert a plain, readable information into a secure form that can only be read using a special password or key
see DES, PGP, SSL

end user person that will use a program or product that a developer is creating

Energy Star standard and logo on a monitor, computer or other electrical device; the standard means that the product has been specially designed to save electricity: if it is switched on but has not been used for a while it will shut off some parts of the electrical circuits to save electricity. For example, many monitors will shut off power after five minutes of inactivity to save electricity

engine part of a software package that carries out a particular function; for example, a search engine is the part of a multimedia title that lets a user search for text in a multimedia book

Enter key key on a keyboard (on the right-hand side) that produces a carriage-return code when pressed by a user; the Enter key is used in a wordprocessing package to end a paragraph of text or enter a new line, it is used with an operating system (such as DOS) to execute a command
see also CARRIAGE RETURN, COMMAND LINE

enumeration method of identifying resources or objects using a unique number

environment electronic space in which you work when you use your computer. When you switch on your PC and it loads DOS or Windows, it creates an 'environment' for you to work in. The environment can be changed to suit your needs - by defining its characteristics such as colour or wallpaper - and by setting up a standard printer, keyboard and fonts that can be used

environment variable special container within the computer's environment that holds information that a program can use. For example, if you are on a network there might be an environment variable set with your user name, another with the location of the program you are using. As a user you would not normally see or use these variables.

EPP ENHANCED PARALLEL PORT standard that defines the way data can be transferred at high speed through a parallel port connector (at the back of your computer); a standard parallel port can transfer data at around 150Kb per second, wheras an EPP port can transfer data at around 500Kb per second
compare with USB

EPROM ERASABLE PROGRAMMABLE READ-ONLY MEMORY memory component that can be programmed using a special electrical signal and it will retain this information even without electrical power; to erase the information, the component is normally placed under an ultraviolet light source
see also FLASH ROM, ROM

EPS ENCAPSULATED POSTSCRIPT method of saving a formatted page or document to a file; the file contains PostScript page description commands. EPS is used as the filename extension for a file that contains PostScript commands - for example, 'PAGE1.EPS'
see also POSTSCRIPT

erase (i) tool in a graphics or paint program that sets an area of an image to the same colour as the background, effectively removing it - just like a pencil eraser; (ii) to permanently remove a stored file from disk
see also DELETE

error box or message small window that pops up to tell you an error has occurred - for example, if you have tried to do something that the program does not understand, or if an error has occurred in the program

error correction technique used to correct any errors that have been introduced during transmission; high speed modems now have error correction systems built-in to ensure that the data received is correct
see LAPM, MNP, V42

errors (in a program) problems caused by mistakes that have not been corrected by the software developer who created the program. In a commercial program that you buy from a dealer there should be very few

errors; if you do come across a strange error message, telephone the dealer
and he can advise as to whether this is a bug or a mistake on your part. Bugs
are the reason that software companies release patches (which fix a
particular bug or error in a program - these are normally available free from
the manufacturer or can downloaded from the manufacturer's web site)
see also BUG, PATCH

Esc key key on a PC keyboard, in the top left-hand corner, that is
sometimes used to cancel an action. In Windows, pressing the Esc key is the
same as selecting the Cancel button. If you press Alt-Esc within Windows
you will cycle between any program windows that are currently running

escape character ASCII code number 27 that is used to send control
data to some printers or programs

escape sequence method of switching a Hayes-compatible modem
into command mode by sending the three characters '+++' allowing a user
to enter new commands whilst still online
see also AT COMMAND SET

ESDI ENHANCED SMALL DEVICE INTERFACE standard
specification that defines how a disk drive or tape drive is connected to a
computer; this specification is now rarely used, the popular choice is either
IDE or the SCSI control system
see also IDE, SCSI

Ethernet standard used for networking; Ethernet defines the type of
cable, signal and language used if you connect several computers together.
Normally refers to transmission of packets of data at 10Mbits/second over
co-axial cable with BNC connectors. It defines how the packets of data are
formed, using IEEE standard 802.3; variations include the 10Base-T
standard that uses twisted-pair cabling, 100Base-T that transmits at
100Mbps and various proprietary high-speed networks
see also 10BASE-T, CHEAPERNET, TOKEN RING

Eudora electronic mail program used to send, receive and manage
messages sent over the Internet; there are two versions of this popular
product - a free, entry-level version and a more powerful commercial
version

even parity way of transmitting data over a communications link that
provides a very basic way of checking for transmission errors; the
communications software counts how many '1is there are in each block of
data it will transmit and sets an extra check bit to ensure that there is an
even number of '1is in the data. If you are setting up your communications
software to dial into a bulletin board system or online service, you will need
to know whether the service requires even or odd parity. Communications
software packages like HyperTerminal in Windows 95 let you set the parity
to either even or odd

event action that occurs during the course of time; Windows works by responding to events. For example, if you click on the mouse button, this generates a button down event, then a button up event; if you press a key, it generates a key-press event, and so on. Windows waits for events and then responds to them - it wonit do something until you tell it to do so. This type of program is called event-driven.

e-wallet feature of new web browsers that lets you enter a range of different ways of paying for your shopping. You might include your credit card and e-cash, then open your e-wallet when you visit a shop. It's one future method of managing spending on the net.

Exchange application supplied with Windows 95 that provides features that allow you to manage your communications including electronic mail and fax. Exchange can control a fax modem to send and receive fax messages; it can send and receive electronic mail messages with other PCs linked together in a network and it can send and receive messages to users linked to the Internet via either CompuServe or a dial-up Internet account. If you want to use Exchange to provide electronic mail for a small network then you can use the software supplied, however if you want to support several servers or postoffices you will need to upgrade to the commercial package, Exchange Server, that provides a wider range of features for larger networks and company sites. Exchange has now been replaced by Microsoft Outlook and Outlook Express.
see OUTLOOK

extended data output memory
see EDO MEMORY

EXE file three-letter filename extension that indicates that a file is a program and can be run. If you start a DOS window from Windows (or if you are already in DOS) type 'DIR' and you will see the names of all the files stored in the current directory on your hard disk. To the right of the file name is the three letter filename extension that describes the type of file. DOC means document, WAV means Wave or sound file, EXE means executable - a program file that can be run. To run a file with an EXE extension, type in its name (you do not need to add the EXE suffix) and press return.

executable (file) file containing the instruction data that makes up a program; to run the program, in Windows double-click on the icon or file name

execute to run a command or program on a computer

exit to leave, quit or stop running a program on a computer. If you are using Windows, you can press the Alt key and F4 together to exit the program, or choose the File/Exit menu option

expanded memory   extra RAM memory fitted to your computer that is located at an address above 1Mb, but that uses special software to fool your computer into thinking that the memory is located below 1Mb and so can be used by any application. The special software that carries out the deception is called an expanded memory manager and needs to be loaded before you run any other applications. If you are using Windows it will work out for itself how it should best use the memory fitted to your PC
see also   EXTENDED MEMORY, MEMAKER

expansion bus   series of electrical wires that carry the signals between the main processor chip in your PC and the other components, such as the video display card, the disk drive or serial port.

expansion card   set of electronic components fitted to a small piece of plastic that can expand the functionality of your PC. For example, if you want to connect your PC to a network, you will need to add the electronic components that control the way signals are sent over the network cable - this is done by buying a network expansion card. You can fit several expansion cards to a PC by plugging them into an empty expansion slot. To do this, you will need to open up your PC: you can easily damage the sensitive electronic components, so follow the instructions in your computer's manual.

expansion slot   connector fitted to the motherboard that lets an expansion card connect to the expansion bus of a computer. The electrical signals from the expansion bus can be read by the expansion card.

expert system   program that lets a computer imitate an expert for a particular human activity. For example, some expert systems carry details of every type of medical symptom and link these to the cause

Explorer   program supplied with Windows 95 that lets you manage all the files stored on a disk. With Explorer you can copy files, move files from one folder to another, create new folders, and rename or delete files and folders. Explorer can also view folders on other PCs in a network. To start Explorer, click on the Start button, then choose Programs/Explorer. Windows 3.1x users have a similar utility called File Manager that is in the Accessories group.

export   to convert a file from its native format to another format so that it can be read by a different program. For example, if you have written a letter in Microsoft Word, and want to give it to a friend who uses Wordperfect for Windows, you need to export the Word document to a Wordperfect format file using the File/Save As option in Word.

extended binary coded decimal interchange code (EBCDIC)
numerical system used mainly on IBM computers in which each number represents a different character or symbol, similar to the ASCII system

extended character set set of 128 special characters that includes accents, graphics, and symbols. Each font has a different set of extended characters; to see the range and to use a particular character in the set, start the Character Map utility that is provided with Windows. The normal range of characters - A to Z, numbers and punctuation - each has a code assigned called its ASCII number. For example, 'a' has an ASCII code of 97 in any font. The ASCII codes are only defined for the code numbers between 0 and 127. The characters represented by the ASCII codes between 128 and 255 are the special characters. If you want to enter any character into a document, in WordPad say, you can directly type in its ASCII code number rather than using the Character Map utility. For example, if you are writing a letter in French, you would need the é (e with an acute accent) character. This has an ASCII code of 233; to enter this, hold down the Alt key and enter 0233 on the numeric keypad, release the Alt key and the character will appear.

extended memory section of main memory in your PC that lies above the 1Mb mark. The first 640Kb of memory is called conventional memory, the next 384Kb is called upper memory and any memory above 1Mb is called extended memory. The difference between extended memory and expanded memory is that any software program can use expanded memory, since it does not realise that it is using it (the memory manager fools the software), but software needs to be specially written to be able to use extended memory
see also EXPANDED MEMORY, EMS

extension (in a file stored on a disk) filename has the main name and a three letter code at the end that generally indicates the type or format of the file. For example, a filename in MS-DOS might be LETTER1 with the extension DOC; this is written with a full-stop separating the two parts of the name 'LETTER1.DOC'. The three-letter extension, DOC, indicates that the file is a document. Similarly, BMP means a bitmap graphic file, EXE means an executable program file and so on. In DOS and Windows 3.1x, the total length of the filename cannot exceed 11 characters, with a three letter extension this leaves just eight characters for the filename. In Windows 95 this has been changed and you can enter long file names.
see also LONG FILENAME

external something that is not fitted inside a computer's casing

external modem a modem that is in its own case with its own power supply and connects to the computer using a cable; most modems are internal (they are fitted inside the computer case and are plugged into an expansion connector) but external modems have the advantage that they can be easily moved from one computer to another.
see also MODEM

extranet an internal company network (an intranet) that has a connection to the public Internet and allows users to gain access via the Internet; often used to provide access to people in the company who are working away from the office. A normal intranet does not normally allow access via the public Internet and includes security measures that protect against hackers and unauthorised users.

Ff

facsimile
see FAX

fan electrical device that blows cool air onto a heat-sensitive device or that circulates cool air within a computer's case. If your computer is fitted with one of the newest processor chips, then you probably have two fans inside your computer's case: one glued on top of the processor chip itself to ensure that the processor remains cool and the other, larger, fan fitted to the back of the computer case to circulate cool air over the components inside the computer

FAQ FREQUENTLY ASKED QUESTIONS web page or help file that contains common questions and their answers related to a particular subject

FAT FILE ALLOCATION TABLE data file that is stored on a disk and that contains the name, size, date and location of all the files that are stored on the disk. When you open a document in a wordprocessor, the wordprocessor asks DOS to open the file - it does this by looking through the file allocation table to find the position on the disk where the file is stored. The FAT is hidden, so you cannot see it, nor can you easily delete it - without it you cannot retrieve any of the information stored on your disk. Sometimes, the FAT can get corrupted - to remedy this problem run SCANDISK (a utility supplied with Windows) or a commercial disk recovery program

fault tolerance the ability of a computer or an electronic device to continue to operate even if there is an unexpected fault or failure in a part of its hardware or software. For example, many server computers have two disk drives, one with an exact copy of the data stored on the other (called a mirror); if one disk drive fails or develops a fault, the second drive is used instead without any loss of data.

fax *or* **facsimile functions** PCs can send and receive fax transmissions to and from any normal office fax machine. To send or receive a fax from your PC you will need a special modem that can handle fax data. If you want to send handwritten notes, you will also need a scanner - letters and graphics created on your PC can be sent directly via the fax modem. To control the modem, you will also need special fax software; Windows is supplied with several utilities that allow you to send and receive faxes (Windows 95 uses the Exchange program to receive faxes). If your

computer receives a fax, it is stored as an image, which you can then view
on screen or print out. If you want to send a fax, there are several ways of
doing this: the easiest is to install the fax modem as a type of printer. If you
want to fax a letter to someone, type the letter in your wordprocessor and
select File/Print - you will see your normal printer listed together with the
fax modem. Choose the fax modem and you will be asked to type in the fax
telephone number of the recipient.

fax group   method of defining the basic features of a fax machine or
modem: groups 1 and 2 are old and rarely used now, group 3 is the most
common standard used today, groups 3bis and 4 provide higher speed and
better resolution of transmission

fax modem   modem that can be used to send and receive faxes to and
from a standard fax machine as well as being used as a modem to connect to
other computers
see also   MODEM

FDD
see   FLOPPY DISK DRIVE

FDDI   FIBRE DISTRIBUTED DATA INTERFACE   ANSI standard for a
high-speed transmission system that uses fibre optic cable and can transmit
data at up to 100Mbps; the cable is arranged in a dual-ring topology and is
normally used to connect servers together; FDDI II is an extension to FDDI
standard to allow transmission of analog data (such as sound and voice) in
digital form together with other digital network data

fibre distributed data interface
see   FDDI

field   (in a database) individual container that can hold a particular type of
information. For example, if you have a contacts list of your customers,
each entry is called a record and the various parts of each record are called
fields - there would be a separate field for the name, address, telephone
number and so on.

FIFO   FIRST IN FIRST OUT   method of arranging a queue so that the
first item placed in the queue is the first one to be processed

file   collection of information stored on a hard disk or floppy disk; the file
has a name that identifies it and could be a letter, a spreadsheet or a
program. To see the files that are stored on a disk, either type in the 'DIR'
command at the DOS prompt or, if you are using Windows, start the
Windows Explorer utility
see also   DIR, DOS, WINDOWS EXPLORER

file attributes
see   ATTRIBUTES

file format way in which data is stored in a file. For example, every document created within Word for Windows is stored as a Word format file that includes special codes to tell Word how the margins are setup, the fonts that are used and if any images are included. Each type of program stores information in its own file format - this means that it is difficult to read a file that is been created by a different program to the one you are using. To get round this, you can either use the import function of a program or use one of the standard file formats that let you exchange data between different programs.

file locking method of preventing two users from trying to alter the contents of a file at the same time; the first user locks the file and can make any changes he wants, the second user must wait until the first user has finished using the file and has unlocked the file before he can make his changes. File locking is carried out automatically by any software program that runs on a network and is used by more than one person at a time

File Manager program supplied with Windows 3 that lets you manage all the files stored on a disk. With File Manager you can copy files, move files from one directory to another, create new directories, and rename or delete files. To start File Manager, open the Accessories group and double-click on the icon. Windows 95 and later includes a more sophisticated program, Windows Explorer.
see also EXPLORER

file properties (in Windows 95) attributes that are assigned to a particular file, including its name, date that it was created, owner and so on which are all stored in the file's properties page. To view these properties, highlight the file with a single click from within Windows Explorer and click on the right-hand mouse button - now choose the Properties menu option to view the file's properties page

file server
see SERVER

file sharing feature that allows users on two or more computers connected via a network to access one file stored on a computer. If you want to share a file with other users on the network, you normally need to share the folder or directory in which the file is stored; if more than one user will share the file at the same time, you will need to set the file attributes so that the Share attribute is switched on

file transfer to send a file from one computer to another, normally over a serial connection such as a modem link or cable between a desktop and laptop PC.

file transfer protocol
see FTP

filename unique name that identifies a file stored on disk. In DOS, a filename is made up of eight characters plus a three character filename extension that defines the type of file. For example, a letter might be called LETTER1.DOC. In Windows 95/98 you can enter long file names that are not limited to eight characters so the same file could be called 'Letter to Roger re proposal'. You can use most characters in a filename, except for a space. It is also possible to have two or more files with the same filename, but stored in different directories or folders on a disk
see also EXTENSION, LONG FILENAME

filter (i) function in a database program that selects a group of records from the database according to a particular feature, for example, if you want to display all records where the country field is equal to France you would use the filter function (in Microsoft Access, select the Filter menu option). If you want to find a single record you would use the search function; (ii) feature of a program that lets you convert data from one format to another, for example, you can filter 1-2-3 spreadsheet files using the Import function of Microsoft Excel so that Excel can read the file correctly (in this context, filter is normally called Import); (iii) (in an email program) feature that will automatically move, copy or forward new email messages based on a set of rules you have defined (for example, move all messages with the word 'project' to the new projects folder

Find utility program supplied with Windows 95 that will search through any disk - on your PC or, if you are connected to a network, on any other PC - for a particular file, folder or computer; to use the Find function, select the Start/Find menu option

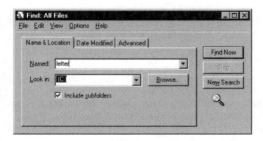

Windows includes a search feature, Find, that can locate files by name or content.

finger (on the Internet) software program that will retrieve information about a user based on their electronic mail address; the program does this by asking DNS servers for more information about the location of the user
see also DNS

firewall security system fitted to a server connected to the Internet; if you connect your main office server to the Internet to provide a web server, or if you connect your web server computer to the office server without a firewall, then any user on the Internet could gain access to your office server by getting around the very basic WWW security functions. To stop hackers gaining access to your internal office network via an Internet connection, you should fit a firewall. The firewall could be sophisticated software that checks the address of each user that tries to access your server and blocks any unknown users, or could be a hardware device that prevents sensitive information travelling between the office server and the WWW server. If you are connecting your desktop computer to the Internet using a modem, there is a very slight risk that someone could get into your computer whilst you are connected - but this does not warrant a firewall. If your office is permanently connected to the Internet (for example, to provide electronic mail) then there is more of a risk and you should install a firewall system

firmware a read-only memory (ROM) device that contains data or software; for example, an EPROM or ROM chip that has data or a program stored on it is firmware

flame (on the Internet) to send a rude or angry message to a user; normally in response to an offensive action, a controversial article, or a spammed article (an article that has been posted to multiple newsgroups)

flash ROM electronic memory component that contains data that can normally only be read, but does allow new data to be stored in the memory using a special electrical signal; this type of memory component is now often used to store the BIOS or configuration information for a modem or PC card storage device. Normally, this configuration information is used to setup the modem each time it is switched on, but if the manufacturer improves the features of the modem, the user can upgrade the functions of his modem by storing this new configuration data in the Flash ROM rather than replacing the chip or the entire modem
see also PC CARD, ROM

flat screen display monitor that has been manufactured with a flat, square-edged front to the monitor; older monitors often had a curved front to the display which meant that the image could appear distorted at the edges. To provide a flat screen, a monitor has to be manufactured using complex glass-blowing techniques and electronics within the monitor - which is why these monitors are often more expensive

flatbed scanner scanner in which the original artwork to be scanned is placed face down on a sheet of glass; a lid is closed over this and the scan-head is moved (below the sheet of glass) across the artwork using accurate motors, converting the image into a graphics file that you can view on your computer. Flatbed scanners are more accurate than hand-held scanners and are normally more expensive.

floating point system of writing a number using a decimal point; for example, '134' is an integer wheras '134.567' is a floating point number. These numbers are more difficult for a computer to manipulate so some computers can be fitted with a coprocessor chip that is dedicated to handling floating point numbers

floppy disk convenient, portable storage device that stores information on a thin, flexible disk. The disk is coated with a magnetic material that is rather like an audio cassette tape. The information is stored on the disk as a series of magnetic signals using a disk drive. The flexible disk is protected from scratching within a rigid plastic case with a sliding window on one side to allow the disk drive access to the surface of the disk. There are two standard sizes of floppy disk - a larger 5.25-inch disk can store 1.2Mb of data and is now rarely used. The more robust and smaller 3.5-inch disk can store 1.44Mb of data and disk drives of this size are fitted to almost every new PC.

flow control method of controlling the transfer of data between two devices (for example, between a computer and modem); there are two types of flow control - hardware flow control (also called CTS/RTS) uses the hardware to manage the transfer; software flow control (also called XON/XOFF) requires the software to generate and decode special messages sent with the data, it is slower than the hardware system

FM FREQUENCY MODULATION to change the frequency of one signal according to another signal. Often used as a method of representing data through changes in the frequency of a signal (the carrier); often used as a method of carrying data over fibre-optic or telephone cables (for example, many modem standards use FM to transmit data)

FM synthesizer way of creating sounds by combining base signals of different frequencies; for example, sound cards using this technique create sounds of a piano, drum or guitar by combining different frequencies at different levels to recreate the complex sound of a musical instrument. *compare with* WAVETABLE

focus (i) to adjust a monitor so that the image that is displayed on the screen is sharp and clear; (ii) a particular window or field that is currently ready to accept a user's command - for example, if there are several check-boxes displayed in a window on screen, when you move to one of the check-boxes using the Tab key or mouse, this check-box is the focus and your actions control this particular box, not the others. In Windows, the object that currently has the user's focus has a dotted line around it.

folder (i) (in Windows 95) name for a directory; a folder can contain files or other folders - just like a filing cabinet; (ii) (in an email application) container for mail messages that helps the user organise his messages; many email applications provide a feature called rules that allow the messages to be automatically placed in folders according to a set of user-defined rules. For example, if a message arrives regarding project X, you can create a rule that will automatically move this message in the folder for all messages to do with project X

see also DIRECTORY, RULES

Windows supports folders that can contain files or other folders to help organise the contents of a disk.

font set of characters that are all in the same typeface. For example, labels in Windows are normally displayed in a font called Helvetica or Arial - the characters do not have serifs (the pointy bits on the edges of the letters). In Windows there are TrueType fonts that can be printed and displayed in almost any size, and printer fonts that can be printed in a range of pre-defined sizes.

see also DOWNLOAD

Fonts Folder (in Windows) location for all the fonts that are currently installed on your PC; to add a new font or to view the existing fonts, open the folder by clicking on Start/Settings/Fonts.

foobar term used by programmers to refer to whatever is being discussed. For example, if a programmer is explaining how a graphic program works, he might refer to an example graphic file that stores the image as 'foobar.gif' - it does not really exist but is just an example. Many programmers refer to example variables or example user details as foobar. You will often see this term used in books and lessons about software and systems

footer information at the bottom of a page, typically the author's name, copyright, date or page number. Microsoft Word allows you to add footers to each page - select the View/Footers menu option

compare with HEADER

footprint size of a computer's case on the desk

for your information (FYI) document file that contains general

background information related to the Internet or the TCP/IP protocols; specific technical information is normally contained in RFC documents
see also RFC

foreground colour colour used to display text or information on top of any background image; for example, if you are creating a presentation, you might set the background image to a graduated blue with your company's logo in one corner. The text for each slide of the presentation is called the foreground text and would be displayed in a contrasting colour
see also BACKGROUND

form series of commands within HTML that allow a developer to ask a user to select choices or enter text; for example, if you want to allow a user to request a printed catalogue from your web site, you would create a form with fields that allow the user to enter their address - together with a button to submit the form to the web server for processing. In this case, the form processing would simply be to send the details by electronic mail to the network manager. Another example of a form is used by the search engines, such as Yahoo! and AltaVista; when you type in the words you want to search for, you are entering text in a form, which is sent to the search engine when you press the submit button
see also APPENDIX, CGI, HTML, PERL

form factor the size and shape of a device, normally used to refer to a computer's motherboard or other printed circuit board. For example, the motherboard (the board that holds all the main componenets in a computer) tends to be the size of the first IBM desktop PC computer (full form factor) or smaller.

form feed to advance the paper in a printer to the top of the next page or sheet; if you are using a laser or inkjet printer this has the effect of ejecting the current piece of paper

format to arrange text and define margins, columns, include special fonts or embolden text in a wordprocessor or DTP program.

format a disk to prepare a new disk so that files can be stored on it - you need to format any disk before you can use it: use the Format command from File Manager or Explorer.

forward to send an email message that you have received on to another user

fps FRAMES PER SECOND number of individual frames of a video sequence that can be displayed each second to give the impression of movement. This number depends a lot on the power and speed of your PC. To give the impression of smooth, continuous (also called full-motion) video your PC needs to display at least 25 separate frames each second. If the frames are small, there is not too much data to update; however, if the

frame is large - for example, a large window display - then the PC has to update the hundreds of thousands of pixels that make up each image 25 times per second. To do this needs a fast graphics adapter or special video display hardware. If you want to experiment with video clips, start the Media Player tool and load any sample file that has an AVI extension.
see also MPEG

FQDN FULLY QUALIFIED DOMAIN NAME full domain name, for example 'pcp.co.uk' is a fully qualified domain name that can be used to identify a server; 'pcp' is just the hostname

fractal complex geometric shape that repeats itself within itself and so always appears the same however much you magnify a part of the image. Fractals are used to compress images and to create interesting mathematical patterns.

fragment piece of information that has had to be split up into several smaller units of information before being sent over the Internet; the receiver will re-assemble these units into the correct order

fragmentation problem that can occur when a file is stored on a disk: the operating system (DOS) normally tries to save it in one contiguous block. However, if your disk is very full, there might not be enough room to save the entire file in one block, so DOS splits the file up and stores the separate sections in any available gaps on the disk. This spread of bits of files over the disk is called fragmentation. It is not dangerous, but it will slow down your disk access time since the disk head has to move to several different parts of the disk to make up the entire file. Windows includes the Disk Deframenter utility (Start/Programs/Accessories/System Tools) that will go through the entire disk and sort it all out so that all the files are in complete blocks. You should try to run this program every month or so to keep your disk drive at peak performance.
compare with DEFRAGMENTATION

frame (in HTML web pages) set of commands (developed by Netscape and now supported by most web browsers) that allow the main window of a browser to be split into separate sections, each of which can be scrolled independently; most new or sophisticated web pages use frames to present lots of information clearly
see also HTML, APPENDIX

frame (in communications) standard unit of information (also called a packet) that contains a header with the destination address and sender's address followed by the information and a trailer that contains error detection information

frame (in animation) one single image within a sequence of different images that together show movement or animation. Each frame is normally slightly different from the previous one to give the impression of movement

frame buffer   electronic memory that is used to temporarily store one frame of an animation; normally used to regulate and provide a smooth delivery of image data retrieved from the hard disk before they are displayed on screen.

frame relay   communications protocol used to ensure that data is delivered correctly over a packet-switching system (such as X.25)

free WAIS   non-commercial version of the WAIS search index server
see WAIS

freeware   software that can be used on a permanent basis without charge.

front-end   part of a software program that a user sees and interacts with. The front-end has to be carefully designed to be clear, simple and straightforward to use

front-end processor   processor or server that manages the communications within a network or a server that manipulates (or formats) data before sending it on to the main server for processing
see also BACK-END PROCESSOR, SERVER

ftp   FILE TRANSFER PROTOCOL   system used to transfer files between two computers linked via the Internet or two computers both running Unix linked via a network; software is used to transfer files between computers; this system is part of the suite of TCP/IP protocols (that includes email and web page delivery)
see also ARCHIE, BITFTP, TCP/IP, TELNET

ftp mail
see BITFTP

full duplex   two devices that can send and receive (talk and listen to) data at the same time; almost all modems allow full duplex data transmission over a telephone line, using different frequencies depending on whether the data is sent or received

full text search   to carry out a search for a word or item through the entire text of a database or multimedia application rather than limit the search to a particular section, chapter or field.

full-motion video
see FPS

function   series of commands or program instructions that carry out a particular job and can be called by a user or from within a program; for example, if you are writing a Javascript script in a web page to convert kilograms to pounds, this set of instructions is called a function

function key   one of several special keys placed along the top of a PC keyboard that have different uses according to different applications. For example, most applications use the F1 key to display help information and Alt-F4 to quit an application

FYI FOR YOUR INFORMATION document file that contains general background information related to the Internet or the TCP/IP protocols; specific technical information is normally contained in RFC documents *see also* RFC

Gg

gaming gear   accessories (for a computer) that are designed to increase the enjoyment of playing a computer game; for example, a joystick for action games or a steering wheel and foot pedals for a driving game

gated   GATE DAEMON   (pronounced 'gate-dee') software that redirects network traffic (normally Internet traffic) according to a set of rules; it can also be used to limit access to a site or to route traffic to another site
see also   ROUTED

gateway   (i) (in electronic mail) software program or combination of server and software that links two different electronic mail systems together so that mail messages can be transferred from one system to another; for example, if you are using an network electronic mail product within your company, you would need to fit a gateway function to allow messages to be sent and received to users on the Internet; (ii) (in networks) device that passes packets of data from one type of networking system, computer or application to another system; (iii) (in an email system) software that will transfer messages from one electronic mail standard to another, for example from an Internet standard to a local area network standard; (iv) (in a web page) method of transferring information that a user has entered into a form on a web page to a server-based application
see also   CGI, MAIL GATEWAY

gateway interface
see   CGI

Gb   GIGABYTE

generic   something that is compatible with a whole family of hardware or software products from one manufacturer.

geotargetting   method of analysing what a visitor to your website is viewing or doing and deducing their location, then displaying custom content or advertisements accordingly; for example, if they ask for the weather in Seattle, you could display banner advertisements from taxi companies in Seattle.

GET method   (used in HTML for CGI access) method of transferring information between a web page (that uses the HTML form GET command) and a server-based application
see also   CGI, HTML, PUT

GHz GIGAHERTZ measure of frequency equal to one billion cycles per second

GIF file GRAPHICS INTERFACE FORMAT commonly-used format for storing images and bit-mapped colour graphics; originally developed for the CompuServe on-line system but now one of the most popular formats for images stored on the Internet; most paint programs can read and write to the GIF file format. One extended version of the GIF file format, called animated GIF, allows several images to be stored in one file - these separate images are then displayed in cycle and can be used to create simple animations (many animated or flashing buttons on the Internet are created in this way)
see also ANIMATED GIF, TRANSPARENT GIF

gigabyte (Gb) measure of memory that is equal to 1024 megabytes of storage capacity; gigabyte is often wrongly used to mean 1000 megabytes

gigahertz (GHz) measure of frequency equal to one billion cycles per second

glitch minor error in receiving data accurately or a fault with a program

global something which covers everything; for example, a global search and replace will replace all occurrences of a word in an entire document.

Gouraud shading mathematical equation that is used to create shading within a three-dimensional scene. The equation is applied to each side of each object and produces a gradual change in colour to give the impression of light and shade.

Gopher (on the Internet) system that allows a user to find information and files stored on the Internet using a series of typed commands; has now been replaced by website-based search engines that index documents on websites across the web, such as Excite (www.excite.com); see the appendix for lists of other popular sites
see also ARCHIE, SEARCH ENGINE, VERONICA, WAIS

GPF GENERAL PROTECTION FAULT an error condition that occurs in Microsoft Windows and causes an application to crash; new versions of Windows try and minimise the effects of this type of error. A GPF error is normally caused by insufficient memory or by using an incompatible peripheral or device driver, or an error in a software program.

GPRS GENERAL PACKET RADIO SERVICE standard system for wireless radio and mobile telephone communications that is due to replace the existing GSM (Global System for Mobile Communications) system; GPRS supports high-speed data transfer rates of up to 150Kbps compared to the GSM limit of 9.6Kbps. When mobile telephones and other wireless devices, such as PDAs, use the GPRS system, it will make mobile access to the Internet and email much faster.

graphical user interface (GUI) (pronounced 'gooeey') interface between an operating system or a program and the user; this defines a way of representing files, functions and folders with little images (called icons). Windows is a GUI that makes it easier to operate a PC. Before Windows you had to type in commands at a command prompt to control the computer, with a GUI such as Windows you can use a mouse to point and click on an icon using the mouse rather than typing in the file name - which is far easier to learn and use.

graphics any form of pictures or lines that can be displayed on screen or printed out. Refers to shapes and patterns rather than to text characters

graphics accelerator special card that fits inside your computer and uses a dedicated processor chip to speed up the action of drawing lines and images on the screen. In a normal PC, it is the main processor chip that has to carry out all the calculations to display a line on screen - at the same time as looking after the keyboard, mouse, disk drive and memory. By adding a graphics accelerator card you can speed up the reaction time of graphics software such as Windows, CAD or paint programs.

graphics adapter electronic components on a circuit board that connected to the motherboard of your computer; these components are used to convert software instructions into electrical signals that control the text and images that are displayed on the monitor

graphics file file stored on a disk that contains data that describes an image

graphics library set of basic functions provided by a graphics output device (such as a graphics adapter card or printer) that can be used by programmers and so avoid having to write complex routines. For example, a graphics library might provide a function that draws a line between two given points - the programmer can simply use this function rather than implement his own mathematical equation to calculate how to draw a line between two points.

gray scale *or* **grey scale** range of shades of grey used in an image

greeked text characters that are displayed as a dotted rather than individual characters; this is often used by DTP programs when displaying text in a very small type size. Greeked text is only meant to give an impression of the characters rather than a readable display

grid matrix of evenly spaced horizontal and vertical lines that help you align and measure drawings. The grid lines are not printed but serve only as a guide in drawing or DTP applications.

grid snap feature of drawing and DTP applications that will, when you are drawing a line or image, automatically limit the position of the cursor to a point on the grid, making it easier to align drawings and lines on screen.

group collection of files or icons within a separate window in the File Manager screen of Windows 3; this term is not used in Windows 95/98

Group 3
see FAX GROUP

GSM GLOBAL SYSTEM FOR MOBILE COMMUNICATIONS
the most popular system used for wireless cellular telephone communications throughout Europe, Asia and parts of North America. This system allows eight calls to share the same radio frequency and carries the digital data that represents voice signals transmitted by each user's telephone. The main drawback of GSM is that it does not offer very fast data transfer rates which has become more important as users want to access the Internet and read email via a mobile telephone connection. GSM provides data transfer at up to 9.6Kbps, but it is due to be replaced by the GPRS system that can support high-speed data transfer at up to 150Kbps.
see also GPRS, MOBILE PHONE, PCS

GUI
see GRAPHICAL USER INTERFACE

gutter (i) the blank space between two adjacent columns of text; (ii) the blank space or inner margin between two facing pages.

Hh

H
see HEXADECIMAL

hacker (originally) someone who was fascinated by computers and tried to program them as efficiently as possible or explore how they worked; now normally used to refer to someone who is trying to break into a secure computer system for criminal purposes - such as someone trying to discover a way into a bank's central computer.

halftone way of representing tones in a printed image: a photograph is made up of continuous tones which a computer cannot represent, instead the photograph is converted into millions of groups of tiny dots - often too small for the eye to see - in which a group of small dots shows up as a light area and a group of large dots as a dark area. If you want to print any photograph, either on your laser printer or with a commercial printer, you will need to convert the photograph into a halftone image. If you are using a scanner to read in the photograph to a graphics file on your computer, it will carry out this conversion automatically. In the case of a commercial printer, he will do the conversion for you before printing.

hand-held device that is small enough to be held and used, such as a palm-top computer
see also PALM COMPUTER, PDA

hand-held scanner small hand-held device, rather like a large mouse, that is used to scan small photographs and line drawings and convert these into graphic images that can be used on your computer. The scanner plugs into a special controller card in your PC and works using a row of light-sensitive cells along its bottom surface. When you move the scanner (by dragging it by hand) over an image, it reads the amount of light reflected from the image or photograph and converts this into a form which can be displayed on your computer
compare with FLATBED SCANNER

handle (in a graphics or DTP program) small square that is displayed on the edge of a frame or object or image; if you move the mouse pointer over the handle and click and drag with the mouse, you will resize or move the object.

handshaking series of signals that are sent between two communication devices (such as two modems linked by telephone) to establish the way in which they should send and receive data.

hang slang term that means your computer has stopped responding because of a temporary fault. Some programs, which are not tested thoroughly are liable to stop at unpredictable times and hang the computer. This means that you cannot do anything else except to switch off your PC and start again. Any data typed in since the last time you saved the document would be lost.

hard copy printed document or copy of an image that is stored on computer.

hard disk (drive) rigid magnetic disk that is able to store many times more data than a floppy disk and usually cannot be removed from the disk drive that is located inside your PC. In most PCs the hard disk drive is called drive C:, wheras the floppy disk drive is called drive A: or B:. A hard disk drive can normally store several hundred million bytes (or characters) of information, whereas a floppy disk can only store 1.44Mb

hardware physical unit, hard disk, monitor or electronic circuit that is part of a computer system.
compare with SOFTWARE

hardware compatibility method of designing two different computers (or computers from different manufacturers) so that each can use the add-on hardware of the other without any changes. A prime example is the standard PC you are probably using - it is based on an original design by IBM and now all PCs are hardware compatible which means you can buy a network card or graphics adapter from any PC manufacturer and you can be reasonably sure that it will work correctly in your standard PC and that both the software and hardware will function correctly.
see also BACKWARDS COMPATIBLE, EISA

hardware dependent something that will only work on a particular type or configuration of hardware. For example, network software will only run and work properly if it can detect that a network adapter has been fitted into your PC.

Hayes AT command set standard set of commands used to control a modem from a communications program; Hayes is a manufacturer of modems that allow you to send data over the telephone line to another computer; it standardised the software commands that allow a computer to control a modem and these commands (also known as the AT command set) means that any communications software can control just about any modem, as long as both are Hayes-compatible. For example, the command ATD123 means dial the number '123'

Hayes-compatible modem modem that supports the range of commands in the standard Hayes AT command set

HCI HOST CONTROLLER INTERFACE

HDD
see HARD DISK

head special transducer that can read or write data from the surface of a magnetic disk. The head is just like the playback head in a cassette recorder and skims just above the surface of the disk as the disk spins using tiny wings that allow it to fly above the disk's surface

head crash fault that occurs when the access head in a hard disk drive touches the surface of the spinning disk; a head crash is rare and generally caused by a sharp knock - such as dropping a computer - and will cause data to be lost from the hard disk

header (i) (in a document) text that appears at the very top of each page; for example, the header might contain the chapter name and the page number. Most wordprocessors and DTP applications let you define whether you want headers (in Word for Windows, look in the View menu under Header/Footer option). The line of text that runs along the bottom of each page is called the footer; (ii) part of a message that contains the recipient is address, sender's name and any delivery options

heat sink a metal device with fins and ridges that helps reduce the temperature of an electronic component device by transferring (or dissipating) the heat into the air; all large electronic chips, such as the CPU in a computer, need a heat sink - they would get too hot and be damaged without one. Some heat sinks also include a built-in fan to increase the amount of heat that they can dissipate. An active heat sink includes a fan, a passive heat sink has no fan.

help function in an application that displays explanatory text on screen to explain how to use the software or how to use a particular function. Context-sensitive help displays explanatory text about the particular control or command you are using rather than about the general program. Most software applications running under Windows on a PC link the help text to the F1 key.

help key particular key on the keyboard that is linked to the help system of a software. Most Windows applications on a PC have standardised on the F1 key as the help key - press this key at any time and the software will display explanatory text that should help you understand the function or command you are puzzling over.

helper application program that works with a web browser to increase the functionality of the browser and displays its information in a separate, smaller window outside the main web page; for example, if you want to view Adobe Acrobat pages from your web browser you will need to get the Adobe helper application that will then be used to view the pages; a

'plug-in' provides similar functions as a helper application, but displays its information within the main web page (for example, if a plug-in is used to display a video sequence, this appears as part of the web page displayed in the web browser, if a helper application is used then the video is displayed in a separate pop-up window)
see also BROWSER, PLUG-IN

Hertz (Hz) measure of the frequency of a signal in cycles per second

heterogeneous network network that uses many different protocols and server software and types of hardware platform
compare with HOMOGENOUS NETWORK

Hewlett Packard Hewlett Packard is a company that makes, amongst other things, a range of laser and ink-jet printers.

Hewlett Packard LaserJet brand name for a printer model produced by Hewlett Packard. The LaserJet has its own language called PCL that defined the way characters and graphics were printed on the page. This language has now become one of the two standards for sending data from a computer to a laser printer - the other language is called PostScript. Many laser printers are LaserJet compatible. This means that if you setup Windows so that it is configured to support an HP LaserJet printer, it will work with any LaserJet compatible printer.

hexadecimal (*or* hex *or* H) hexadecimal is a way of representing numbers in base 16. Normally we use decimal numbers (base 10), but a computer uses binary numbers (base 2) which can be either a zero or a one. For convenience, computer programs and data are normally converted and displayed in base 16. Hex uses the letters A..F to represent the numbers 10-15 and if you ever see a number with an 'h' after it, such as 45h, this means that it is in base 16.

hidden files files that have had their Hidden attribute set so that they are not displayed and cannot be easily deleted; these files can be listed by changing the view options in Windows Explorer or by changing the Hidden attribute using the ATTRIB command or by changing the Properties page for the file
see also ATTRIBUTE, PROPERTIES

hierarchical filing system a way of storing files and folders within other folders on a disk. It makes it far easier to manage groups of files rather than storing all the files in one place - just like a filing cabinet which has different drawers, files and folders.

hierarchical routing method of directing network traffic over a complex network by breaking down the structure of the network into separate levels - each level is responsible for directing traffic within its area; for example, the Internet has a three-level hierarchical routing system in which the backbones can direct traffic from one mid-level to another, the mid-levels can direct traffic from one server site to another and each server site can direct traffic internally

high density floppy disks that can store either 1.2Mb for a 5.25-inch disk or 1.44Mb for a 3.5-inch disk; high density disks normally have an 'HD' symbol printed on one corner and have two sliding tabs on two corners. This differentiates them from double density disks that cannot store as much information

high memory area (HMA) (small) area of memory in a PC that can be used by some programs. The HMA is 64Kb of extended memory that sits above the 1Mb limit and can only be accessed if you load a special HMA driver (which is done automatically for you when you install Windows 95). Note that HMA is not the same as high memory, which is a more general term that refers to a section of memory located between 640Kb and 1Mb marks

high resolution screen or printer that can display fine images, normally refers to a display with a resolution of at least 640x480 or a printer that can print at a resolution of 300dpi
see also DPI, RESOLUTION

highlight to select a word or section of text in a document by moving the mouse pointer over the word and double-clicking on the mouse button. In Word for Windows, a double click will highlight the word you are over, a triple-click will highlight the line and a quadruple click will highlight the paragraph. You can tell that the text is highlighted because it normally appears in reverse (white text with a black background).

history feature of some applications that keeps a log of the actions you have carried out or the places within a hypertext document that you have visited or the sites on the Internet that you have explored. You can then return to any point you had previously visited by looking at the history list.

hit (i) a request from a user's browser to view a page or image on your website. Often misleadingly used as a measure of the popularity of a website or a measure of the number of visitors - it will not provide any of this information, you'll need to analyse your site's access log files to find these details. The problem occurs because as each element within a web page is displayed, it generates a 'hit'. If your home page has three pictures and some text, every user will generate four hits in your access log; (ii) data that matches your search criteria

HMA
see HIGH MEMORY AREA

Home key key on a PC keyboard (in the group above the four cursor control keys) that will move the cursor to the start of the current line. Some wordprocessing programs will move the cursor to the start of the document if you press the Home key twice.

home page opening page of a web site (normally stored in a file called index.html); if you enter a web site address into your web browser, it will automatically open the home page. For example, if you enter 'www.microsoft.com' you will actually see the home page of this site that is stored in a file called index.html.

hop path taken by a packet of data as it moves from one server or router to another; when you send information over the Internet (or a wide area network) your data will probably have to travel via several servers to reach its destination

hop count number of hops required to send information from one computer to another over the Internet

horizontal scroll bar bar displayed along the bottom of a window that indicates that there is more information than can be displayed in the window. You can move horizontally to display the rest of the information by clicking on the arrow buttons at each end of the scroll bar.

host computer that stores the web site you want to access; the host will have its own IP address and a domain name

host adapter device that is used to control SCSI devices; for example, if you want to add a CD-ROM drive to your computer; you will also need to install a special controller card (that is called the host adapter)

host address or host number
see INTERNET ADDRESS

host name name given to a web site on the Internet; for example, www.pcp.co.uk is the host name for the Peter Collin Publishing web site. When you type in this host name, also called the site address, the text is converted by a DNS server to its unique IP address that uniquely identifies the site
see also DNS, DOMAIN NAME, IP ADDRESS

hosting service company (normally called an ISP) that provides storage space on its web server for you to store the pages that form your web site; the company also maintains the server and its connections to the Internet
see also ISP

hot key way of selecting a menu option or command by pressing two or more keys at the same time. For example, instead of selecting the File/Save menu option, most Windows programs use a hot key shortcut of Alt-S (the Alt key and the S key pressed at the same time) to do the same thing. Another useful hot key shortcut is Alt-F4 which will quit any Windows program.

hot link   word or image or button in a web page or multimedia title that
moves the user to another page when clicked
see also   HYPERLINK

hot plugging *or* **hot swapping**   feature of a computer that lets you
plug in or remove a device while the computer is running; the computer's
operating system software automatically detects the change and alters its
configuration. To support hot plugging the computer needs a special
connection and operating system software that can manage this feature;
currently USB, IEEE and PC-Card ports support hot plugging. For example,
if you plug a PC-Card modem into a PC-Card slot, your computer will
automatically detect this change and will let you use the modem

hotspot   (in a multimedia title) area of an image that does something if
you move the mouse pointer onto the area and click on the mouse button.
Normally, you can tell that there is a hotspot in an image because the mouse
pointer changes shape from an arrow to a hand. For example, if the
multimedia title displayed a picture of a guitar, there could be a hotspot over
each string which would play the sound of the string being plucked when
you clicked on the hotspot.

HP
see   HEWLETT PACKARD

HP-PCL   series of commands (developed by Hewlett Packard) that allows
any application to control any of the HP range of printers. This set of
commands, or language, is built into all the LaserJet and DeskJet printers. If
you buy a printer that is LaserJet-compatible and your software does not
directly support this particular printer, set the software to HP LaserJet mode

HTML   HYPERTEXT MARKUP LANGUAGE   series of special codes
that define the typeface and style that should be used when displaying the
text and also allow hypertext links to other parts of the document or to other
documents. HTML is normally used to create documents for the World
Wide web - the graphical part of the Internet. A document coded in HTML
can be displayed on any viewer software that understands HTML - such as a
WWW browser. For a list of the main HTML tags, see the Appendix.
see also   BROWSER, INDEX PAGE, HYPERTEXT, WWW

HTTP   HYPERTEXT TRANSFER PROTOCOL   commands used by a
browser to ask an Internet web server for information about a web page;
when you enter a site name into your browser (for example,
www.pcp.co.uk) the browser then has a conversation with the remote web
server and asks it to send the file that contains the home page; this
conversation is carried out using HTTP commands and the remote server
that is being asked questions by your browser is called an HTTP server

HTTPd   HYPERTEXT TRANSFER PROTOCOL DAEMON

web server that carries out the functions required to process forms, image maps, authentication and searching
see also DAEMON

hub device that connects together several terminals or computers to form an electrical network allowing data to transfer between each device; for example, if you want to connect ten computers together in your office, you would probably use 10BaseT cable to link each computer to a small box called the hub. The hub creates an electrical connection between each computer

hue colour of an image or pixel

HyperTerminal (in Windows) communications program that is included with Windows 95 and allows you call a remote computer via a modem and transfer files. It is not meant to be used to access the Internet, it is more useful when used to access bulletin boards or other on-line services.

hyperlink word or image or button in a web page or multimedia title that moves the user to another page when clicked

hypertext (i) (*Internet*) a way of linking one word or image to another page; when the user selects the word or image, he jumps directly to the new page. This is the basis of navigating around the WWW - if you click on an underlined word in a web page, it will link you to another section of the page or to another page; (ii) (*multimedia*) a way of organising information in a multimedia title: certain words in the text include a link to another part of the book or to another document. When the user clicks on the word, he is moved to another part of the document or book.

hypertext markup language
see HTML

hyphenation and justification feature of most wordprocessing and DTP programs that will align a line of text so that both ends are level with the left and right margins. It will either split a long word over two lines (hyphenation) or will add tiny spaces between words to pad a line to fit.

hypertext transfer protocol
see HTTP

hypertext transfer protocol daemon
see HTTPD

Hz
see HERTZ

Ii

I-beam cursor (in Windows) flashing cursor shaped like a capital letter 'I' and used to indicate that you are can edit text on screen. For example, if you use a Windows wordprocessor, the mouse pointer turns into an I-beam cursor when you move it over the main page and returns to an arrow shape when you move it over the menu bar or other controls.

IAB
see INTERNET ARCHITECTURE BOARD

IANA
see INTERNET ASSIGNED NUMBERS AUTHORITY

IBM INTERNATIONAL BUSINESS MACHINES currently, the biggest computer company in the world, IBM developed the first PC based on an Intel processor and now sells a range of desktop and laptop computers as well as its traditional large mainframe computers.

IC
see INTEGRATED CIRCUIT

ICMP INTERNET CONTROL MESSAGE PROTOCOL an extension to the Internet Protocol (IP) - used to manage the transfer of almost all data over the Internet - that provides error detection and control messages; for example, the Internet command 'ping' uses ICMP to test if a named node is working correctly and displays any errors.
see also IP, PING

icon (in a GUI, such as Windows) small graphic symbol or picture that is displayed on screen and used to identify a command or file. For example, many wordprocessors use an icon of a magnifying glass on a button to indicate that this button will start a search function. Within Windows, each application you install has its own program icon and its data files often use the same icon - for example, the Microsoft Excel program has a large X as its icon that is displayed in Explorer or FileManager.

ICQ (pronounced 'I-seek-you') software program (developed by Mirabilis) that supports instant messaging and allows two or more users to send messages to each other via the Internet that are instantly displayed on the other person's screen.
see also INSTANT MESSAGING

IDE INTEGRATED DRIVE ELECTRONICS standard that defines the way in which a hard disk and its controller connect together and operate. Most home PCs are fitted with an IDE controller and IDE-compatible hard disk drive within the casing. This is not normally important until you want to expand your hard disk capacity or add another disk drive. PCs used as network servers or those used for power tasks, such as CAD, often use the rival SCSI standard that is more powerful than the IDE standard. The two, naturally, are not compatible.

IE
see INTERNET EXPLORER

IEN
see INTERNET EXPERIMENT NOTE

IETF INTERNET ENGINEERING TASK FORCE large group of network designers, researchers, programmers, vendors and engineers that work together to improve and develop the Internet (further information is at www.info.isoc.org)

IIS
see INTERNET INFORMATION SERVER

IGMP INTERNET GROUP MANAGEMENT PROTOCOL standard that helps manage how data is transferred during an IP Multicast operation in which one server computer sends each packet of data to several destinations at the same time - useful when broadcasting a lot of data to several different recipients. (The IGMP standard is defined in RFC1112)

IGP INTERIOR GATEWAY PROTOCOL protocol that distributes information to gateways (now normally called routers) within a particular network

IMA
see INTERNET MERCHANT ACCOUNT

image editor software that lets you edit, change or paint new parts of an image. For example, professional designers might use an image editor to remove any blemishes from a photograph that has been scanned in or an internet designer could use an image editor to draw art and pictures for a web page. Windows has its own basic image editor (that is also a paint program), called Paint - it is stored in the Accessories folder

iMac a personal computer developed by Apple Computer that has a stylish transparent casing that houses the monitor and main computer system with the mouse and keyboard as the only other separate items

imagemap graphic image that has areas of the image defined as hotspots to link to another web page; an image map can either be created with special HTML commands that define the coordinates of the areas and are interpreted by a user's web browser (this is called a client-side image map) and is the usual method of creating an imagemap, the alternative is to use a special program that runs on a web server. The Peter Collin Publishing web page (www.pcp.co.uk) uses an imagemap to provide the index on the left of the screen

IMAP INTERNET MESSAGE ACCESS PROTOCOL standard that defines how messages can be read; this standard (currently at version four) provides an alternative to the POP3 standard. The IMAP standard stores a user's messages on a shared server (for example, at your ISP) and allows a user to connect from any computer and read, send or manage messages. In contrast, the POP3 protocol downloads all messages from a shared server onto the user's computer. This makes it very difficult for a user to access messages from different computer - for example, if you are travelling. Note: regardless of whether IMAP or POP3 is used to read messages, the SMTP protocol is normally used to send messages
see also POP3, SMTP

import (in an application) function that allows you to use a data file produced by another program and stored in another format in your application. For example, if you use Microsoft Word and want to read a document written with WordPerfect, you will need to choose the import menu option in Word and tell Word that it should convert the WordPerfect codes to native Word codes and formats. The opposite is export.

InBox (in Windows) feature of the Windows messaging system (Exchange) that can gather together all your electronic messages including mail sent over the network, fax messages and mail sent over the Internet. All these messages are stored in your personal InBox. Once you have installed Exchange youill see a new icon on your Desktop called InBox; double-click on InBox to send messages or to read new messages.

index list of subjects with related web sites

index.html filename that is normally used to store the home page on any web site on the Internet
see HOMEPAGE

industry standard architecture
see ISA

INF file configuration file supplied by a hardware manufacturer to allow Windows to correctly install the device or peripheral

infra-red link system that allows two computers or a computer and a printer to exchange information using an infra-red light beam to carry the data. Many new laptop computers now have an infra-red connector that allows you to exchange information with a desktop or printer without having to use cables
see also IRDA

INI file   configuration file used in Windows 3.x and earlier that tells Windows how to load and run an application; the INI file could contain the working directory, user name, and user settings
see also   REGISTRY

initialization string   series of AT commands sent to a modem to configure it before it is used

ink   (in a paint or design program) colour that will be used when drawing; most paint programs display two colours on screen - one is the ink, the other is the paper: the ink is the colour when drawing and the paper is the colour used when erasing a part of a drawing. You can normally change the ink to any other colour in the palette.

ink-jet printer   light, quiet and relatively cheap printer that produces printed output by sending a stream of tiny drops of electrically charged ink to the surface of the paper. The movement of the drops of ink is controlled by an electrical field to define the shape of each character, drop by drop. There are few moving parts (so it is very quiet) but the quality, although better than a dot-matrix printer, is not as good nor as fast as a laser printer.

inline plug-in
see   PLUG-IN

input   to transfer information into a computer; for example, if you type text on your keyboard you are actually inputting data into the computer. Another example is to use a scanner or to use a mouse to draw on screen - both are examples of computer input.

Ins key   key on a PC keyboard that switches the typing mode between insert and overwrite. If you are in overwrite mode, any existing characters will be overwritten with the new text you type in. If you are in insert mode any existing characters are moved along automatically to make space for the new characters. Most wordprocessors tell you which mode you are in by displaying 'OVR' for overwrite and 'INS' for insert in the status bar at the bottom of the screen.

install   process of copying and setting up an application program onto your hard disk. The steps normally include copying the files from the floppy disks or CD-ROM (on which the application is sold) onto your hard disk, then configuring the options for your requirements.

instant messaging   A feature that lets you type in and exchange messages with one or more other people connected via the Internet; each person runs special software that tells them when a friend or colleague has connected to the Internet and is available to receive messages. When you type in a message, it is sent instantly to the other user. There are currently several different standards and types of software; one of the most popular is provided by AOL.

instruction cache   memory area within a processor chip that contains the next instruction that the processor has to execute - the instruction is placed there by the pre-fetch unit

integer   mathematical term used to describe a whole number, such as 12, 135 or 987. An integer cannot have fractions or decimal points

integral   feature or hardware device that is already built into the program or computer. For example, most computers are fitted with a floppy disk and internal hard disk drive as standard. Both these are integral to the computer system

integrated circuit (IC)   tiny electronic device consisting of a small piece of a crystal of a semiconductor onto which are etched a number of microscopic electronic components. Together, these electronic components form a circuit which carries out a function. For example, the central processor of a computer is a very complex integrated circuit that can perform mathematical operations on numbers.

integrated drive electronics
see IDE

integrated services digital network
see ISDN

Intel   company that manufactures integrated circuit components and was the first company to develop a commercially available microprocessor (the 4004); Intel also develops the range of 80x86 processors and the Pentium processor that are used in many PCs.

intelligent   software program that can respond to situations in a similar (although limited) way to that of a human. For example, some doctors now use computers that ask the patient simple questions and can deduce the possible ailment and treatment - this is a basic form of intelligence.

interactive   multimedia title that allows the user to control the progress through the book. Instead of the software showing page one, then two, three and so on, the user can move around and click on hypertext links and hotspots that move him around the book in a random order

interface   (i) electronics that provides a connection between two devices, often used to refer to the connector; for example, a printer interface allows a computer to be connected to a printer; (ii) see GUI

interior gateway protocol (IGP)   protocol that distributes information to gateways (now normally called routers) within a particular network

interlace   method of building up an image on a display using two passes over the entire screen - each pass displays alternate lines. Although this system requires two passes, each only displays half the information in a shorter time than one complete pass, so reducing the appearance of flicker.

interleave method of storing data on alternate tracks on a hard disk drive to slow down data transfer rates to match a slower processor. Many hard disks store information in non-consecutive sectors on the disk; for example a file might be stored in sectors 100, 102, 104 and 106. Hard disks are configured with an interleave to slow down their performance and allow a slower computer to keep up with the amount of data that is being transferred. The number of sectors skipped is called the interleave factor; for example, a disk drive saving a file to sectors 4, 6, 8, 10 has an interleave factor of two. Fast computers run the hard disk with no interleave factor, since they can cope with the fast flow of data to and from the hard disk.

internal (something) inside the computer or inside the computer's case
compare with EXTERNAL

international standards organisation
see ISO

Internet international network that links together thousands of computers using cable links and allows data to be transferred between each computer using the TCP/IP protocols; these computers are called the servers and are rather like a local telephone exchange - individual users can then use a modem to connect to the server computer from their home and so have access to the entire world network. A user can send electronic mail over the Internet and transfer files and text from one computer in London to another in New York - all for the price of a local phone call to your nearest server. The World Wide web is an enhancement to the Internet and provides a graphical front-end to the different databases and servers that are available. In order to connect to the Internet, you will need a modem and an account with a server - normally called an Internet service provider (ISP) or point-of-presence provider - together with some special software. You will be given a unique ID name that will (like your telephone number) identify you to any other user in the world together with an access telephone number that allows your modem to connect to their server. No one person or company controls the Internet. NOTE: historically, the Internet was developed by the US department of Defense under its ARPANET project and was originally called an Internetwork
see also ARPANET, DIALUP, DNS, ISP, TCP/IP, WWW

Internet address unique number that identifies the precise location of a particular node on the Internet; this address is also called an IP address and is a 32-bit number usually written in dotted decimal format; it used by the TCP/IP protocol and is normally of the form '123.33.22.32'; a domain name system is used to convert a domain name (such as 'petercollin.com') into its full Internet address

Internet architecture board (IAB) group that monitors and manages the development of the Internet; it includes the IETF and the IRTF

Internet assigned numbers authority (IANA) group that assigns unique identifying numbers to the different protocols and network products used on the Internet

Internet-draft (I-D) draft documents produced by the IETF that often lead to RFCs

Internet engineering steering group (IESG) group that reviews Internet standards and manages the IETF

Internet engineering task force (IETF) large group of network designers, researchers, programmers, vendors and engineers that work together to improve and develop the Internet (further information is at www.info.isoc.org)

Internet Explorer (IE) web browser developed by Microsoft, currently available free, that allows a user to view web pages; it supports many features including ActiveX applets. To download a copy, visit the Microsoft website (www.microsoft.com)
compare with NETSCAPE

Internet Information Server; (iiS) Internet web server software developed by Microsoft

Internet merchant account (IMA) business bank account that allows the business to accept credit card payments via the Internet; many businesses have a merchant account, allowing them to accept credit card payments by telephone or mail, but still need a separate IMA to accept payments via the net.

Internet message access protocol
see IMAP

Internet number
see INTERNET ADDRESS

Internet protocol (IP) protocol used to carry data over the Internet; it is part of the TCP/IP protocol suite
see also PROTOCOL, TCP/IP

Internet relay chat
see IRC

Internet research steering group (IRSG) group that manages the Internet research task force; part of the Internet Society

Internet research task force (IRTF) group that considers the long-term technical objectives and standards for the Internet; part of the Internet Society

Internet Society an organisation that looks after maintaining and enhancing the Internet; it is not linked to any government nor company so provides an independent view of the future of the Internet. It is made up of committees, such as the Internet Advisory Board and the Internet Engineering Task Force, that are responsible for developing and approving new Internet standards

Internet service provider
see ISP

Internet telephony system that allows someone to make a telephone call using the Internet to carry the voice signals; this is particularly appealing if you have low-cost dial-up access to the Internet, since it allows you to make long distance calls for the low-price you pay for your Internet connection. To make a telephone call, you need a computer with a sound card fitted and a microphone and loudspeaker plugged in; special software manages the connection and transfers the voice data over the Internet to the person you are calling. Some systems let you call and speak to anyone else connected to the Internet who is using the same software. More sophisticated software links you to a real telephone exchange and lets you call any normal telephone number and so speak to anyone in the world. This type of system normally charges an extra fee to manage the link to the real telephone exchange, but this is still often very much cheaper than the cost of a normal long-distance telephone call.

InterNIC organisation that was originally responsible for managing the way domain names are registered, assigned and paid for by organisations. Recently, the system has changed to allow a group of companies in different countries to manage the registration and payment process

interrupt electronic signal that diverts the central processor in your computer from one task to another. For example, if the processor is looking after the printer and you move your mouse, this will generate an interrupt signal that tells the processor to look after the mouse actions.

interrupt request
see IRQ

intranet private network of computers within a company that provide similar functions to the Internet - such as electronic mail, newsgroups and the WWW, but do not have the associated security risks of making the information public or linking the company to a public network

invalid input to a program that is not appropriate. For example, if you are prompted to enter the date and you enter a name by mistake, this invalid response will be rejected.

IP INTERNET PROTOCOL protocol used to carry data over the Internet; it is part of the TCP/IP protocol suite
see also TCP/IP

IP address unique 32-bit number that defines the precise location of a

computer connected to a network or the Internet using the TCP/IP protocol
see also DNS, TCP/IP

IP multicast process of sending out one set of data to several recipients simultaneously

IP spoofing method of gaining unauthorised access to a computer (or network) by pretending to be an authorised computer or device; each device on the network has its own unique address (its IP address) and many security systems block or allow access to networks based on the computer's IP address. A hacker needs to find out which IP address is allowed (or trusted), then modifies the header information in the data packets from his computer to include this IP address and so allowing access to the target computer. Newer routers and firewalls use a range of techniques to spot this scheme and block the data.

IPng INTERNET PROTOCOL NEXT GENERATION a new version of the Internet Protocol (IP) that allows more computers to connect to the Internet and supports more data traffic
see also IP

IPsec IP SECURITY a set of security protocols that allows information to be transferred securely over the Internet and will be primarily used to setup and support secure virtual private networks (VPNs). The system works with packets of data at the IP layer and supports two types of public-key data encryption. The first, called Transport mode encrypts the data within a packet, but does not touch the header information (that contains the destination address, subject and source of a packet); a second mode, Tunnel mode, provides a greater level of security by encrypting all of the packet, including the header information.
see also HEADER, PACKET, PUBLIC-KEY ENCRYPTION, VPN

IRC INTERNET RELAY CHAT system that allows many users to participate in a chat session in which each user can send messages and sees the text of any other user

IRSG
see INTERNET RESEARCH STEERING GROUP

IRTF
see INTERNET RESEARCH TASK FORCE

IRQ INTERRUPT REQUEST signal from a device to the central processor that asks the processor to stop what it is doing and look after the needs of the signaling device

ISA INDUSTRY STANDARD ARCHITECTURE standard method of designing the expansion bus within a computer that allows any compatible expansion card to work in any PC that has an ISA bus. The ISA bus was the only bus design used in almost all PC-compatible computers and is sometimes called an AT bus and transfers data 16 bits at a time, which slows down newer faster processors that work with 32 bits of data. Because of this, this bus has been superseded by bus designs that provide faster data transfer

see also   EISA, LOCAL BUS, PCI, MCA

ISAM   INDEXED SEQUENTIAL ACCESS METHOD   efficient and commonly used method of indexing the contents of a database

ISAPI   INTERNET SERVER APPLICATION PROGRAM INTERFACE

(on a Windows NT server) set of commands and procedures that allow web server software to access other applications on the same server running Windows NT

ISDN   INTEGRATED SERVICES DIGITAL NETWORK   system that allows data and voice signals to be transmitted over a digital telephone line using an ISDN adapter. ISDN normally transmits data at 64Kbps - much faster than a normal modem - and makes a call and connects very quickly: you can dial and connect within a tenth of second using ISDN, wheras it could take over a minute using a traditional analog telephone line. An ISDN connection works in a similar way to a normal telephone call: you dial the ISDN telephone number and connect, this is different from ADSL or a leased line that provides a permanent digital link between two points

see also   ADSL, DIAL-UP, LEASED LINE

ISO OSI reference model   INTERNATIONAL STANDARDS ORGANISATION OPEN STANDARDS INTERCONNECT

official definition of the way a network is organised; the definition describes seven layers of network function from the lowest layer (physical), which deals with physical connections such as the wires, connectors and electrical signals; to the highest layer (application), which provides the user interface to the lower levels. OSI offers guidelines for developers enabling them to design networks and related products which can talk, regardless of their make and use.

ISP   INTERNET SERVICE PROVIDER   company that provides one of the permanent links that make up the Internet and sells connections to private users and companies to allow them to access the Internet. If you want to access the Internet you will (in most cases) have to have an account with an ISP. The ISP normally has very fast fixed links to other ISPs on the Internet and provides telephone access numbers for users to dial in with a modem or ISDN adapter. When you subscribe to an ISP you will be assigned a user name which will be your electronic mail address; for example, if you have an account with the XYZ ISP company, you might have a mail address of 'simon.collin@xyz.co.uk'. The ISP will also provide a list of telephone access numbers (called POPs - points of presence) that are used to dial into the ISPis computer using your modem. In order to connect to the Internet, you will need a dialer utility that dials the telephone access number, support for the TCP/IP protocol (included in Windows and Macintosh System) and a web browser and electronic mail program.

Jj

jack connector plug that has one central pin; usually used to connect audio equipment - for example, a microphone or speakers are connected to a sound card using a jack plug

jaggies slang term for the jagged edges that are visible along the sides of curves, graphics or round characters. Jaggies occur because the printer can only print individual dots rather than smooth lines.
see also ANTI-ALIASING

Java programming language derived from C++ developed by Sun Microsystems that is used to create small applications designed to enhance the functionality of a web page; for example, if you want to add multimedia effects to your web page, you cannot carry out these functions with standard HTML commands, so you could write a small Java program, called an applet, that is automatically downloaded by the user's browser and run on the user's computer. In order to run a Java applet, the user needs a web browser that supports Java, such as Microsoft IE 3 or Netscape Navigator. A Java applet is a self-contained program file that is downloaded separately from the web page and run on the user's computer; a JavaScript program is a series of commands included within a web page HTML file and executed by the web browser.
see also ACTIVEX APPLET, VBSCRIPT

Java Beans software system (developed by Sun Microsystems) that provides objects within the Java programming language, that is similar to COM and CORBA and can work with both these standards

Java Database Connectivity (JDBC) programming interface standard that allows a Java program to access external data sources; similar to the ODBC interface

JavaScript set of programming commands that can be included within a normal web page (that is written using HTML commands); the JavaScript commands carry out a function to enhance the web page - such as providing the time of day, animation or form processing. A Java applet is a self-contained program file that is downloaded separately from the web page and run on the user's computer; a JavaScript program is a series of commands included within a web page HTML file and executed by the web browser. To write JavaScript you need to learn the script commands and then use an editor to add them to your web page file; to create a Java

application you need a program compiler and programming skills
see also ACTIVEX APPLET, VBSCRIPT

JDBC
see JAVA DATABASE CONNECTIVITY

Jet database engine software developed by Microsoft that is used in most of the Microsoft applications; for example, the Microsoft Access database management application uses the Jet database engine to carry out its commands; Jet is normally only accessed by other applications and is not directly used by a user

jitter fault on a monitor that manifests itself with very annoying, tiny movements of the characters displayed.

joystick device that lets you control the movement of a cursor by tilting an upright rod. Usually used for games. In order to use a joystick, you will need to fit a joystick controller card inside your PC. The first PCs had joystick ports fitted, but now it is common for the sound card to provide the joystick port. The port itself looks like a serial port connector with nine pins arranged within a D-shaped surround.

JPEG JOINT PHOTOGRAPHIC EXPERTS GROUP standard that defines a way of storing graphic images in a compressed format in a file on disk; JPEG is a complex way of storing images in a compressed format so that they take up a fraction of the disk space of the uncompressed image.
see also GIF, MPEG

JScript version of JavaScript developed by Microsoft

jukebox CD-ROM drive that can hold several CD-ROM discs and select the correct disc when required

justify to align text so that both the left and right hand margins are flush and level. This is normally an option on your wordprocessor and is carried out automatically - the wordprocessor inserts tiny spaces between the words to make each margin level.

Kk

Kb *or* **Kbyte** KILO BYTE measure of the data capacity of a storage device that is equal to 1024 bytes. A more comprehensible way of imagining this is that in a document, each byte normally represents one character so one Kbyte is equal to 1024 characters
see also BINARY, MBYTE

Kbps KILO BITS PER SECOND measure of the amount of data that a device can transfer each second. A fast modem can transfer data at a rate of 33.6Kbps, wheras an ISDN adapter can transfer data at a rate of 64Kbps

kern to adjust the space between pairs of characters so that they are printed closer together. For example, in a monospaced character set each character takes up the same width. This looks odd when you have an 'i' next to an 'l', so most character sets kern pairs of letters so that they look better when printed. Some sophisticated wordprocessors and DTP programs let you adjust the kerning between pairs of characters manually.

key one of the individual buttons that make up your keyboard.

key combination/shortcut combination of two or more keys that carry out a function when pressed at the same time. For example, the key combination Alt-S normally saves the file you are working on in any Windows program; Alt-F4 will exit the program you are using. To use these key combinations, hold down the Alt key (lower left, beside the spacebar) and press the second key.
see also SHORTCUT

keyword word that you type into a search engine to find information.

K56flex communications standard developed by Hayes, Pace and other manufacturers for a range of high-speed modems that can transfer data at 56,000 bits per second
see also V SERIES, X2

KHz (i) measure of the frequency of a sound that is equal to one thousand cycles per second. The higher the number, the higher pitched the sound. Normal speech has a very limited frequency range - mostly between 300Hz and 2.4KHz, wheras music and other sounds can be heard at far higher and lower frequencies; (ii) You will also see KHz mentioned in the specification of a sound card. This can define two separate functions for the sound card: the first is the range of frequencies that the sound card can output and the second, and more usual use, is the frequency at which the sound card takes samples of a sound when recording it onto your disk. A sound card looks at the level of a sound (from a microphone) thousands of times each second and so builds up a picture of the sound. The more times it takes a sample, the more accurate the recording - and the number of times the sound card takes a sample per second is described in KHz. A good sound card would cope with 22KHz or 44KHz samples - 22,000 or 44,000 samples each second.

Kilostream   leased line connection supplied by British Telecom that provides data transfer rates of 64Kbit per second
see   LEASED LINE

LI

L1 cache LEVEL ONE CACHE small section of high-speed memory that is built into the processor chip to improve the speed and flow of data transfer
see also CACHE, L2 CACHE

L2 cache LEVEL TWO CACHE high-speed cache memory that is normally fitted to the computer's motherboard or, in the case of some custom processors, such as the Intel Celeron processor, which includes 128Kb of cache memory built into the processor chip itself
see also CACHE, L1 CACHE

L2TP LAYER TWO TUNNELING PROTOCOL network protocol (an extension to the PPP protocol) that allows the data from small Virtual Private Networks (VPN) to be transferred over a network (such as the public Internet) by enclosing the network packets from the VPN within a special packet that can then travel over the Internet (a process called tunneling)
see also TUNNELING, VIRTUAL PRIVATE NETWORK

label (i) paper label stuck to the outside of a floppy disk on which you can write; (ii) text name assigned to a disk normally during formatting; this name appears at the top of any DIR command or within the MyComputer window. To assign a new name in Windows, highlight the floppy disk icon and select its properties window and type in the new volume name; in DOS, use the LABEL command

LAN LOCAL AREA NETWORK way of connecting several computers together within an office or building so that you can exchange files or messages with another user on another computer that is connected to the local area network. To setup a local area network, each PC needs a network adapter fitted inside it and each then needs to be linked together with cable. A wide area network is similar to a local area network, but links computers that are miles apart - even those in different countries.

landscape document/orientation layout of a piece of paper in which the longer edge is horizontal. This is useful if you want to print out a wide spreadsheet or image. Documents and letters are almost always printed with the paper in Portrait format - the long edge vertical. You can change the orientation of the paper through Page Setup menu option of your wordprocessor or spreadsheet program: if you select landscape format, the

software then tells Windows to rotate the text before printing it.
compare with **PORTRAIT**

language Windows can support different foreign languages; in most
cases, the foreign country has not only a different set of accented characters
but also a different keyboard layout. For example, the UK and USA use the
QWERTY keyboard layout (this describes the first keys on the top left hand
row), whereas France uses the AZERTY layout. If you want to use a
different language for display and printing you will have to change the
language setup for both the font used to support the accents and the
keyboard layout for Windows. If you want to use some Central European or
Asian languages, you will need to buy new fonts for Windows

LAPM LINK ACCESS PROCEDURE FOR MODEMS error detection
systems for modems, defined by the CCITT, and included within the CCITT
V.42 standard
see V-SERIES

laptop small portable computer that can be carried around; a laptop
normally has a clam-shell construction with a fold-down lid that houses the
screen, a keyboard (often slightly smaller than full-size) and a floppy disk
and hard disk drive. An internal battery pack provides power for a few
hours' use. Most new laptop computers include colour screens and as much
computing power as a desktop but with the convenience of being portable.

laser printer printer that produces very high quality text and graphics
using a laser beam. The beam draws the characters as tiny dots - normally
300 or 600 dots per inch - onto a special drum; the drum then attracts a fine
black powder (called toner) to these dots which is then transferred onto a
sheet of paper. The final stage is to heat the toner which melts it onto the
paper forming a permanent printed image. A laser printer is more expensive
than almost any other type of printer, but is generally faster and produces
excellent print quality. The other types of printer include ink-jet printers that
are slower and do not have such high quality print. There are also
dot-matrix printers which are very noisy and have poor quality output, but
are cheap and are the only type of printer that can handle multi-part invoices
or other similar stationery.
see also INK-JET, DOT-MATRIX

LaserJet brand name for a printer model produced by Hewlett Packard.
The LaserJet has its own language called PCL that defined the way
characters and graphics were printed on the page. This language has now
become one of the two standards for sending data from a computer to a laser
printer - the other language is called PostScript. Many laser printers are
LaserJet compatible. This means that if you setup Windows so that it is
configured to support an HP LaserJet printer, it will work with any LaserJet
compatible printer.

latency time taken for data to travel across a network or the Internet from the sender to the destination

launch a program to start a program. You can launch a program by double-clicking on its icon within Windows or by typing in the program name at the DOS prompt. Within Windows 95, you can launch a program by typing in the program name from the Start/Run menu command

layer one part of a complex system, such as an operating system or network protocol; for example, the TCP/IP protocol suite has five layers that each carry out a different task; the OSI/ISO network model has seven layers

layout (i) (keyboard) arrangement of the keys on a keyboard; different countries have different keyboard layouts - the UK and US have a standard QWERTY layout which refers to the order of the first keys on the top left-hand corner of the keyboard. Other countries have different key layouts according to their accents and local requirements. If you want to change the keyboard layout of your PC, you can plug in a different keyboard and configure Windows to support this - using the Control Panel icon in Windows 3.1 or the Start/Settings menu option in Windows 95 or later; (ii) (paper) way of using a sheet of paper; there are two basic layouts for any printed page: with the long edge horizontally which is called landscape or with the long edge vertically which is called portrait.
see also LANDSCAPE, PORTRAIT

LCD screen LIQUID CRYSTAL DISPLAY SCREEN technology used to create thin displays normally used in laptop or PDA computers; there are three types of LCD screen available: a monochrome screen, a colour DSTN screen and a colour TFT screen. The monochrome screen has a thin light source behind the screen that glows. This is the cheapest type of LCD screen available for laptop computers and provides a reasonably bright, clear display. The two colour LCD screens are now a standard feature of laptops. A DSTN screen is cheaper but does not have such good colour or contrast as a TFT screen.

LCP
see LINK CONTROL PROTOCOL

LDAP LIGHTWEIGHT DIRECTORY ACCESS PROTOCOL new standard that provides directory services over the Internet; derived from the X.500 standard, LDAP is beginning to be included in many Internet applications and provides a way of organising, locating and using resources over the Internet listed within its database

leading space between lines of text printed or displayed. It is usual to measure the leading between two lines of text in points - one point is equal to 1/72nd of an inch. If you increase the leading between lines of text, the lines are often clearer to read and nicer to look at.

leased line   permanent communications link between two sites; companies that want to setup their own Internet server in-house would normally choose a leased line between their offices and the ISP (Internet service provider). Two ISPs could use a fast leased line to connect to each other to transfer data. A leased line provides a permanent link with no call charges, unlike ISDN, however it is more expensive to install. If you are planning to install your own WWW server in your company, it will probably be cheaper to install a leased line than pay the call charges for an ISDN connection
see also ISDN

LED LIGHT EMITTING DIODE   electronic component that emits light when an electrical current is passed through it. LEDs are often used as indicators on computers and printers or, in some cases, are used as the printing element in a printer instead of a laser
see also LASER PRINTER

left-handed mouse   configuration of a mouse so that the function of the two buttons are reversed; if you are left-handed you can swap the functions of the two keys using the setup software supplied with the mouse or by using the Settings function of Windows

left-justify   to print or display a paragraph of text with the left-hand margin aligned and the right-hand margin of the text ragged.

legacy   older technology or a previous version that is still supported in new developments to allow existing applications and hardware to still be used

level one cache
see L1 CACHE

level two cache
see L2 CACHE

licence agreement   legal document that accompanies any commercial software product and defines how you can use the software and, importantly, how many people can use the software. Unless you buy a network version of a software product, the licence allows one person to use the software - copying the software is illegal. If you want several people to use the software or if you want to use the software on a network, then you need to buy a multi-user licence.

light emitting diode
see LED

lightweight directory access protocol
see LDAP

line row of characters on a screen or printed on a page

line noise unwanted interference on a telephone or communications line that causes errors in a data transmission

line spacing number of blank lines that are printed between each line of text. This dictionary, for example, is printed with a single line spacing. If you print with double-line spacing each line of text is separated by a blank line.
compare with LEADING

link hypertext link from one web page to another; this could be a hotspot (an image) or a section of text (normally displayed in a web browser as blue and underlined text) that will move the user to another page when the user clicks on it
see also HYPERLINK, IMAGEMAP

link control protocol (LCP) protocol used to create a link between two computers to allow information to be transferred - provides similar functions to the PPP protocol but includes better security and authentication
see also PPP

linked object one piece of data that is referred to in another file or application. For example, if you open a spreadsheet program and a wordprocessor in two adjacent windows and drag the spreadsheet data into your document, Windows actually creates a link between the two files. The spreadsheet file is called an object and is linked into the document in your wordprocessor.
see also OLE

linking information (in Windows) feature that allows you to insert data from one application into a another application using its OLE function. For example, you can include a spreadsheet inside a document, which is then automatically updated whenever the spreadsheet changes.
see also OLE

Linux (normally pronounced 'lee-nucks') a version of the UNIX operating system originally developed by Linus Torvalds, who then distributed it free of charge over the Internet. Enthusiasts and other developers have extended and enhanced the software, normally also publishing their software free of charge. Linux has a very enthusiastic and loyal following and is one of the most popular operating systems for developers and people running web-based applications. Unlike many other operating systems, such as Microsoft Windows, the Linux software runs on a range of different types of computer hardware including the PC and Macintosh.

list box number of items or options displayed in a list; for a long list you can scroll up and down through the list using a scroll bar

listserv *or* **listserver**   server on the Internet that sends a newsletter or articles to a list of registered users; there are tens of thousands of listservers on the Internet that cover all sorts of subjects, from computing to Spanish, teaching to travelling. If you want to keep up to date with a specialist subject, join the related listserver. Any user can submit information that might be useful to the other users and this information is sent automatically by email to all registered users on the list. Anyone can become a member of a list; see sites such as www.liszt.com that catalogue all the lists available. The management of a listserver is normally carried out by a majordomo: if you want to subscribe to a list so that you start receiving information, send a message to the majordomo at the list address
see also AUTOMATIC MAILING LIST, MAJORDOMO

Lithium-Ion battery   a type of rechargeable battery that provides high output power in a compact and lightweight unit; this type of battery is often used in mobile telephones, PDAs and lightweight laptop computers. The main advantages of Lithium-Ion batteries is that they are light, powerful, and do not suffer from memory effect. However, they tend to be more expensive than the older NiCad or NiMH batteries.
see also MEMORY EFFECT, NICAD, NIMH

Live3D
see VRML

local   (i) (hardware device) that is attached to your computer; (ii) (software) an application that is running on your computer.

local area network (LAN)   way of connecting several computers together within an office or building so that you can exchange files or messages with another user on another computer that is connected to the local area network. To setup a local area network, each PC needs a network adapter fitted inside it and each then needs to be linked together with cable. A wide area network is similar to a local area network, but links computers that are miles apart - even those in different countries.

local bus   expansion bus within a PC that allows data to travel around the computer very fast. Normally, you would use the local bus to connect a graphics adapter to your computer to get the best possible performance when displaying images.
see PCI, VL-BUS

LocalTalk   networking standard used by Apple Macintosh computers to connect Apple computers together in a local area network. If you want to connect your PC to a Macintosh network, you need to get a LocalTalk network adapter and software for your PC.

log file   (i) file that contains a record of actions; (ii) (on a web server) file that contains details of the visitors to a web site, recorded automatically

with the visitor's DNS address, time and the name of the web page that they viewed
see also ACCESS LOG

log on command that tells the network you want to use the network resources. Normally, you need to enter your user name and password which is then verified by the network software before allowing you to access the resources

log off to stop using a network and work individually. Your computer is still physically connected to the network, but you have told the network software that you do not want to use the network features or resources. Log off can apply either to a local area network or to an online system, such as CompuServe or MSN. In the case of the latter two, you log off and disconnect by hanging up the phone line to the online service.

logic (i) Boolean algebraic operations that determine the outcome of binary numbers based on conditions; (ii) term sometimes used to describe low-level programming commands
see also BOOLEAN

login to enter your user name and password that allows the computer to check that you are an authorised user of the computer or network and permit you to use the resources

login script series of instructions that are automatically run when you log into a network. For example, if you log into your office network in the morning by typing your name and password, the login script might remind you of important information or just display 'good morning'

logoff steps that you carry out to stop using a computer or network, usually a single command like 'bye' or 'shutdown'

long filename feature of Windows 95 that lets you give files a long name (up to 254 characters long). Before Windows 95 was released, file names were limited to a maximum of just eight characters. For example, before your letter would be called 'MEMO27.DOC' now you can call it 'memo to Simon about project delta'. If you try and access files that have a long filename within an older version of MS-DOS that does not support this feature, then the filenames are shortened with a ~ symbol but can still be accessed correctly
see also EXTENSION

loopback test test mode for a modem in which any information sent to the modem from a local computer is immediately sent back to prove that the connection between the computer and modem is working

low memory memory locations from zero up to 640Kb.
see also HIGH MEMORY, EXPANDED MEMORY

low-power standby   energy saving feature of laptop computers and many monitors connected to a desktop. If you do not use the computer for a few minutes, it will shut down some parts of the electronics - normally the hard disk drive and the screen or monitor. When you start typing or move the mouse, the computer switches these parts back on to normal power levels.
see also   ENERGY STAR

LPT   LINE PRINTER   acronym that refers to the main parallel printer port on a PC
compare with   COM

lurk   to join an online conference, discussion group or chat room and listen to the messages without contributing anything yourself. Most discussion forums don't mind lurking, since it helps to build confidence from new users and lets someone check the content before joining in, however some chat rooms do not approve of lurking and immediately identify anyone joining to discourage people who do not contribute to the forum.

Mm

M MEGA- prefix meaning an amount equal to 2^{20} or 1,048,576

m MILLI- prefix meaning an amount equal to one thousandth

Macintosh personal computer developed by Apple; the Macintosh originally used the Motorola 68000 series of processor but now uses the PowerPC processor; it runs the System operating system that provides an easy-to-use graphical interface. The software is not naturally compatible with the Microsoft Windows operating system and the hardware is not naturally compatible with an IBM PC. However, special software or hardware can be fitted to allow a Macintosh to run Windows and Windows-based applications.
see also IMAC, POWER PC

macro series of commands or operations that are named and can be run at any time. For example, if you always carry out a series of operations on your text to turn it into a monthly report (perhaps, changing the font, adding a table, searching and replacing one character for another), then you could record a macro to do all these functions automatically. Almost all wordprocessor and spreadsheet programs can record and playback macros and Microsoft has taken this one step further by including the VBA (Visual Basic for Applications) programming language into its main applications such as Word and Excel to allow you to create complex macros

macro virus type of virus that is stored as a macro attached to a document or email message. Most advanced software applications, such as Microsoft Word (wordprocessor) or Excel (spreadsheet) or Outlook (email software) provide a macro language that lets users extend the application and automate features. However, as macro languages become more advanced and powerful, they also provide an opportunity for someone to create a macro that can delete files or corrupt data when run.

A macro virus will run when the document is opened; some viruses are benign, others carry out malicious damage on your files and data. The virus will also try and spread to other compatible documents and applications on your computer, so that any new documents you create are also infected.

The latest wave of macro virus attacks has targetted the Microsoft Outlook email software; the virus uses the macro feature of Outlook to re-send itself to all the email addresses stored in your email address book. The last major macro virus created so much extra network email traffic on the Internet that many servers were overloaded.

The best way to avoid a macro virus is to regularly run virus detection software that can check and remove viruses attached to documents and new email messages.

magnetic storage method of storing information as magnetic changes on a sensitive tape or disk, such as a floppy disk or hard disk
compare with CD-ROM, RAM

magneto-optical recording type of disc that stores data on an optical disc. It is similar to a CD-ROM, but the difference is that you can write to and erase data from an MOR disc many times. A magneto-optical disc can store over 600Mb of data.

mail
see ELECTRONIC MAIL

mail application programming interface
see MAPI

mail-enabled application application from which it is possible to send mail without specifically calling up your email package. Lotus is mail-enabling new releases of its Windows packages to automatically call up cc:Mail; WinMail supplies macros to mail-enable standard applications.

mail exchange record (MX record) (in an electronic mail system) information stored in the DNS (a database that helps locate a domain name on the Internet or a Unix network) that tells a mail system how to deliver a mail message to a particular domain (for example, mail sent to 'smith@pcp.co.uk' will be sent to the 'pcp.co.uk' server by the MX record, the local server then has to send the message to the user 'smith'

mail gateway software program or combination of server and software that links two different electronic mail systems together so that mail messages can be transferred from one system to another; for example, if you are using Lotus cc:Mail as the electronic mail product within your company, you would need to fit a gateway function to allow messages to be sent and received to users on the Internet. LAN email systems normally use one of three main standards (MAPI, MHS or VIM) to send mail messages - if you are sending mail from a LAN email system to the Internet the mail gateway needs to convert this standard to one of the Internet mail standards (such as POP3 or SMTP) before it can be delivered

mail merge to automatically include the address details from a database into a standard (or form) letter. For example, if you want to tell all your customers that your prices of goods are increasing, write one standard form letter and then include the name and address fields from your customer database. Almost all wordprocessor programs let you carry out a mail merge with an external database.

mail server computer that stores incoming mail and sends it to the

correct user and stores outgoing mail and transfers it to the correct
destination server on the Internet

mail transfer agent (MTA)   software program that manages the way
electronic mail messages are transferred over a network; a user would never
normally see this software and would use an email application (the mail
user agent) to create and read messages. On computers running the Unix
operating system and the Internet the 'sendmail' software is the most
popular mail transfer agent
see also   EMAIL, MAIL USER AGENT, MAPI, POP3, SMTP

mail user agent (MUA)   software used to create and read electronic
mail messages; this software creates a message in the correct format and
standard and passes this to the mail transfer agent that is responsible for
transferring the message over the network
see also   EMAIL, MAIL TRANSFER AGENT, MAPI, POP3, SMTP

mailbox   storage location that contains a user's mail messages; if you are
using electronic mail sent via the Internet, the mailbox will be on a mail
server computer at the ISP. To read your mail messages, you need email
software that can communicate with the mail server computer to send the
messages
see also   EMAIL, MAIL TRANSFER AGENT, MAPI, POP3, SMTP

mailing list   (in electronic mail) list of email addresses of users that
receive information on a regular basis from a company or person or other
people on the list; an Internet mailing list allows any member of the list to
send a message to the list, which will then automatically distribute a copy of
this message to all other members of the list; mailing lists are very popular
and provide a convenient method of distributing information or maintaining
discussions on the Internet
see also   LISTSERV, OPT-IN MAILING LIST

main memory   main electronic storage area outside the processor chip
that is used to store data and instructions for the software that is being run.
For example, a PC might have 64Mb of RAM (electronic memory
components) that forms the main memory for the computer. It might also
have other memory, such as 128Kb of cache memory built into the
processor itself

majordomo
see   LISTSERV

management information services
see   MIS

MAPI   MAIL APPLICATION PROGRAMMING INTERFACE   set of
standards (developed by Microsoft) that defines how electronic mail is sent
and delivered

mapping representing the network directory path on a remote computer with a local drive letter, enabling a user to view the contents of the remote directory by simply typing in the drive letter rather than the often long and complex directory path. If your computer has a floppy disk drive (drive letter A:) and a hard disk drive (drive letter C:), you could map drive letter E: to point to a directory path on a disk drive of another computer on the network.

mapping representing a network printer connected to another computer on a network with a local printer identifier, so a user can treat the remote network printer as if it is directly connected to their computer.

mapping transforming a two-dimensional image into a three-dimensional form that can then be rotated or manipulated.

margins blank spaces at the top, bottom, left and right of a printed page.

marquee text that moves slowly across the screen, used as a special feature of a web page; many web page design software applications provide a Java applet that will produce this effect or you can use a JavaScript program to display a marquee

maths coprocessor specially designed processor chip that is designed to help the main processor in a computer by carrying out calculations with floating point numbers, speeding up mathematical operations
see also COPROCESSOR

maximise (in Windows) command that increases the size of a window so that it fills the entire screen. In Windows 3.x you can maximise any window by clicking on the Maximise button - the up arrow at the very top right-hand corner of the window. In Windows, click on the middle of the three buttons in the top right-hand corner of the window

Mb *or* **Mbyte** MEGABYTE measure of the data capacity of a storage device that is equal to 1,048,576 bytes (which is equal to 2^{20}). Megabytes are used to measure the storage capacity of hard disk drives or main memory (RAM).
see also BINARY, KBYTE

MCA MICRO CHANNEL ARCHITECTURE design of an expansion bus connector inside the PS/2 range of IBM computers. The MCA bus provides 32-bit data transfer, is fast, but requires a special type of adapter that is more expensive than standard adapters.
see also EISA, EXPANSION BUS, LOCAL BUS

MCI MEDIA CONTROL INTERFACE commands that allow any program control multimedia, such as a sound card or video clip. You never see raw MCI commands, but you might see them referenced - the Media Player and Sound Recorded applets within Windows work by sending out MCI commands.

MDRAM MULTIBANK DYNAMIC RANDOM ACCESS MEMORY high performance memory normally used in video adapter cards to provide fast graphic display

media (i) something that stores or carries information - it is a rather vague term, but in computing it generally refers to diskettes or CD-ROM discs; (ii) information that is used within a multimedia presentation and can be sound, graphics, or video.

media control interface
see MCI

Media Player utility program supplied free with Windows that allows you to control installed multimedia hardware including video disc or audio CDs or playback multimedia files including sound, animation and video files. To run this program, select Start/Programs/ Accessories/Multimedia from the Windows toolbar

meg slang term for a megabyte.

mega- prefix meaning 2^{20} or 1,048,576

megabyte
see MB

megaflop MILLION FLOATING POINT measure of the speed of a processor calculated as the number of mathematical calculations it can carry out per second

megahertz
see MHZ

Memmaker software utility supplied with some versions of Microsoft MS-DOS and used to automatically configure the computer's memory settings to provide optimum performance

memory device that can store information, but generally used to refer to electronic components that can store data and are used to provide the RAM in your computer that is used to run the software. Electronic memory chips only 'remember' data for as long as electricity is supplied. This is not the same as disk storage which is long-term data storage on magnetic media. *see also* EPROM, DRAM, FLASH RAM, RAM, ROM

memory chip electronic component that stores binary data *see also* EPROM, DRAM, FLASH RAM, RAM, ROM

memory effect feature of nickel-cadmium (NiCad) rechargeable batteries where the battery's capacity to hold charge is reduced if the battery

is recharged before it has been fully discharged. For example, if a battery is half-charged when it is recharged, it appears only to have the capacity to carry the new half-charge rather than a full charge (it seems to have a memory for the last level of its charge). This problem was particularly noticeable on older NiCad batteries, but modern NiCad batteries suffer very little from this effect; other types of battery, such as the newer Lithium Ion battery, do not suffer from memory effect.
see also LITHIUM ION BATTERY, NICAD, NIMH

memory expansion to add more electronic memory chips to your computer; your PC needs memory to run software programs and Windows needs as much memory as possible - 8Mb of RAM is a reasonable quantity.

memory management unit
see MMU

menu list of options available in a program
see also DROP-DOWN, PULL-DOWN

menu bar line of options available that run along the top of a window; when one of the words in the menu bar is selected, a further list of options is displayed beneath the word (this is called a drop-down menu). For example, almost all Windows programs have a menu bar that starts with the word 'File'. If you select the word File, it displays a list of menu options that include Open, Save and Exit.

menu driven software that is operated by selecting options from menus rather than by typing in a command word
compare with COMMAND LINE

menu item single choice displayed in a menu

menu shortcuts key combination of two or more keys that are the same are selecting a menu option. For example, if you want to save the document you are working on in your wordprocessor, you can either choose the File menu and pick Save from the list or press Ctrl-S which is the standard menu shortcut.
see also HOTKEY, SHORTCUT

message box small window that is displayed on screen to warn you of an event or condition or error. For example, if you try and save a document with the same name as an existing file, a message box pops up to ask if you want to change the filename or replace the existing file with the new one.

meter - power supply utility within Windows 95 displayed as an icon in the bottom right-hand corner of the status bar that indicates how much power is left in your laptop's battery and whether your laptop is running from a battery or mains electricity power

MFM MODIFIED FREQUENCY MODULATION system of recording

data onto a magnetic hard disk
compare with RLL

MHS MESSAGE HANDLING SERVICE store-and-forward message
transfer mechanism used mainly by Novell; this system allows electronic
mail messages to be sent between users on a network or to users on remote
networks
compare with MAPI, VIM

MHz MEGAHERTZ measure of the frequency of a timing signal that is
equal to one million cycles per second. The higher the number, the faster the
clock that is generating the timing signal. This normally refers to the main
clock that sets the timing signal for the processor chip in your PC. The
faster the timing signal, the faster the processor will run and so the faster
your software will run; current high-performance processors use a clock that
has a frequency of 300MHz - the original PC used a clock with a frequency
of just 4.77MHz

micro- (prefix) means one millionth

micro outdated term that refers to a personal computer

Micro Channel Architecture MCA design of an expansion bus
connector inside the PS/2 range of IBM computers. The MCA bus provides
32-bit data transfer, is fast, but requires a special type of adapter that is
more expensive than standard adapters.
see also EISA, ISA

microfloppy name for the 3.5-inch floppy disk

microphone device that converts sound waves into electrical signals. In
order to record speech or sound on your PC you need a sound card that can
convert and store electrical signals and a microphone that converts sound to
electrical signals.

microprocessor
see CPU

Microsoft software publisher that created Windows, MS-DOS, Word,
Excel and many other applications. It dominates the software world for both
the PC and Macintosh.

Microsoft Exchange electronic mail and fax management software
supplied with Windows 95, now replaced by Microsoft Outlook and
Outlook Express

Microsoft Exchange Server program that runs on a server under
Microsoft Windows NT and provides sophisticated groupware functions
using the Exchange client software supplied with Windows 95

Microsoft Fax series of programs supplied with Windows 3.1 and 95
that let you send and receive fax transmissions from your PC. The Fax

software also lets you create coversheets for the fax transmissions.

Microsoft Internet Explorer web browser developed by Microsoft, currently available free, that allows a user to view web pages; supports many features including ActiveX applets
see also NETSCAPE

Microsoft Network (MSN) online service that was launched by Microsoft to provide information, weather, database links to the Internet and electronic mail especially for Windows 95 users. The software required to access MSN is built-into Windows 95.

Microsoft Outlook application that provides a range of features to manage email, fax messages, contacts, diary appointments, notes and projects

Microsoft Outlook Express free version of Outlook that is normally used for email; it has fewer extra features for managing contacts and appointments

Microsoft Windows operating system developed by Microsoft designed to make PCs easier to use; Windows is a GUI (pronounced gooeey) - a graphical user interface. It lets you control the computer using a mouse and represents files and folders as icons on screen. Before Windows was developed, PC users had to type commands into MS-DOS. The current version is Windows 95 that includes features to allow access to the Internet, allow users to send and receive fax and electronic mail messages
see also GUI, WINDOWS

MIDI MUSICAL INSTRUMENT DIGITAL INTERFACE special interface that lets your computer control musical instruments, such as a synthesizer, keyboard or drum machine. To create a MIDI setup you need a MIDI interface for your PC - which is often part of a sound card - and a cable that runs to your musical instrument.

MIDI file file stored on your PC that contains musical notes and sound information that can be sent via a MIDI interface card to a musical instrument. MIDI files can also contain information that describes the type of sound played as well as the note - for example, to inform the synthesizer to sound like a piano or trumpet.

MIDI Mapper program that is supplied with Windows 3.1x and that allows experienced MIDI users to change the way in which musical notes are sent to each instrument that is connected to the PC. For example, you could use the MIDI Mapper to re-direct all the notes meant for the drum machine to the electronic piano.

millennium compliance PC that has been built to work correctly into the year 2000; this feature should be part of all new PCs and ensures that the computer's BIOS and internal clock will recognise the year 2000 and leap

years within the next millennium. To prevent any problems, you need a
compliant PC and you also need compliant software
see Y2K, YEAR 2000

milli- (m) prefix meaning one thousandth

million instructions per second
see MIPS

MIME MULTIPURPOSE INTERNET MAIL EXTENSIONS
standard that defines a way of sending files using electronic mail software.
MIME allows a user to send files over the Internet to another user without
having to carry out any other encoding or conversion actions. MIME was
developed to get around a problem of many electronic mail systems that
could only transmit text which is stored in a 7-bit data format; programs,
multimedia, graphics and other files are stored using an 8-bit data format.
To send a binary file by email before MIME would require that you first
encode the file then send it as a text mail message; the recipient would then
have to decode the text file back to its original state

minimise to shrink an application window down to an icon so that the
application is still running in the background, but is not the active window.
To do this, click on the first of the three buttons in the top right-hand corner
of the window (or in Windows 3.1x, select the down-arrow button in the top
right-hand corner of the window). Minimising an application allows you to
run several applications at the same time, minimising the ones you are not
using. In Windows 95 and later versions, the application shrinks down to an
icon on the status bar; you can switch back to the application with a single
click on the icon. In Windows 3.1x the minimised applications appear as an
icon in the bottom left hand corner of the screen. To go back to the
application, double-click on the minimised icon.

MIPS MILLION INSTRUCTIONS PER SECOND measure of
processor speed that defines the number of instructions it can carry out per
second
compare with MEGAFLOPS

mirroring method of improving fault tolerance in a network. In a
mirrored disk system, two separate hard disks are connected to the same
controller. The same data is duplicated on the two drives by one controller.
This offers a cheaper, but less secure, fault tolerance than disk duplexing.

MIS MANAGEMENT INFORMATION SERVICES department in a
large company that runs the computer systems

MMU MEMORY MANAGEMENT UNIT electronic component in a
computer that manages the way in which data is stored in different RAM
chips

MMX MULTIMEDIA EXTENSIONS (Intel Pentium processor chip) that includes components that are used to improve the performance when dealing with multimedia and communications; typically, these improvements allow the processor to manage many different data sources at the same time, improving the way it can handle image processing, video, speech

see also INTEL, PENTIUM

mnemonic key sequence that is a shortcut to a menu option or function in an application. For example, pressing the Alt and F4 (written Alt-F4) keys at the same time will exit an application. Similarly, Ctrl and S (Ctrl-S) will save new changes to a document within a Microsoft application

MNP set of error-control standards developed by Microcom Inc. and adopted into the CCITT V.42 standard. MNP allows a modem or communications program to detect transmission errors and request a resend.

MNP 2-4 error-correcting communications protocol developed by Microcom Inc. and adopted into the CCITT V.42 standard. MNP allows a modem or communications program to detect transmission errors and request a resend.

MNP 5 communications standard that provides data compression, providing up to 2-to-1 compression (though averaging less).

MNP 10 error correcting communications protocol that can transfer data accurately even over poor-quality telephone connections. It adjusts rapidly to changing line conditions to get the best throughput. MNP 10 has been adopted for cellular modems.

mobile phone *or* **cellular phone** small, portable device that lets someone make and receive telephone calls; older mobile phone standards transmitted the user's voice as an analogue radio signal, current phones convert the voice to digital data and transmit this via a radio signal. New mobile phones provide data and messaging services as well as basic telephone functions: some include built-in modems to provide dial-up access to the Internet, many allow text messages to be transmitted to other phone users and some incorporate an electronic diary, organiser and address book. Current mobile telephones transmit information using the GSM, PCS or GPRS standard and can provide basic Internet access using WAP and GPRS

see also BLUETOOTH, GPRS, GSM, PCS, SMS, WAP

modal (in Windows) window that is displayed and that does not allow you to do anything outside it. For example, dialog boxes are normally modal windows - you have to reply to the dialog box before you can continue with the application.

modem device that connects your computer to a telephone line and allows you to dial and connect to an ISP - and so gain access to the Internet

(the word comes from 'modulator' and 'demodulator'). A modem works by converting your computer's data into sound signals that can be sent along a phone line. New communication systems (like ISDN, ADSL and cable modems) do away with this conversion and send information in its native digital format to provide much higher transfer speeds. Some modems are internal - you have to open your PC and fit the modem into a free expansion slot. Most modems are external and plug into the serial port of your computer. Current modems can transfer data at 56,000 bits per second, which is roughly equivalent to one and a half pages of A4 text every second. Most modems now also offer fax features that allows you to send and receive text and images to other fax machines. Lastly, many newer modems provide voice-mail features that allow your computer to work as a sophisticated answering machine
see also DIAL-UP, ISP, TELEPHONY

moderated mailing list mailing list in which someone reads all the material that has been submitted before it is distributed to the users on the list

moderated newsgroup newsgroup in which someone (the moderator) reads all the material that has been submitted before it is published in the newsgroup; most newsgroups are not moderated and anyone can write anything - moderated newsgroups usually have a '-d' after their name

moderator person responsible for reading messages sent to a mailing list and editing any messages that do not conform to the rules of the list, for example by deleting commercial messages

modified frequency modulation
see MFM

monitor device that displays the text and graphics from your computer. It looks and works rather like a TV set. Images are displayed as tiny dots on the screen (the smaller and closer the dots, the sharper the image). If you do a lot of design or DTP, you might consider a screen that is bigger than the normal 15-inch (which is normally measured across the longest diagonal).
see also MULTISYNC MONITOR.

monochrome monitor monitor that can only display black, white and grey text and images.

monolithic driver driver software that has a range of different functions or applications within one program
see also DRIVER

monospaced font font in which each character has the same width, making it easy to align tables and columns. In Windows, the monospaced font is called Courier.

morphing special effect used in multimedia and games in which one image gradually turns into another. For example, a tiger might gradually turn into a bucket over a few seconds.

motherboard main circuit board within your computer. If you open your PC (with the mains electricity unplugged), youill see the motherboard at the bottom of the case. It is normally varnished green to protect the tiny connections and has the main electronic components and connectors soldered onto it.

Motorola company that designs and makes the 68000 range of processors that are used in Macintosh and Atar' computers. Its latest processor is the PowerPC chip that is used in workstations and Apple Macintosh computers *see also* INTEL

mouse small, hand-held device that is moved on a flat surface to control the position of a pointer on screen. A mouse normally has two buttons. In Windows, the left-hand button selects text or starts an application. The right-hand button displays options for the item. If you want to change a file so that it can only be read, and not written to, move the pointer to the file name (in Windows 95 Explorer) and select the file with a single click on the left-hand button. Now click once on the right-hand button to display the properties for this file.

mouse acceleration feature of some mouse driver software that will move the mouse pointer at different speeds according to the speed (not the distance) at which you move the mouse. For example, if you move the mouse slowly, the pointer will move slowly to allow you to carry out delicate tasks; if you move the mouse suddenly, the pointer will accelerate and move much further and faster

mouse-driven software that is controlled using a mouse rather than by typing in commands.

mouse driver special software that converts the movement of a mouse into position signals that inform Windows of the new position of the pointer on screen.

mouse pointer (in Windows) small arrow that is displayed on screen and moves as you move the mouse. The pointer is used to select and start applications. It can also change shape to an 'I' beam pointer.

mouse sensitivity ratio of how far the pointer moves on screen in relation to the distance you move the mouse - high mouse sensitivity means that a small movement of the mouse results in a small movement of the pointer

mouse tracking inverse of mouse sensitivity: high mouse tracking means that a small movement of the mouse results in in a large movement of the pointer, useful if you want to move around the screen quickly, but do not want to do detailed work

movie file file stored on disk that contains a series of images that make up an animation or video clip.

moving pictures expert group
see MPEG

MP3 MPEG AUDIO LEVEL 3 way of encoding digital audio data into a compressed data format that is approximately one twelfth the size of the original without perceptible loss of quality. MP3 files (that normally have the file name extension 'MP3') are now one of the most popular ways of storing and distributing music over the Internet. Because MP3 files are compact and easy to copy, they are relatively quick to download and very easy to distribute - which is causing problems for the original artists who are trying to protect their copyright material. Once you have an MP3 file you can listen to it by opening it and playing it with special software on your computer or by transferring it to a dedicated pocket-sized device that stores the file in its memory, has no moving parts and but can play back CD-quality music.

MPC MULTIMEDIA PC old set of minimum requirements for a PC that will allow it to run most multimedia software. Generally refers to PCs that have 4Mb or more of RAM, a 486SX processor or better, at least a 160Mb hard disk, a CD-ROM XA drive, 16-bit sound card and MIDI port.

MPEG MOVING PICTURES EXPERT GROUP group of developers that have defined a series of standards to improve audio and video quality but at the same time increase data compression so that the audio or video information takes less space but retains its quality. MPEG is often used to compress video clips and its derivative standards MPEG audio level 3 (MP3) provides one of the most popular ways of compressing and storing audio information, whilst JPEG provides a popular way to store compressed still images.
see also JPEG

MPPP MULTI-LINK POINT TO POINT PROTOCOL communications protocol used with ISDN to link the two B-channels in a standard ISDN adapter to create a transmission channel that can transfer data at a higher speed

ms MILLISECOND one thousandth of a second, often used to measure the time taken for hard disk access
see also ACCESS TIME

MS-DOS MICROSOFT DOS operating system software developed by Microsoft that controls and coordinates the basic functions of your computer. If you are running Windows 95 or later, the functions of MS-DOS have been integrated into Windows. If you are using Windows 3.1x or do not have Windows, then you are relying on MS-DOS (or a

similar product from IBM called PC-DOS) to control the computer.
see also OPERATING SYSTEM

MSN
see MICROSOFT NETWORK

MTA MAIL TRANSFER AGENT software program that manages the
way electronic mail messages are transferred over a network; a user would
never normally see this software and would use an email application (the
mail user agent) to create and read messages. On computers running the
Unix operating system and the Internet the 'sendmail' software is the most
popular mail transfer agent
see also EMAIL, MAIL USER AGENT, MAPI, POP3, SMTP

MTBF MEAN TIME BETWEEN FAILURES specification for new
electronic equipment, such as a new hard disk, that specifies the number of
hours (often tens of thousands) for which the equipment can be used before
it is expected to go wrong.

MUA MAIL USER AGENT software used to create and read electronic
mail messages; this software creates a message in the correct format and
standard and passes this to the mail transfer agent that is responsible for
transferring the message over the network
see also EMAIL, MAIL TRANSFER AGENT, MAPI, POP3, SMTP

MUD MULTI-USER DUNGEON adventure game played by multiple
users over the Internet

multi-part stationery stationery that has several sheets laid together
that produce copies without carbon paper. Donit forget that only impact
printers, such as dot-matrix or daisy-wheel printers, will print correctly with
multi-part stationery.

multibank dynamic random access memory
see MDRAM

multicast to transmit one message to a group of recipients; this could be
as simple as sending an email message to a list of email addresses or posting
a message to a mailing list. It can also refer to more complex transfers such
as a teleconference or videoconference in which several users link together
by telephone or video link. A broadcast, in comparison, refers to the process
of sending a message to anyone who could receive the message rather than a
select group of recipients. Narrowcasting is very similar in concept to a
multicast, but is normally used to refer to the concept, wheras multicast
refers to the technology used.
see also BROADCAST, MAILING LIST, NARROWCAST

multifrequency monitor
see MULTISYNC MONITOR

multimedia combination of text, images, video, sound and animation within an application.
see also MPC

multimedia extensions
see MMX

multimedia-ready PC that has all the extra equipment requirement to run most multimedia software. Normally, this means that it runs the Microsoft Windows operating system, is fitted with a CD-ROM drive, large hard disk, 8Mb of RAM and a sound card with speakers.

multipurpose Internet mail extensions
see MIME

multiscan monitor
see MULTISYNC MONITOR

multisession compatible CD-ROM drive that can read PhotoCD discs or other discs that have been created in several goes. For example, if you save one photograph onto a PhotoCD disc on Monday and another two on Tuesday, you have created a multisession disc. When buying a CD-ROM drive, make sure that it is multisession-compatible.

multisync monitor monitor that can be plugged into different types of computer and display different graphic resolutions. For example, if you have a normal desktop PC with S-VGA graphics (at a resolution of 800x600 pixels) and want to plug this monitor into your laptop computer, which uses an older EGA standard, the monitor will only display the images if it is multi-scan and can automatically switch between resolutions.

multitasking ability of Windows to run several programs at once. For example, under Windows you can sort a database address list while typing in a letter. The trick is that Windows actually switches repeatedly and very rapidly between the tasks, giving you the impression that they are running in parallel.

multithreading to run several different parts of a complex application at the same time to improve overall performance

music chip special electronic component on a sound card that creates the sounds which are then amplified and played back through speakers; some music chips create sounds from pre-recorded samples, others generate each sound according to your music software

musical instrument digital interface
see MIDI

My Computer icon that is normally in the upper left-hand corner of the screen on a computer running Windows 95 and contains an overview of your PC. If you double-click on this icon, you will see all the peripherals

that are connected to your PC including hard disk, floppy disk, CD-ROM and any printers
see also DESKTOP

MX record MAIL EXCHANGE RECORD (in an electronic mail system) information stored in the DNS (a database that helps locate a domain name on the Internet or a Unix network) that tells a mail system how to deliver a mail message to a particular domain (for example, mail sent to 'smith@pcp.co.uk' will be sent to the 'pcp.co.uk' server by the MX record, the local server then has to send the message to the user 'smith'

Nn

n NANO- prefix that means one billionth, often used to indicate the speed or access time of memory chips

name description given to a file, folder, printer or computer on a network. If you want to change the name of folder in Windows, move the pointer over the name and click once. Wait a couple of seconds and you will be able to type in a new name.

name registration
see DOMAIN NAME REGISTRATION

name resolution process of converting a domain name into its numerical IP address
see also DNS

name server computer on the Internet that provides a domain name service to any other computer
see DNS

namespace group of unique names; for example, in a small office network the namespace might include 20 users, in the Internet the namespace runs into hundreds of millions

naming services method of assigning each user or node or computer on a network a unique name that allows other users to access shared resources even over a wide area network.

nano-
see N

nanosecond
see NS

Napster software that allows users to share MP3-format music files over the Internet (these MP3 files are usually a personal recording of a commercial artist); the software, developed by Shawn Fanning, lets anyone download music from any another Napster users' computer. Once installed, the free software searches your hard disk for any MP3 music files, then allows other Napster users online to access these files from your hard disk, via the Internet. Because it allows music to be copied and shared very easily, Napster has become unpopular with the recording and music industry.

narrowcast
see MULTICAST

NAT NETWORK ADDRESS TRANSLATION   system that allows a
local area network to work with two sets of IP addresses for each computer
or node in the network. The first set of addresses is used for internal traffic
and the second set (often just one or two addresses) is used for external
traffic, for example when accessing resources on the public Internet via a
router. This system provides basic security against external attacks, for
example using IP spoofing. Its main purpose is that it allows the local area
network to use as many IP addresses as are required, but only using a
minimal number of public IP addresses (that must be registered and
allocated by an organisation such as InterNIC)

National Center for Supercomputing Applications (NCSA)
organisation that helped define and create the world wide web with its
Mosaic web browser

NC
see NETWORK COMPUTER

NCSA NATIONAL CENTER FOR SUPERCOMPUTING
APPLICATIONS
organisation that helped define and create the world wide web with its
Mosaic web browser

NDIS NETWORK DRIVER INTERFACE SPECIFICATION   standard
software interface that is used by network adapters to communicate with the
Microsoft Windows operating system

near-letter quality NLQ   printer that is almost as good as a traditional
typewriter. This now covers just about all printers except some cheap or
very fast dot-matrix printers that still look 'dotty'.

nerd (slang term for a) person who is obsessed with computers and rarely
talks or thinks about anything that is not technologically exciting
see also GEEK

NetBIOS NETWORK BASIC INPUT/OUTPUT SYSTEM   low level
software interface that lets applications talk to network hardware. If a
network is NetBIOS compatible, it will respond in the same way to the set
of NetBIOS commands, accessed from DOS by the 5Ch interrupt. NetBIOS
was the de facto standard, thanks to a lack of international standards, but its
limitations and age now make it near redundant.

netiquette   set of unofficial rules that define good manners on the
Internet

Netscape   software company that has developed a wide range of web
browser and web server software for use on the Internet and intranets

Netscape Navigator   one of the most popular web browsers that still dominates the marketplace; includes many features including a news reader, and supports Java applets (to read details of the newest developments, visit the www.netscape.com site)
see also   BROWSER, HTML, INTERNET EXPLORER, JAVA

NetView   network management architecture developed by IBM. Information about the way the network and nodes are working is sent to a central computer that provides reports that help a network manager spot any warning signs

NetWare   network operating system, developed by Novell, that dominates the local area networking market; one central server computer runs the NetWare software and other workstations connect to this server to share files, resources and printers
see also   NETWORK OPERATING SYSTEM

network   way of connecting several computers and printers together so that they can exchange information. To set up a network, each PC needs a network adapter and a cable that forms the connection between each; there are two basic types of network: a peer-to-peer network in which each computer can share its own files with other computers, or a server-based network which has a main dedicated computer to which all the other computers are connected
see also   NETWORK NEIGHBORHOOD, PEER-TO-PEER, SERVER

network adapter   board that plugs into an expansion socket inside your PC and converts data into electrical signals that are then transmitted over an electrical cable to other computers on a network; if you want to link three computers together so that they can each share files and resources, you have to fit a network adapter into each computer and link each with cable

network address   part of an IP address that defines the main network on which the domain is located: for class A networks this is the first byte of the address, for class B networks it is the first two bytes and for class C networks it is the first three bytes. The rest of the IP address forms the host address

network address translation
see   NAT

network computer (NC)   new type of computer that, it is predicted, will change the way computers are used. The network computer is designed to run Java programs and access information using a web browser. It has a small desktop box that does not have a floppy disk drive, instead it downloads any software it requires from a central server. Network computers are simpler and cheaper than current PCs and Macintosh computers, and are designed to be easier to manage in a large company.

network drive disk drive that you can access, but that is physically located on another PC on the network. To Windows, it appears to be just another disk drive - although its icon shows a tiny cable running beneath it. To view the network drives that are currently mapped to your computer, use the Network Neighborhood utility
see also MAPPING

network file system (NFS) network protocol developed by Sun Microsystems that allows a computer to share its local disk drives with other users on a network and is now used as a standard across most of the Internet

network interface card (NIC)
see NETWORK ADAPTER

Network Neighborhood utility that is part of Windows 95 that allows you to view and manage connections to your computer; if Windows 95 detects that you are connected to another computer, it will display the Network Neighborhood icon on your Desktop. This utility shows the other computers linked into the network and allows you to share the files stored on their disk drives or use a network drive or printer.

network news transfer protocol (NNTP) standard method of distributing newsgroup information over a Unix-based network (typically, the Internet), the NNTP is one of the protocols within the TCP/IP protocol suite and provides a way of creating, reading and distributing messages within newsgroups over the Internet. If you are reading the messages (called postings) in a newsgroup, the software is using the NNTP protocol to retrieve the messages
see also NEWSGROUP, NEWSREADER

network operating system (NOS) software that carries out all the functions required to support a network; the network operating system software normally runs on a dedicated server computer and each user's computer is linked to the server. The NOS manages the way in which files and printers are shared and ensures that unauthorised users cannot access the resources. The two main network operating systems used with PCs are Novell NetWare and Microsoft Windows NT/AS. Peer-to-peer networks do not use a dedicated server running network operating system software, instead each computer runs network software
see also PEER TO PEER

network printer printer connected to a computer that is also connected to a network, allowing you to use the printer as if it were connected directly to your PC

network server dedicated computer that runs network operating system software; the network server forms the centre of the network, with all the other computers connected to the server. Each computer can store files on the server's disk drive, or can print to a printer connected to the server. Small networks are often setup as a peer-to-peer network in which each computer can share files with others on the network. Large networks use a main network server that can be easily managed centrally

network time protocol (NTP)   protocol that provides an accurate time signal to computers on the Internet based on an atomic clock; allows local computers to synchronise their clocks

newbie   refers to someone who is a new user to the Internet

newsgroup   feature of the Internet that provides free-for-all discussion forums; newsgroups are one area within what is often called Usenet - a newsgroup lets anyone discuss a particular topic and there are over 15,000 different newsgroups that cover just about every subject available. Newsgroups are one of the most active parts of the Internet: you can read messages from other users, comment on them or submit your own message. To view newsgroups you need a connection to the Internet, either via an ISP or an on-line service such as CompuServe; you will also need special news reader software that lets you view the newsgroups together with the articles in each group. The Netscape Navigator web browser provides these functions as part of the software and Microsoft provides utilities to view newsgroups from within its IE web browser and within its Outlook and Outlook Express email software.
see also   ALT, BIZ, COMP, NNTP, USENET

news reader   software that allows a user to view the list of newsgroups and read the articles posted in each group or submit a new article; the software uses the NNTP protocol to create and read messages in the newsgroup
see   NEWSGROUP, NNTP

NFS
see   NETWORK FILE SYSTEM

NIC
see   NETWORK INTERFACE CARD

NiCad battery   NICKEL-CADMIUM BATTERY   type of rechargeable battery used in laptops but now superseded by the NiMH battery. NiCad batteries suffer from a problem called 'memory effect' which gradually reduces their ability to retain charge; to remove the memory you should condition a battery by running it right down so that it has no charge, before re-charging it
compare with   LITHIUM-ION BATTERY

NiMH battery   NICKEL METAL HYDRIDE BATTERY   type of rechargeable battery now used in laptops; has better charge-carrying ability than a NiCad battery, is quicker to charge and does not suffer from 'memory effect'

NLQ
see NEAR LETTER QUALITY

NNTP NETWORK NEWS TRANSFER PROTOCOL standard method of distributing news messages on the Internet, the NNTP is one of the protocols within the TCP/IP protocol suite and provides a way of creating, reading and distributing messages within newsgroups over the Internet
see also NEWSGROUP

node device that is connected to a network, such as a computer or printer

noise unwanted random signal that sounds like hissing on a recorded sound.

non-interlaced method of building up an image on a display using one pass over the entire screen
compare with INTERLACED

nonmaskable interrupt electronic signal from a device that cannot be ignored by the processor, normally generated by an important device, such as a reset button

nonvolatile memory that can retain information even when electrical power is not supplied to the device; a magnetic disk is nonvolatile, wheras a RAM chip is a volatile memory

NOS
see NETWORK OPERATING SYSTEM

notebook computer small portable computer that is normally designed as a folding clam-shell with a hinge at one edge, a flat LCD screen and a small keyboard. Notebook computers are normally lighter than laptops and have a smaller screen and keyboard.

ns NANOSECOND one billionth of a second, used to measure the access speed of RAM memory

NSFnet a wide area network developed by the National Science Foundation (NSF) to replace ArpaNet as the main government-funded network linking together universities and research laboratories. NSFnet was a crucial stepping-stone in the development history of the Internet; it was closed down in 1995 and replaced by a commercial high-speed network backbone that formed one of the foundations for the current commercial Internet

NT
see WINDOWS NT

NTFS
see WINDOWS NT FILE SYSTEM

NTP
see NETWORK TIME PROTOCOL

NTSC NATIONAL TELEVISION SYSTEM COMMITTEE governing body responsible for defining the video and television standards used in the USA

null modem cable special cable that lets you link together two computers via their serial ports so that they can exchange files.

NumLock key key on the top-left of the numeric keypad that switches the keypad between cursor control actions and number entry

NVRAM NON-VOLATILE RANDOM ACCESS MEMORY memory that can permanently retain information

Oo

o/p
see OUTPUT

object something that exists within an computer's user interface or operating system; for example, a folder is an object; a section of text, graphics, part of spreadsheet, even, in some cases, users and printers are objects.

object linking and embedding (OLE) system within Windows that allows information created and formatted in one application to be used directly within another, different application; for example, you can create a spreadsheet, then switch to a wordprocessor and insert the spreadsheet file into the document. To insert objects, select the Edit/Paste Special menu command and you will see a list of the types of object that you can include. Windows currently uses the OLE2 specification that allows greater flexibility and power when linking objects between applications

object-oriented method of creating software so that each part of the program is a separate object that works independently and can respond and react to other objects or events that occur in the system; for example, under Microsoft Windows, a window is an object, each menu option is an object. When you select a menu option, this sends a message to the program code that controls the menu object, which can then respond correctly

Object Packager utility included with Windows 3.x that lets you convert data from an application that does not support OLE so that it can be used as an OLE object in another application; this is redundant in Windows 95 since all programs for this platform support OLE

OCR OPTICAL CHARACTER RECOGNITION software application that can covert bitmap text stored in an image file (i.e. the result of scanning in a page of text) into characters that can be edited with a wordprocessor.

octet term used in networking to refer to eight bits of information used in some non-standard systems in which a byte (normally eight bits) is not eight bit long

OCX file extension of an ActiveX component or add-in that is used by an application (such as a web browser or custom application) running under Windows 95 or 98

ODBC OPEN DATABASE CONNECTIVITY software interface that

allows an application to access any compatible data source; the standard was developed by Microsoft but is used by many different developers as a standard method of providing access to a wide range of databases

odd parity way of transmitting data over a communications link that provides a very basic way of checking for transmission errors; the communications software counts how many '1is there are in each block of data it will transmit and sets an extra check bit to ensure that there is an odd number of '1is in the data. If you are setting up your communications software to dial into a bulletin board system or online service, you will need to know whether the service requires even or odd parity. Communications software packages like HyperTerminal in Windows lets you set the parity to either even or odd
see also EVEN PARITY, PARITY

OEM ORIGINAL EQUIPMENT MANUFACTURER company that produces equipment (e.g. a computer) using basic parts made by other companies

offline printer that is switched on, but is not ready to accept data. For example, if your laser printer runs out of paper, it normally automatically switches to offline mode until you insert more paper; it then switches back to online mode and continues printing. To stop printing at any time, press the online button to switch offline.

OK button (in Windows) button displayed on screen with the label 'OK'. If you click on this button, you accept the choice or options.

OLE
see OBJECT LINKING AND EMBEDDING

online (i) modem that is connected to another modem via a telephone line and is currently transferring information; (ii) a printer that is ready and waiting to print

online help help screen displayed about a particular function of a program

OnNow new standard that provides a way of integrating power management and control within all types of computer; the main benefit of OnNow is that it allows the development of a computer that is dormant but will be ready to use almost immediately after it has been switched on, unlike current computers that can take a minute to configure and load the operating system

open (i) to access a file and read its contents using an application. Most Windows applications will read a file via the File/Open menu option. ; (ii) to look inside a folder to view the list of files or sub-folders stored within it - open a folder with a double-click

open file file that is currently being read from or written to by an application or another user on a network

operating system software that controls and coordinates the actions of the different parts of your computer. In older computers, the operating system is called MS-DOS. In new PCs, Windows is the operating system that manages the screen, keyboard, disks and printers.

open systems interconnection (OSI) standard theoretical model of a network that is created from seven different layers each with a different function; this model provides the basis of almost all networks in use

operator symbol that defines a mathematical action, for example 'x' is the multiplication operator.

optical character recognition
see OCR

optical disc flat, plastic disc that can store data in the form of tiny holes or bubbles created in a central layer using a laser. Some optical discs can be written to several times, others, like a CD-ROM, are manufactured with the data in place and cannot have data written onto them.

optical mouse older-style mouse that uses a light sensor beneath the mouse to detect movement. The mouse is moved over a special mouse mat which has tiny location dots printed onto it.

opt-in mailing list list of email addresses in which each recipient has specifically asked to receive advertising email messages - normally so that they can keep up to date with a topic or industry. If you buy an email mailing list, make sure that it's an opt-in list.

OR Boolean function that is often used in searches to ask the search engine to find text that contains any of the search words; for example, if you enter 'dog OR cat' the results will include all documents that contain the words dog or cat
see also AND, BOOLEAN

orientation way in which a piece of paper is held; for example, portrait orientation is with the longer edge vertical; landscape orientation is with the longer edge horizontal.
see also LANDSCAPE, PORTRAIT

origin start of a counter or ruler; if you are using a paint or drawing program, the positions are normally measured from the origin which is in the top left hand corner of the work.

original artwork or photograph that has been scanned or copied.

original equipment manufacturer
see OEM

orphan first line of a paragraph printed at the bottom of a column, with the rest of the paragraph printed at the top of the next column.

OS
see OPERATING SYSTEM

OS/2 operating system developed by IBM that provides a powerful, multitasking graphical environment; OS/2 is currently in a version called Warp that looks similar to Microsoft Windows. Currently, applications written for OS/2 will not run under Windows, however Windows applications can run under OS/2 Warp

OSI OPEN SYSTEMS INTERCONNECTION standard theoretical model of a network that is created from seven different layers each with a different function; this model provides the basis of almost all networks currently in use

OSPF OPEN SHORTEST PATH FIRST protocol that allows a network to calculate the shortest route between two points, used when sending information from one node or computer to another. Each node has a basic map of the entire network and communicates with every other node in the network to send information about its local links; this allows any node to look at its internal map and calculate which route its should use when transmitting information. The protocol is widely used to provide fast, efficient networks, but does require considerable computing power at each node.

outline font font that is described by geometric shapes and lines, which can be scaled to any size without losing sharpness. Windows includes TrueType fonts that are outline fonts and can be printed in any size. *compare with* BITMAP FONTS

outliner software application that lets you organize your thoughts, ideas and their structure. Each headword can have many sub-sections beneath it - these too can have sub-sections or bullet points and you can view all the sections or just the headwords.

output anything that is produced by your PC - for example, a printout or sound.

Overdrive processor chip that is used as a more powerful replacement for a conventional Intel 80486 processor

overlay (i) strip of paper that is placed above the function keys on the keyboard to describe their function in a particular application; (ii) electronic device that will convert a video camera or TV signal so that it can be displayed in a window on screen

overlay card
see VIDEO GRAPHICS CARD

Pp

p PICO- one trillionth

packet basic unit of data sent over the network during intercommunication. A packet includes the address of the sending and receiving stations, error control information and check procedures, and, finally, the information itself.

packet Internet groper
see PING

packet switching method of sending a series of packets of information over a network in which each packet does not necessarily have to travel via the same route from originator to destination; the software sending the information decides the route over the network for each packet and the receiving software re-assembles the packets in the correct order

page (i) block of memory used in a memory management scheme; data can be stored in individual pages of memory and moved to and from the hard disk as and when required, the memory management software uses pages of memory to get around the 640Kb limit of MS-DOS; (ii) one section of a document; (iii) one screen of information
see also EXPANDED MEMORY, VIRTUAL MEMORY

page break point at which one page of text stops and the next starts. In many wordprocessors, you can insert a page break by pressing Ctrl-Enter.

page description language (PDL) series of codes and keywords that describe to a printer where and how to print text and graphics. When you print from a wordprocessor, Windows normally generates a complex series of page description language codes that are then sent to the printer
see also PCL

page design
see WEB PAGE DESIGN

page down key (PgDn) key that moves down one page in a wordprocessor

page impression a measure that's used to count how many times a web page has been displayed to a visitor to a website. Normally used as a crude counter for the number of visitors to a site and not as realistic as analysis of your website's access log.
see also ACCESS LOG, BANNER ADVERTISEMENT, IMPRESSION

page preview function within a wordprocessor or other application that lets you view the way the printed page, text, graphics and margins will look before they are printed.

page printer printer that prints a page in one go; generally refers to a laser printer; an ink-jet or dot-matrix printer creates a printed page one line at a time and they are called line printers.

page requests a measure of the number of pages viewed in a day, providing an indication of the popularity of your website. For a true indication, you should use special software to analyse your site's access logs and count the number of individual visitors - after all, a visitor might view several pages.

page setup options within an application that let you define the margins, paper orientation and paper size for the document.

page up key (PgUp) key that moves up one page in a wordprocessor

pages per minute (ppm) number of standard A4 text pages that a printer can print out each minute. A standard laser printer can print between 6-12 ppm, whereas a slower and cheaper ink-jet might manage 2-3ppm.

paint program program that lets you draw, cut, paste and edit a bitmap image. There are normally a series of tools that include a spray-can effect, and tools to draw circles, boxes and lines. Sophisticated paint programs can be used to edit scanned photographs and to adjust colours and remove any hair-line scratches or blemishes. A paint program cannot support vector graphics, instead it will only work with a bitmap image
compare with VECTOR

Paintbrush/Paint application supplied with Microsoft Windows that lets you create or edit bitmap images
see also BITMAP

palette range of colours that can be used in a paint program or printed on a colour printer

palm computer tiny computer that is about half the size of a paperback book; it does not contain a keyboard, but uses a touch-sensitive screen and character recognition to allow the user to enter information and control applications. Normally used for contact management, calendar and email. One of the most popular products is the 3Com Palm computer that runs its own operating system software and and a range of palm computers that can all run the Windows CE operating system software

palmtop computer tiny computer that is normally about the same size as a paperback book and contains a compact keyboard, screen and storage. For example, the Psion Organiser is a palmtop computer with a keyboard and screen that will run database, wordprocessor and spreadsheet

applications.
see also WINDOWS CE

paragraph section of text between two carriage returns. In Word, a double click will select a word, a triple click selects the line and four rapid clicks selects the paragraph.

parallel port connection at the back of your PC that lets you connect your computer to a printer. A parallel port sends data to the printer over eight parallel wires wrapped into one cable and are therefore eight times faster than a serial connection in which the data is sent sequentially.

parameter information that defines an option or function. For example, if you type in 'DIR /P' at the MS-DOS prompt, the '/P' parameter instructs the DIR command to list all files, pausing between each full screen.

parent folder folder that contains other folders.

parity method of checking for errors in a data transmission; there are two systems - odd and even parity. The number of bits equal to '1' in a section of data are counted by the sender and an extra bit is set according to this number. In an error detection system that uses even parity, the extra bit is set to create an even number of bits
see also EVEN PARITY, ODD PARITY

parity bit extra bit that is set according to the number of '1' bits in a section of data

partition way of dividing a hard disk into separate chunks that can then be addressed by separate disk drive letters. For example, if you buy a large 4Gb hard disk, you might find it convenient to split it into four 1Gb partitions that are then called C:, D:, E:, and F:.

password secret word or phrase that is associated with your user name and confirms your identity. If you subscribe to an online service, such as CompuServe, you will have a public user name and number and a secret password that only you know.

paste to insert a section of text or other information that was previously copied or cut onto the Clipboard. For example, to move a section of text in a document: select the text, choose Edit/Cut, move to its new location and choose Edit/Paste.

Paste Special to insert a special object within a document; Windows allows you to insert sound, images, or data from other applications (such as a spreadsheet) into a document. To insert a special object, select Edit/Paste Special
see also OLE

patch small program that will fix an error within a larger program.

path series of directories or folders that locate a particular file. For example, if a file is in a sub-folder LETTERS within a parent folder SIMON, on drive D:, its full path is D:\SIMON\LETTERS

PC PERSONAL COMPUTER normally refers to an IBM-compatible computer that is based on an Intel processor. Originally, the term referred to an IBM PC that used an 8088 processor with 512Kb or 640Kb of memory - now this means any computer that runs MS-DOS or Windows; in some cases, PC also means any small computer including the Apple Macintosh.

PC-97 basic requirements for the hardware of a PC system that can run the Windows 95 operating system

PC-98 basic requirements for the hardware of a PC system that can run the Windows 98 operating system

PC Card electronic device, about the same size as a thick credit-card, that can be plugged into a PCMCIA adapter to provide a particular function; for example, PC Cards are available that provide a modem, network adapter, extra memory or hard disk drive functions
see also PCMCIA

PC-compatible software or hardware that will work on a standard IBM-compatible computer that uses an Intel processor and has standard ports and expansion slots.

PCI PERIPHERAL COMPONENT INTERCONNECT high-speed local bus designed by Intel that runs at 33MHz and is most often used in Pentium-based personal computers for network or graphics adapters. This high-speed connection on the motherboard of your PC can be used by components that need to exchange large chunks of information at high speed. For example, a graphics adapter could communicate with the processor and main memory at high speed over a PCI connection.
compare with VESA

PCL PRINTER CONTROL LANGUAGE type of page description language that was created by Hewlett Packard and is used in almost all its printers and those of many of its competitors.

PCM PULSE-CODE MODULATION way of storing sounds in an accurate, compact format that is used by high-end sound cards.

PCMCIA PERSONAL COMPUTER MEMORY CARD INTERNATIONAL ASSOCIATION
specification that defines a way of creating tiny peripherals that can be used on laptops and notebook computers; the PCMCIA standard defines the adapter and technology; a PC Card is inserted into a PCMCIA adapter to provide a particular function; the PC Card looks like a fat credit card and has a connector at one end; it fits into a slot in a notebook or laptop and can provide a tiny hard disk drive, modem, network adapter and many other functions and provides a way to expand the functions of a notebook

PCS PERSONAL COMMUNICATIONS SERVICE refers to second generation digital cellular mobile telephones; the term was defined by the Federal Communications Commission (FCC) to cover cellular mobile telephones transmitting digital signals using the CDMA, GSM or TDMA standards.
see also CELLULAR TELEPHONE, GSM, MOBILE TELEPHONE, SECOND GENERATION

PC/TV a personal computer that can receive, decode and display standard television images

PCX file method of storing a bitmap graphic image file on disk. The standard is widely used and is a convenient way of exchanging graphic files between different paint programs.

PD
see PUBLIC DOMAIN

PDA PERSONAL DIGITAL ASSISTANT palmtop computer that aims to provide all your day-to-day computing and communication requirements. This normally includes a wordprocessor, diary, database, email links, modem and fax within a device the size of a paperback book. Well known examples are the Apple Newton, the Psion Organiser and the 3Com PalmIII
see also PALM, PALMTOP

PDF PORTABLE DOCUMENT FORMAT file format used by Adobe Acrobat
see ADOBE ACROBAT

PDL
see PAGE DESCRIPTION LANGUAGE

peer single computer linked to a peer-to-peer network; each peer computer can share files or resources on other peer computers and can make its own resources available to the other computers on the network

peer-to-peer network way of connecting several computers together within an office or building so that you can exchange files or messages with another user on another computer that is connected to the network; this system does not use a central, dedicated server; instead each computer is connected to the next in line and each runs network software that allows it to share the resources of any other computer on the network. For example, if you have four computers running Windows you can connect them together to form a simple peer-to-peer network to allow the four users to share files, share a printer and exchange electronic mail messages - all using the networking functions built into Windows
see also NETWORK SERVER

pen computer small, handheld computer that does not normally have a keyboard, instead a user operates it using a pen to draw or point on the

sensitive display; many PDAs, such as the Apple Newton, now use a pen to allow a user to write text directly on to the screen; Microsoft has also developed a version of Windows (called Windows CE) that can be used in these handheld computers and operates with a pen rather than a mouse.
now usually called PALM COMPUTER

Pentium   processor developed by Intel and used in high-performance PCs. It replaced the 80486 and is compatible with all the older 80x86 processor range, and provides high-speed processing power; however this processor has been replaced by newer designs including the Pentium Pro and Pentium II

Pentium Pro   high-performance processor developed by Intel; this processor replaced the original Pentium

Pentium II   currently the most powerful in the Pentium range of Intel processors; unlike earlier Pentium processors, the Pentium II is now supplied in a special cartridge that fits into a special expansion slot on a compatible motherboard. Earlier Pentium processors fitted into a standard square processor socket and so could be upgraded, a Pentium processor cannot be easily upgraded to a Pentium II

peripheral   any add-on item that connects to your computer, such as a printer or modem.

peripheral component interconnect
see PCI

Perl PRACTICAL EXTRACTION REPORT LANGUAGE
programming language normally used to create CGI programs that can process forms or carry out functions on a web server; for example, if you want to add a form or search function to your web server, you could write a program using the Perl language - this program is run by the web server
see also CGI

permanent swap file   (in Windows) file stored on your hard disk, made up of contiguous disk sectors, which is used to store temporary data and pages from the virtual memory system that is used by Windows. If you start several programs running, for example Paint, WordPad and a big application such as Microsoft Excel, then Windows will use virtual memory (which is actually the permanent swap file stored on the disk) to store the programs that it cannot fit into the real RAM chips installed in your PC. Windows 3.x supports either permanent or temporary swap files, but a permanent file is faster - you can change the size and the file type from a temporary to a permanent swap file using the Control Panel icon in Windows, and selecting the Enhanced/Virtual Memory option. A general rule is that a permanent swap file is faster than a temporary swap file, but it takes up a section of disk space. A temporary swap file is deleted after it is been used, which is important if you are running short of disk space.

Windows 95 and later versions prefer to keep control of the swap file internally and does not allow a user to vary the size of the permanent swap file

personal computer
see PC

Personal Computer Memory Card International Association
see PCMCIA

personal digital assistant
see PDA

personal information manager (PIM) software that helps a user to organise their diary, appointments, address book and projects; Windows includes the Schedule+ PIM utility that provides diary and address book features and Microsoft Office includes the more sophisticated Outlook program that combines these features with electronic mail

personalizing term used by Microsoft that means you can change the settings of Windows from their default. For example, you can change the background wallpaper to display a different image behind your windows or you could change the colours of the title bars, the font used by Windows and so on. To make these changes, use the Start/Settings menu item in Windows or the Control Panel icon in the Main program group of Windows 3.1x.

perspective appearance of depth in an image in which objects that are further away from the viewer appear smaller - there is a new range of cheap 3-D software programs that let you add perspective to your images or to text.

PgDn
see PAGE DOWN KEY

PGP PRETTY GOOD PRIVACY encryption system developed to allow anyone to protect the contents of their email messages from unauthorised readers; this system is often used when sending credit card or payment details over the Internet

PgUp
see PAGE UP KEY

phase alternation line (PAL) standard for television transmission and reception using a 625-line picture transmitted at 25 frames per second; PAL provides a clearer image than NTSC and is used in most of Europe, except for France which uses SECAM. The USA and Japan use NTSC

Phone Dialer utility supplied with Windows 95 that allows you to dial telephone numbers from the comfort of your computer. In order to use this utility, you need to have a modem installed and connected to the telephone network, plus a normal telephone handset to use once you have dialed the number.

phoneme one small sound, several of which may make up a spoken word; used to analyse voice input to recognise words or to produce speech by playing back a sequence of phonemes

phono connector or RCA connector plug and socket standard used to connect audio and video devices; the male plug has a 1/8-inch metal central core that sticks out from within the centre of an insulated core. If you have fitted a sound card to your PC you will see two phono connectors on the back plate. These let you connect your sound card directly to your HiFi or tape recorder.

phosphor substance that produces light when excited by some form of energy, usually an electron beam. Phosphor is used for coating the inside of a monitor (the cathode ray tube); a thin layer of phosphor is arranged in a pattern of tiny dots on the inside of the screen and produces an image when scanned by the picture beam. In a colour screen there are three tiny coloured phosphor dots (coloured red, green and blue) arranged in a group; the different colours you see displayed are a mix of the light from the three dots.

phosphor dots individual dots of red, green and blue phosphor on the inside of a colour screen

phosphor triad group of three individual phosphor dots (representing red, green and blue) that together form a single pixel on a colour screen.

PhotoCD standard developed to store 35mm photographic slides or negatives in digital format on a CD-ROM. The PhotoCD is normally created at the same time as the photographic film is developed - by digitizing each frame at a resolution of 2048x3072 pixels with 24bit colour (together with a lower-resolution preview image file); one PhotoCD can hold 100 photographs. To read a PhotoCD disc, the CD-ROM drive must conform to the CD-ROM XA standard. If all the images are recorded onto the PhotoCD at the same time, then the disc can be read by a single-session drive; if further images are recorded onto the PhotoCD at a later date, then the disc can only be read by a multi-session CD-ROM drive (developed by Kodak and Philips). If you want to display photographs on your PC, the simplest and cheapest way is to use the PhotoCD system. Take photographs with a normal colour film and ask for a PhotoCD disc when you take the film in to the chemist (this service is normally only from the bigger chemists or photographic shops). You will receive the pictures as normal together with a CD-ROM which has graphic files of the pictures and can be accessed from your CD-ROM drive.

photorealistic computer image that has almost the same quality and clarity as a photograph; for example, images stored on a PhotoCD are photorealistic since they are scanned at a resolution of 2048x3072 pixels in 24-bit colour

phototypesetter device that can produce very high-resolution text on photo-sensitive paper or film; the phototypesetter, rather like a large laser printer, normally uses the PostScript page description language and can generate type at 2,540 dpi; if the device is capable of outputting text and half-tone images, it is normally called an image setter. If you want to produce a professional-looking newsletter or brochure, you would send a disk of the files to a bureau that has a phototypesetter machine; the bureau will produce a printed version that you can then give to a printer.

pica (i) measurement equal to 12points (0.166 inch); (ii) width of characters in a typeface, usually 12 characters to the inch

pico- (p) prefix meaning one trillionth

picture element
see PIXEL

PIF
see PROGRAM INFORMATION FILE

PIM
see PERSONAL INFORMATION MANAGER

pin metal wire or metal conducting leg on a chip or other electronic device

pincushion distortion fault with a monitor that causes the distortion of an image displayed in which the edges curve in towards the centre. Some monitors have controls to adjust the display to get rid of pincushion distortion - otherwise if a straight line or edge of a window displayed close to the edge of the monitor appears curved you should return the monitor to the manufacturers.

PING PACKET INTERNET GROPER software utility that will test the path to a particular node on a network or Internet to ensure that all the route is working correctly; the test works by sending a test packet of information to the host and waiting for the reply

pipe to create a link between two programs running on a computer so that the output of one program is sent as input to the other; in MS-DOS you can create a pipe between two DOS utilities using the '|' symbol

pipeline burst cache secondary synchronous cache that uses very high speed memory chips (with access speeds of around 9ns); the main feature of this type of cache is that it transfers large amounts of data in bursts during a CPU clock cycle

pipelining (i) method of executing several instructions in parallel to increase performance. Some new high-performance computers use pipelining or pipeline memory to try and boost performance by executing several instructions at once; (ii) to carry out more than one task at a time: for example, to compress and store an image on disk as it is being scanned

pirate to illegally copy commercial software applications

pitch (i) number of characters which will fit into one inch of line, when the characters are typed in single spacing (used on line-printers, the normal pitches available being 10, 12 and 17 characters per inch); (ii) frequency of a sound

pixel or picture element smallest single unit or point on a display or on a printer whose colour or brightness can be controlled. A monitor normally has a resolution of 72 pixels per inch, whereas a laser printer has a resolution of 300-600 pixels (also called dots) per inch.

plain old telephone service
see POTS

plain text text that is not encrypted and so can be read by anyone; once it has been encrypted it is called cipher text

plane (in a graphics image) one layer of an image that can be manipulated independently within a graphics program. Many drawing programs let you create different planes or layers within your drawing and edit the layers independently.

plasma display or gas plasma display display screen using the electroluminescing properties of certain gases to display text; this is a thin display usually used in small portable computers
compare with LCD, TFT

platform type of hardware or combination of hardware and system software that makes up a particular range of computers. For example, the PC-compatible platform usually means a computer that has an Intel-compatible 80x86 or Pentium processor running DOS, Windows 95 or another popular operating system. When you buy a new piece of software, the side of the box normally lists the type of platform that the software requires to run. This might be either the type of hardware, the amount of RAM or the operating system that is required.

platform independence software that can work with different types of incompatible hardware. For example, some software, such as Adobeis Acrobat graphics format, can be displayed on a Macintosh and a PC.

platter one disc in a hard disk drive; a hard disk drive normally has between two and eight separate discs (platters) mounted on a central metal rod (the spindle)

playback to run a multimedia title or view a video clip or listen to a recorded sound

playback head electronic device that reads signals recorded on a storage medium and usually converts them to an electrical signal

playback rate scale factor (i) (in waveform audio) sound played back at a different rate, directed by another application, to create a special effect - created by skipping samples rather than changing the sample rate; (ii) (video displayed on a computer) point at which video playback is no longer smooth and appears jerky due to missed frames; this is determined by the size of the playback window and the power of the processor. The first time you view a video clip on your computer, the software (normally Video for Windows) will analyse the speed of your computer and will work out the playback rate that it should use to display video action that appears smooth.

plotter printing device that creates an image on paper using a pen to draw onto the paper

Plug and Play (PNP) feature of most new PCs that allows the Windows operating system to manage and automatically configure new peripherals. When you plug a new peripheral (a printer or scanner) or adapter card (a new disk controller, network adapter or graphics adapter) into your PC you do not have to configure it or set any switches - when you next switch on the PC, Windows will automatically configure and set up the new peripheral for you. This process works with Windows 95 and later and peripherals that conform to the Plug and Play standard (also sometimes called PNP).

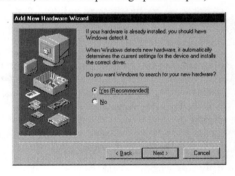

plug-compatible equipment that can work with several different types of computer, so long as they have the correct type of connector. For example, a SCSI hard disk drive will work with any computer that has a SCSI controller card - you could even switch a drive from a Macintosh to a PC.

plug-in program that works with a web browser to increase the functionality of the browser; for example, if you want to view Adobe Acrobat pages from your web browser you will need to get the Adobe plug-in that will then be used to view the pages; a 'helper application' provides similar functions as a plug-in, but displays its information in a separate, smaller window outside the main web page (for example, if a plug-in is used to display a video sequence, this appears as part of the web

page displayed in the web browser, if a helper application is used then the video is displayed in a separate pop-up window)
see also BROWSER, HELPER APPLICATION

PNP
see PLUG AND PLAY

point (i) to move an on-screen cursor using a mouse or arrow keys; see also pointer ; (ii) (typography) a unit of measurement equal to 1/72-inch - normally used to measure the height of a character

point of presence
see POP

point-to-point tunneling protocol
see PPTP

pointer graphical symbol - normally a small arrow - used to indicate the position of a cursor on a display. If you are using Windows, the pointer changes shape according to what you are doing. For example, it is normally an arrow, but would change to an I-beam pointer when you are typing or editing.

pointing device input device that controls the position of a cursor on screen. The most common example is a mouse, which controls the position of a pointer as you move the mouse; other examples are touchpads - common on laptop computers - that move the pointer as you move your finger over a sensitive pad.

point to point protocol
see PPP

policy
see ACCEPTABLE USER POLICY

polygon graphics shape with three or more sides

POP POINT OF PRESENCE telephone access number for a service provider that you can use to connect to the Internet via your modem. Most of the big service providers have dozens of POPs scattered across the country so that you can connect to the Internet with a local-rate telephone call. If you are trying to decide on a service provider, make sure that it has a POP near you or you will have to pay higher telephone charges if you are in Cornwall and its only POP is in Dundee. If you travel, check if the service provider has any POPs overseas or you will have to telephone a UK or home long distance telephone number to get onto the Internet.
see also ISP

POP 3 POST OFFICE PROTOCOL 3 system used on the Internet and some networks to read electronic mail messages stored on a mail server. In a standard setup, a user would have an account with an ISP, the user would dial the ISP and connect then use email software that retrieves new messages by issuing POP3 commands. The SMTP protocol is normally used when sending messages and IMAP provides a more powerful alternative to the POP3 system

see also   EMAIL, IMAP, SMTP

pop-up menu   menu that can be displayed on the screen at any time by pressing the appropriate key, usually displayed over material already on the screen; once the user has made a choice from the menu, it disappears and the original screen display is restored. This rather dry definition is best illustrated with an example, for example, if you use Windows you are probably using pull-down menus (select the Start button or File menu and you are using a pull-down menu) which appears below a menu option. Pop-up menus are used in DOS programs and in a few Windows applications.

pop-up window   window that can be displayed on the screen at any time on top of anything that is already on the screen; when the window is removed, the original screen display is restored. These are most often used to display warning messages or to confirm a choice. For example, if (under Windows) you try and save a file with a name that is the same as an existing file, you will see a pop-up window that asks if you want to overwrite the existing file or change the name - these pop-up windows are often called dialog boxes.

populate   to insert electronic chips into empty sockets on a motherboard, normally to upgrade your computer by adding more memory

port   (i) to transfer an application between platforms; (ii) communications channel that allows a computer to exchange data with a peripheral. On the back of your computer you will see a range of connectors - these are all ports between your computer and the outside world; (iii) (on the Internet) number assigned to each program that runs on a network server; normally you do not need to know this number, but sometimes you might need to access a program directly (such as when using Telnet) and in this case you would access the port

See also   PRINTER PORT, SERIAL PORT.

port replicator   version of a docking station that allows a laptop computer to connected to duplicate the connection ports on the back of the laptop; this allows a user to keep a mouse, power cable, and printer connected to the port replicator and easily insert the laptop to use these ports without having to plug in cables each time the machine is used

portable   (i) (any hardware or software or data files) that can used on a range of different computers. For example, Adobe's Acrobat graphics file format can be viewed on almost any type of computer; (ii) compact self-contained computer that can be carried around and used either with a

battery pack or mains power supply.
see also   LAPTOP

portable document format
see   PDF

portrait   orientation of a page or piece of paper where the longest edge is vertical. If you want to change the way in which a page is printed, you should use the File/Print Setup/Setup option in you application which allows you to change the orientation and size of the paper used.
compare with   LANDSCAPE

post   to submit a message to an online discussion group, newsgroup or mailing list

POST   POWER-ON SELF-TEST   series of checks that are carried out by a computer when it is first switched on and before it loads the operating system (such as Windows)

post office   central store for the messages for users on a local area network; the post office will also ensure that messages are delivered locally and might have a gateway to route any mail to other post offices or mail systems

post office protocol
see   POP3

postmaster   email address of the person nominally in charge of email within a company; if you are having problems reaching a user at a site, try sending a message to the postmaster

PostScript   language used to describe how a printed page will look - including the size, position and style of text and graphics. PostScript was developed by Adobe Systems and offers flexible font sizing and positioning; it is most often produced by DTP systems and used in high-quality laser printers and phototypesetters; Display PostScript is an extension of PostScript that allows PostScript commands to be displayed on a screen so that a user can see exactly what will appear on the printer. An encapsulated PostScript file contains PostScript commands that describe an image or page, the commands are stored in a file and this can be placed on a page; an encapsulated PostScript file often contains a preview image in TIFF format

POTS   PLAIN OLD TELEPHONE SERVICE   simplest, standard telephone line without any special features (such as call waiting or forwarding) and without high-speed digital access, such as ADSL.

power management   software built into laptop computers and some newer desktop PCs and monitors that will automatically turn-off components that are not being used to save energy. Power management is

designed to cut the electrical power supply to a device or peripheral when it is not being used. For example, if the computer has not been used for 10 minutes, the power management software might cut power to the disk drive (which normally spins constantly) or to the monitor. As soon as you hit a key or move the mouse, the power is re-supplied to the device and your computer 'wakes up' again. In a laptop, it is a good way of conserving the battery power and can often double the effective life of a battery.
see also ENERGY STAR

power down to turn off the electricity supply to a computer or other electronic device
see also SHUTDOWN

PowerPC high-performance RISC-based processor developed by Motorola and used in the PowerPC range of Apple Macintosh computers and in some graphics workstations and top-of-the-range PCs and Apple Macintosh computers
see also INTEL, MOTOROLA

power supply electrical device in a computer that converts the mains electrical supply to a steady DC voltage of (normally) 5volts and 12volts that is then used to provide electricity to the disk drives and electronic components in the computer

power up to turn on the electricity supply to a computer or other electronic device

power user user who needs the latest, fastest model of computer because he runs complex or demanding applications

ppm
see PAGES PER MINUTE

PPTP POINT-TO-POINT TUNNELING PROTOCOL protocol that allows a standard local-area network protocol (such as Novell's IPX or Microsoft's NetBEUI) to be sent over the Internet in a transparent manner without the user or operating system noticing, this is used by companies that want to use the Internet to connect servers in different offices

PPP POINT TO POINT PROTOCOL set of commands that allow a computer to use the TCP/IP protocol over a telephone connection. Normally, the TCP/IP will only work over a network, but the PPP system fools it into working over a telephone line. You might wonder what this has to do with you! The TCP/IP protocol is the way in which computers talk to other computers over the Internet, so you need to use the PPP system if you want to connect to the Internet using a modem.
see also LCP

preemptive multitasking feature of some operating systems (notably IBM OS/2 and Microsoft Windows 95 and later versions) that allows them to run several programs at the same time in an efficient manner. The trick is that with preemptive multitasking, the operating system is always in control: it executes a program for a period of time, then passes control to the next program so preventing any one program using all the processor time.

prefetch unit part of a microprocessor that sorts out which instruction and data is next to be processed; it looks in the main memory and the instruction cache and passes the next instruction on to the decode unit.

prescan feature of many flat-bed scanners that carry out a quick, low-resolution scan to allow you to re-position the original or mark the area that is to be scanned at a higher resolution

presentation graphics graphics that have been created to display business information or data. Presentation graphics are normally created in slides that can then be displayed on an overhead projector or direct on a PC monitor. If you are giving a lecture or trying to sell a product or giving a presentation on the latest company sales figures, each slide in the presentation graphics would illustrate a point or would show graphs or images to back up your speech. You can create your own presentation graphics using either a sophisticated wordprocessor or a paint program, but special presentation graphics software makes it easier to create slides and normally includes hundreds of logos and icons to make the slides more exciting.

Presentation Manager graphical user interface supplied with the OS/2 operating system, that is similar to Windows, but includes slightly different utilities

presentation software software application that allows a user to create a business presentation with graphs, data, text and images

pretty good privacy
see PGP

preview to display text or graphics on a screen as it will appear when it is printed out. Wordprocessors, such as Microsoft Word, have a standard view which allows you to type and edit rapidly. However, if you want to see the effect of margins, tables or columns, you would switch to preview mode which shows exactly how the page will look when printed.

primitive (in graphics) simple shape (such as circle, square, line, curve) used to create more complex shapes in a graphics program

print to produce characters on paper using ink or toner

print control code special character sent to a printer that directs it to perform an action or function (such as change font), rather than print a character

print job file in a print queue that contains all the characters and printer control codes needed to print one document or page

print life number of characters a component can print before needing to be replaced. For example, a laser printer toner cartridge normally has a print life of around 5,000 pages.

Print Manager software utility that is part of Microsoft Windows and is used to manage print queues

print modifiers special codes included in a document that cause a printer to change mode, i.e. from bold to italic

print preview function of a software product that lets the user see how a page will appear when printed
see PREVIEW

print queue list of the files waiting to be printed. If you are using Windows, the printing is normally controlled by the Print Manager - a program that will accept any document that an application wants to print and temporarily stores it on disk until the printer has finished the previous document.

Print Screen key special key in the top right-hand side of the keyboard that under DOS will send the characters that are displayed on the screen to the printer. Under Windows, its function has changed and it now copies the screen image to the Clipboard. For example, if you want to produce a manual for other users or want to print part of the Windows screen, press the Print Screen key. Now start the Paint program (from Start/Programs/Accessories) and choose the Edit/Paste menu option. A copy of the image that was displayed on screen is copied into the Paint file and can be printed or edited. If you want to copy an image of the active window (the window that has a dark blue title bar and is currently being used) rather than the whole screen, press the Alt and PrintScreen keys at the same time. To see what you have captured, use the Clipboard Viewer in the System Tools menu.

print server computer in a network that is connected to a printer and stores the print queue with temporary files before they are printed.
see also SERVER

print spooling to automatically print a number of different documents in a queue at the normal speed of the printer, while the computer is doing some other task

printer device that produces text or an image on paper using ink or toner under the control of a computer. There are many different kinds of printer: a daisy-wheel printer is an impact printer that strikes an inked ribbon with a metal impression of a character arranged on interchangeable daisy-wheels. A dot-matrix printer forms characters from a series of tiny dots printed close together; an ink-jet printer produces characters by sending a stream of tiny drops of electrically charged ink onto the paper (the movement of the ink drops is controlled by an electric field); a laser printer is a high-resolution printer that uses a laser source to print high quality dot-matrix characters normally at a resolution of 300 or 600dpi; a line-printer prints text one character at a time, moving horizontally across each line; a page printer composes one page of text, then prints it rapidly (such as a laser printer). A printer is normally connected to the parallel port at the back of your computer, but some printers will connect to the serial port (which is much slower at transferring data to the printer). When you connect a new printer to your PC you must tell the software - Windows - the type of printer you are using. Each printer is controlled by slightly different control codes and so each printer needs a printer driver - a special file that tells Windows how to control this particular printer. Before using a new printer you must install a new printer driver using the Printers icon in the Control Panel. If you are using Windows 95 or 98, it will automatically detect that a new printer has been connected and will try and work out the type of printer.

printer buffer temporary store for character data waiting to be printed; a printer buffer is used to release an application to continue working rather than wait for a slow printer that is printing the work

printer control language
see PCL

printer driver special file that tells Windows how to control a particular printer. For example, a PostScript printer such as a Hewlett Packard LaserJet 4M needs to receive data as PostScript instructions whereas an ink-jet printer needs to receive data as instructions that tell it how to print one line at a time. These differences are translated by the printer driver which sits between Windows and the printer. Windows comes with hundreds of printer drivers supplied - these cover most existing printers - however if a new printer is produced make sure that it is supplied with a Windows printer driver or you will not be able to print! The exception is if the printer is emulating another type of printer. For example, all PostScript printers can use the same basic PostScript printer driver.

printer emulation printer that is able to interpret the standard set of commands used to control another brand of printer

printhead (i) row of needles in a dot-matrix printer that produce characters as a pattern of dots. ; (ii) metal form of a character that is pressed onto an inked ribbon to print the character on paper; (iii) in an ink-jet printer, a plastic cartridge of ink together with a row of tiny holes that is used to squirt the drops of ink onto the paper.

printout final printed page

privacy statement the policy of a company (published on their website) that explains to visitors and customers what the company will (and preferably will not) do with a customer's personal details - such as their email address. Used to reassure customers that you're not about to resell their details as a mailing list.

PRN PRINTER acronym used in MS-DOS to represent the standard printer port. For example, if you are at the DOS prompt (C:\) and want to print a text file, such as the CONFIG.SYS file, you could enter the command 'TYPE CONFIG.SYS PRN' which will send the contents of the CONFIG.SYS file to the printer. This will not work if you have a PostScript printer, which expects data in the form of PostScript commands.

processing series of actions that a computer carries out to arrive at a result

processor *or* **CPU** electronic component that provides all the functions that control your computer and run software programs; a processor contains millions of tiny electronic components that have been designed to carry out basic arithmetic and control functions. A CPU can add or subtract two numbers, move numbers from one memory location to another or control an external device. Each of the actions of a CPU is controlled by an instruction - these are the machine code instructions that are used to create software programs. The specification of a CPU is defined in several ways: its speed (for example, 500MHz) roughly defines the number of instructions that it can process each second - 500 million in this case. The power of a CPU is also defined in its data handling capabilities: a 32-bit CPU can add, subtract or manipulate numbers that are 32-bits wide. A 16-bit processor can only handle 16-bit numbers, so would take twice as long to deal with a big number. Lastly, there are two main families of CPU. The Intel-developed range of CPUs includes the 80x86 and Pentium range. These are used in PCs and are backwards compatible. Other manufacturers, such as AMD, are licensed to manufacture these CPUs and they work in exactly the same way, for example the AMD Athelon processor. The second main family is the 68000 and PowerPC range from Motorola. These are used in Apple computers and are not directly compatible with the Intel range, although the PowerPC can run modified PC operating system software. A new range of processor, the Alpha range has been developed by Digital Equipment Corp. provides 64-bit data handling and can run Microsoft Windows NT
see also CPU, INTEL, MOTOROLA, NUMERIC COPROCESSOR

profile feature of Windows 95 that stores the settings for different users on one PC. This is normally used in companies, but could solve a lot of arguments at home! Each user has his or her own profile that describes how Windows looks and performs for each user. For example, Simon might want shortcuts to an Internet browser on the Desktop, wheras Sue might prefer to keep clear of the Internet and have CD-ROM titles installed as shortcuts. When you switch on the PC, Windows asks for your user name and configures itself according to the settings in the Profile. If you want to try out this feature, make sure that you read the user manuals carefully beforehand for a full explanation.

PROFS   electronic mail standard, developed by IBM, built into OfficeVision, allowing users to send messages over a network
see also   IMAP, MHS, POP3, SMTP

program   (i) complete set of instructions which direct a computer to carry out a particular task. For example, a wordprocessing software package is actually tens of thousands of separate instructions that respond to your various actions (such as printing, spell-check or formatting text). These instructions are written by a programmer who creates the program file that contains all the instructions. A program file normally has an extension of .EXE (or .COM for some programs); (ii) (in MIDI) data that defines a sound in a synthesizer; sometimes called a patch

program group   (in Windows 3.1x) window that contains icons relating to a particular subject or program - it is a convenient way of organising your files. For example, the Accessories icon opens the Accessories program group window that contains icons for the various utilities that are included with Windows, such as Paint, Write and so on. In Windows 95, the program groups no longer exist. Instead, there are program folders and program menu trees. Each program folder becomes a sub-menu of the Start/Programs menu.

program icon   icon that represents a program file; to start the program, move the pointer over the icon and double-click on the program icon.

program information file (PIF)   (in Microsoft Windows) file that contains the environment settings for a particular program; the environment settings include the amount of memory the program requires, the way in which in handles graphics and printers and disk space. Windows normally sets these options to standard values.

program instruction   single word or expression that represents one operation. For example, the program instruction ADD A,B adds the values of A and B. It gets a little more confusing when you consider the types of programming language: high level programming languages such as Visual Basic are easier to use, but each program instruction is actually made up of several low-level instructions.
see also   PROGRAMMING LANGUAGE

Program Manager   (In Windows 3.x) main part of Windows that the user sees; when you start Windows you'll see a background and a main window with icons and smaller windows contained within it. This main window is the Program Manager and it allows you to format a disk, run an application or carry out similar basic housekeeping commands. In Windows 95 or later, Microsoft scrapped Program Manager. Instead, the screen is now taken up by the Desktop. This contains icons for the different disk drives, options to format or view disks and so on.

programmable key key on a keyboard that can be assigned a particular function

programming language description of a series of instructions and commands that can be used by a programmer to create a software application; to write a program with a programming language, a programmer uses software that allows him to enter a series of instructions to define a particular task, which will then be translated to a form that is understood by the computer. Programming languages are grouped into different levels: the high-level languages such as BASIC and PASCAL are easy to understand and use, but offer slow execution time since each instruction is made up of a number of machine code instructions; low-level languages (such as assembler) are more complex to read and program in, but offer faster execution time

Programs menu sub-menu that is accessed from the Start button in Windows. The Programs menu lists all the programs you have installed on your computer and lets you start any program by selecting the menu item. The alternative way to start a program is to open the Windows Explorer utility or the MyComputer icon on the Desktop, double-click on the C-drive icon, select the correct folder for the program and then double-click on the program file.

prompt message or character displayed to remind the user that an input is expected; for example, DOS uses the 'C:\' command prompt to indicate that a command is expected - in the case of DOS, the command prompt also displays the name of the current disk and the name of the current subdirectory. For example, if you change directory to \letters, the prompt will now look like 'C:\letters\'.

properties (In Windows) attributes of a file or object. To view or edit all the properties of a file, select the file (with a single click to highlight the name) and click once on the right-hand mouse button. This displays a small menu of options - select the Properties menu option and you will see the various properties for the object. If the object is a file, you can view or edit the attributes to make the file read-only or hidden. You can also change the name or location of an object.

proportional spacing way of displaying or printing text so that each letter takes a space proportional to the character width (so that 'i' takes up less space than 'm'). This makes the text look neater when displayed, but can cause problems if you want to line up columns; in this case you should either tabulate the text or use a monospaced font such as Courier. *compare* MONOSPACED

protected mode operating mode of an Intel processor (the 80286 or higher) that supports multitasking, virtual memory, and data security *compare with* REAL MODE

protocol set of pre-defined codes and signals that allow two different pieces of hardware to communicate. For example, a simple protocol ensures that data is correctly transferred from a computer to a printer along the printer cable; other protocols ensure that a computer can communicate via the Internet or over a network. A protocol is equivalent to a spoken language. If you cannot get two computers to exchange information, it is likely that they are using different communications protocols

protocol stack separate parts of a protocol, each with a different function, that work together to provide a complete set of network functions

proxy server (i) computer connected to an intranet or Internet that stores copies of files and data held on slower servers and so allows users to access files and data quickly; (ii) a computer connected to a local area network and to the Internet that acts as a gateway, it retrieves web pages from remote Internet servers as required by a user but shields the user (for security) from direct access to the Internet

PrtSc PRINT SCREEN (on an IBM PC keyboard) key that sends the contents of the current screen to the printer or copies a picture of the screen or window to the Clipboard

PS/2 range of personal computers developed by IBM
see also MICROCHANNEL ARCHITECTURE

pseudo-static dynamic RAM memory chips that contain circuitry to refresh the contents and so have the same appearance as a static RAM component

public domain (PD) documents or images or sound or text or programs that have no copying fee or restrictions and can be used or copied by anyone. Public domain is rare, since it means that there is no copyright. More usual is freeware, in which the author retains copyright, but allows distribution and use for free.
compare with SHAREWARE

public key encryption method of encrypting data that uses one key to encrypt the data and another different key to decrypt the data; the key used to encrypt is made public to any one that wants to send you an encrypted message, but you keep the decryption key secret
see also PGP, RSA

publish (i) to produce and sell software; (ii) to design edit, print and sell books or magazines; computers and multimedia have greatly influenced how works are published: desktop publishing (DTP) is the design, layout and printing of documents using special software, a small computer and a printer, while electronic publishing uses computers to write and display information (such as viewdata or CD-ROM titles); (iii) to share a local resource with other users on a network (such as a file or folder) (iv) to place web pages on a web server so that users can view the pages on the Internet

pull to request information from another computer; often used when describing how functions of the Internet work: when a user types in a website address in a web browser, the browser requests the web page by sending a pull request to the web server. The opposite is push where a computer broadcasts information to other computers; some news services use push technology to automatically send out news stories to registered users.

pull-down menu set of options that are displayed below the relevant entry on a menu-bar. If you click on the Start button in Windows 95 or on the File menu in Windows 3.x you will see an example of a pull-down menu.

pulse-code modulation
see PCM, ADPCM

pulse-dialling method of dialling a telephone number that uses a number of pulses to dial a digit. For example, if you dial three, pulse dialling will send three pulses. This is an old-fashioned and slow method of dialling. Just about every telephone exchange can now use tone-dialling which is much faster: each digit has a different tone; a Hayes-comaptible modem can dial the number '123' using tone dialing with the AT command 'ATDT123' or using pulse dialing with the AT command 'ATDP123'
see also AT COMMAND SET, TONE DIALING

purge to empty the contents of the Recycle Bin in Windows 95; click once on the Bin icon, then click on the right-hand mouse button and choose the Empty option.

push (Internet) to send information to a computer or user; normally used to refer to a way of broadcasting information over the Internet. Electronic mail uses push technology to send a message to a user; the recipient has not requested the message, it is sent to the recipient. Some Internet-based news and current-affairs services use push technology to automatically send news stories and headlines to registered users. The opposite is pull technology.
see also CHANNEL, MAILING LIST, PULL

push-button square shape displayed on a screen that will carry out a particular action if selected; a push-button is normally made up of two images: one appears as if the button is protruding from the screen, the second, displayed when the button is selected, that is shaded differently to appear to sink into the screen

Qq

quad-speed drive   CD-ROM drive that spins the disc at four times the speed of a single-speed drive, providing higher data throughput of 600Kbps and shorter seek times. Quad-speed drives are now standard on most new PCs and, for high-performance PCs, have been superseded by six-speed drives.

quantize   (i) to convert an analog signal into a numerical representation; (ii) to process a MIDI file and align all the notes to a regular beat, so removing any timing errors

query   question entered into a search engine to retrieve selected documents from a database

query window   (i) window that appears when an error has occurred, asking the user what action he would like to take; (ii) window that is displayed with fields a user can fill in to search a database

question mark (?)   question mark is normally used in searches and is called a wildcard and means 'any character'. So, 'Print?' will match with 'Print' and 'Prints' but not with 'Printed'. To search for all three of these terms, you could use 'Print??'. Alternatively, you could use the asterisk '*' which means 'any number of any characters'. The question mark is also used in DOS and is useful when finding files that match a certain criteria. It is normally used with the DIR command; for example 'DIR print?.*' will display all the files that start 'print' and have any type of file extension. This would match 'Print.DOC', 'Print.TXT', and 'Prints.TXT'.

queue   collection of documents waiting to be printed

quoting   feature of many electronic mail applications that allows you to reply to a message and include the text of the original message; to distinguish the original text, each line normally starts with a '' symbol

QWERTY keyboard   English language keyboard layout for a typewriter or computer, in which the top line of letters are QWERTY. The French use a different layout with the keys on the top line reading AZERTY.

Rr

radio button circle displayed beside an option that, when selected, has a dark centre; radio buttons are a method of selecting one of a number of options, only one radio button in a group can be selected at any time (select another in the group and the first is deselected)

ragged text that is not straight or aligned and has an uneven edge

ragged left printed or displayed text that lines up flush on the right-hand margin but has an uneven left-hand margin

ragged right printed or displayed text that lines up flush on the left-hand margin but has an uneven right-hand margin

RAID REDUNDANT ARRAY OF INEXPENSIVE DISKS storage device that consists of a set of hard disk drives and is used in high-performance PCs or in network servers. The idea is that instead of using one big disk drive, it is more reliable to use eight cheap smaller drives and add one spare in case of a fault. The whole lot are packaged in a case. RAIDs are all the rage at the moment, so you will see a lot of advertisements with this term. It is not particularly useful for home PCs.

RAM RANDOM ACCESS MEMORY memory that allows access to any location in any order, without having to access the rest first (the memory chips in your PC are RAM, since any location can be accessed by specifying its address; a magnetic tape is not random access, since you must read through all locations before you reach the one you want to access)

RAM cache section of high-speed RAM that is used to buffer data transfers between the (faster) processor and a (slower) disk drive

RAMDAC RANDOM ACCESS DIGITAL TO ANALOG CONVERTER electronic component on a video graphics adapter that coverts the digital colour signals into electrical signals that are sent to the monitor

RAM disk
see SILICON DISK

random access memory
see RAM

range left move text to align it to the left margin

raw information that has not been processed or formatted or organised in a clear way (for access log file produced by a web server is raw data that lists each visitor to a web site, this file then needs to be analysed and formatted to produce useful information)

ray tracing (in graphics) method of creating life-like computer-generated graphics which correctly show shadows and highlights on an object as if coming from a light source; ray tracing software calculates the direction of each ray of light, its reflection and how it looks on an object

RCA connector
see PHONO CONNECTOR

RDBMS RELATIONAL DATABASE MANAGEMENT SYSTEM database software that lets you define how different fields in different files are related. For example, you might have a database of all your products sorted by their code number. Another file has a list of all your customers. A third file could be used for orders and would retrieve the customer details from the customer file and the product details from the product file.

read only file or memory device whose stored data cannot be changed. A CD-ROM disc is read-only, in that you cannot save a new version of a file to the CD-ROM as you could to a floppy disk.

read only attribute attribute bit of a file that, if set, prevents new data being written to the file or its contents edited. If you want to protect a file from being accidentally changed, you could set its attribute to read-only using the ATTRIB command in DOS or using its Properties page in Windows

read only memory (ROM) type of memory device that has had data written into it at the time of manufacture, and now its contents can only be read. A CD-ROM is normally considered a type of read-only memory since files are usually written to it when it is manufactured (in fact, this is changing since you can now buy personal CD-ROM writers).
see also EPROM, FLASH ROM

read/write head
see ACCESS HEAD

readme file file that contains last-minute information about an application; the file is normally stored on the disk or CD-ROM together with the application files

Real system used to transmit sound and video over the Internet, normally used to transmit live sound, for example from a radio station, over the Internet; to use Real Audio, your web browser needs a special plug-in that can be downloaded from www.real.com
see PLUG-IN, STREAMING DATA

real memory actual physical memory chips that can be addressed by a

CPU
compare with VIRTUAL MEMORY

real mode (in an old IBM-compatible PC) default operating mode and
the only mode in which DOS operates; real mode normally means only one
program can be written at a time and in which software can use any
available memory or I/O device
compare PROTECTED MODE, WINDOWS

RealNames system of assigning a trade name or descriptive name to a
website address; for example, if you want to find the web page that covers
Panasonic DVD players, you could type in 'Panasonic DVD' and
RealNames will translate this to the correct website address; the service is
supported by many of the major search engines, portals and web browser
software programs; for more information, visit www.realnames.com.

real time solving a problem in the same amount of time as the time taken
for the problem to occur. For example, an air traffic control computer has to
analyse the position of aircraft and produce real time directions for the path
of each aircraft; if the computer was not working in real time and instead
took minutes to analyse each aircraft position, it would be useless.

real-time animation computer animation in which objects appear to
move at the same speed as they would in real life; real-time animation
requires a powerful processor and a graphics adapter that can display a
sequence of 20 animated images every second

real-time authorization *or* **authentication** online system that can
check the authenticity and validity of a customer's credit card within a few
seconds, allowing the Internet shop to deliver goods or confirm an order
immediately; this feature is particularly important when selling software
that can be downloaded as soon as the credit card payment has been
authorized. In order to provide real-time authorization, an online shop needs
to work with a company that offers automated authorization; it can then link
its shopping cart software to the company's computer to provide the
equivalent of a real checkout till.
see also E-WALLET, SHOPPING CART, SSL

real-time clock clock within a computer that has its own battery and
continues to keep the correct time even when the computer has been
switched off.

reboot to reset your computer, equivalent to a soft reset that restarts the
operating system. The correct way to reboot a PC or Macintosh is to use the
meu option (Start/Shutdown/Reboot in Windows); if you press Ctrl-Alt-Del
in Windows or press the reset button you perform a hard reset that restarts
the computer and the system software

receipt notification feature of many electronic mail applications that will send you an automatic message to confirm that the recipient has received your message

record one complete entry in a database that might contain information in many separate fields; for example, in a customer database, information on each customer would be stored in a separate record, which would be made up of different fields for the name and address and order details

record head or **write head** transducer that converts an electrical signal into a magnetic field to record data onto a magnetic medium

record locking system used in database applications to prevent more than one user changing the contents of a record at the same time as another user is looking at the record

recordable CD
see CD-R

recordset group of records selected from a main database by a filter, search or query

Recycle Bin icon that is displayed on the Windows Desktop that looks like a wastepaper bin. If you want to delete a file or folder, drag it onto the Recycle Bin icon or press the Delete key. The Recycle Bin stores the file or folder for a certain number of days or until you purge the Bin of its contents. The contents of the Bin are not deleted from the disk until you shutdown your computer or choose the Empty option by right-clicking on the Recycle Bin icon.

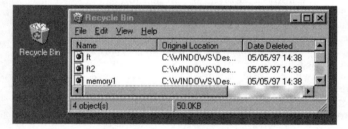

red, green, blue (RGB) (i) high-definition monitor system that uses three separate input signals controlling red, green and blue colour picture beams; (ii) the three colour picture beams used in a colour CRT; in a colour TV there are three colour guns producing red, green and blue beams acting on groups of three phosphor dots at each pixel location

reduced instruction set computer (RISC) type of design of a processor whose instruction set contains a small number of simple fast-executing instructions, that can make program writing more complex, but increases speed of execution of each instruction

redundant array of inexpensive disks
see RAID

refresh (i) process to update regularly the images on a CRT screen by scanning each pixel with a picture beam to make sure the image is still visible. The image on the screen is visible because tiny dots of phosphor shine; the glow from the phosphor only lasts a few tenths of a second and so the dots have to be 'hit' by the electron picture beam again, this process is repeated tens (often 60-70) times per second; (ii) button on a web browser that loads the web page currently displayed from the web server to show any new changes (useful for viewing information that changes rapidly, such as share prices)

refresh rate number of times every second that the image on a CRT is redrawn. The more times the image is redrawn every second, the less you will see flickering in the image - large screens have to be refreshed at a rate of 60-70 times every second to prevent the screen flickering.

region fill to fill an area of a screen or a graphics shape with a particular colour - in the Paint program in Windows there is a paint-can tool that will carry out a region fill of a defined area or shape.

register tiny storage areas within a microprocessor that store the data and instructions that the processor has to carry out

Registry database that forms the basis of Windows 95 and later. The registry contains information about every program that is stored on the disk and the users, networks and preferences. You never actually see the registry, but you might occasionally see an error message such as 'Object not found in Registry' which means some program has not been correctly installed. The registry is the replacement for the old INI files used in Windows 3.x.

rehyphenation to change the hyphenation of words in a text after it has been put into a new page format or line width

relational database database that lets you define how different fields in different files are related. For example, you might have a database of all your products sorted by their code number. Another file has a list of all your customers. A third file could be used for orders and would retrieve the customer details from the customer file and the product details from the product file.

relational database management system
see RDBMS

release version of a product

reliable connection connection between two modems that are both using an error correction protocol to ensure that data is transmitted without errors

remote access to use your desktop PC from another location with a telephone link. You need two computers, each with a modem, and special remote access software (that is built into Windows 95 and later) and this allows you to dial one computer and access the files and folders on its hard disk as if you were there.

remote client a user who is accessing mail without being connected to the mail server's local network. The user can be elsewhere in a WAN, or accessing the mail system via a modem link.

remote control software software that allows one user to connect to use one computer to connect (by modem, Internet or local area network) to another computer and access files, run programs and operate the distant computer as if they were in front of it and using it directly. Remote control software runs on each computer and provides a good way for someone at home to access their office computer or for someone in a technical support department of a large company to access a faulty computer on the office network.

remote procedure call (RPC) method of defining a client-server system in which a user (the client) sends a request to the server that processes the request and returns the answer to the client

REN RINGER EQUIVALENCE NUMBER number that defines the load a device places on a telephone network; any device that can be connected to the telephone network has this load number, if you connect equipment to your telephone system you must ensure that the total of all the REN numbers is less than four

renaming to change the name of a file or folder. In Windows, click once on the file or folder that you want to rename and keep the pointer over the icon. After a couple of seconds the description will be surrounded by a box and you can now edit the name. In DOS use the REN command and in Windows 3.1x use the File Manager utility.

rendering process of colouring and shading a (normally wire-frame or vector object) graphic object so that it looks solid and real

repeat rate number of times that a character will be entered on screen if you press and hold down one key on the keyboard

repeater electronic device that boosts a network signal and re-transmits it to allow the signal to be sent over a greater distance

repetitive strain injury or repetitive stress injury (RSI) pain in the arm felt by someone who performs the same movement many times over a certain period, sometimes experienced by people typing a lot or using the mouse for long periods of time - especially if they are not sitting correctly.

replay   to play back or read back data or a signal from a recording

reply   to answer an electronic mail message; this is often featured as a command in email programs and will automatically take information from the original message and, in the new message enter the correct address, copy the subject line from the original message and preface it with 're:' and insert the text of the original text

request for comment
see RFC

request to send (RTS)   signal used in an RS-232C serial port to control the flow of data from another device (such as a modem); when the computer is ready to receive more data, it sends a RTS signal to the modem that replies with a signal on the CTS pin of the RS-232C connector and then sends the next batch of data to to the computer
see also HANDSHAKE, FLOW CONTROL, CLEAR TO SEND

resample   to change the number of pixels used to make up an image; for example, if you scan an image at 400dpi and your printer is only capable of 300 dpi, you could resample the bitmap image to 300dpi, losing some detail but ensuring that what you edit is printed

reset   to return a system to its initial state, to allow a program or process to be started again; hard reset is similar to soft reset but with a few important differences: it is a switch that directly signals the CPU, while soft reset signals the operating system; hard reset clears all memory contents, a soft reset does not affect memory contents; hard reset should always reset the system if a soft reset does not always work

resolution   (i) number of pixels that a screen or printer can display per unit area; (ii) difference between two levels that can be differentiated in a digitized signal; (iii) degree of accuracy with which something can be measured or timed

resource   device which is available on a network or on a computer that can be used by an application or system software; this is rather a general term and can mean a disk drive on your PC or a printer connected to another computer on a network.

resource sharing   using something that is on another computer connected to the network. For example, if your company has a network of four PCs and one is connected to a printer, if the user of another PC on the network wants to print, he would be sharing this resource.

Restart   function of Windows that performs a soft reset of the operating system: click on the Start button in the bottom left-hand corner and choose

ShutDown, from the options, choose Restart to stop and restart the
Windows software. This function does will not automatically reset all of
your computer's hardware, but only effects the software.
compare with BOOT

restore to get good files and information from a copy to replace files that
have been corrupted on your computer
see also BACKUP

result code reply from a modem in response to an AT command sent to
the modem; the standard result code that indicates that the modem has
understood the command is 'OK'

reverse characters characters which are displayed in the opposite way
to other characters for emphasis (as black on white or white on black, when
other characters are the opposite), often used to indicate you have made a
selection or that you have control over a particular section of text. For
example, in Word, if you click once on a word you place the cursor at that
point. Double-click and the word is selected - indicated by reverse
characters - click three times and the line is selected; click four times and
the paragraph is selected.

reverse video screen display mode where white and black are reversed.

revert to return to the previous version of a document, losing any changes
that have been made since the document was last saved

RFC REQUEST FOR COMMENT document produced by the IRTF
and IETF that contains information about a proposed new standard and asks
users to look at the document and make any comments; each RFC document
is numbered and available to download from many library Internet sites; for
example, RFC 822 describes the specification for electronic mail message
headers

RGB RED, GREEN, BLUE (i) high-definition monitor system that uses
three separate input signals controlling red, green and blue colour picture
beams; (ii) the three colour picture beams used in a colour TV; in a colour
CRT there are three colour guns producing red, green and blue beams acting
on groups of three phosphor dots at each pixel location

RGB monitor high-definition monitor system that uses three separate
input signals controlling red, green and blue colour picture beams; there are
both digital and analog RGB monitors, both produce a sharper and clearer
image than a composite video display; in a colour CRT there are three
colour guns producing red, green and blue beams acting on groups of three
phosphor dots at each pixel location

ribbon cable type of electrical cable that is wide and flat; is is made up
of tens of individual insulated wires glued or bonded together to make them
more convenient to handle. For example, disk drives are connected to the

disk drive controller using a short piece of ribbon cable that is normally 50 wires wide.

rich text text that includes formatting such as bold, italics, etc

rich text format (RTF) way of storing a document that includes all the commands that describe the page, type, font and formatting; the RTF format allows formatted pages to be exchanged between different word processing software

right justify formatting command in a wordprocessor or desktop publishing software that makes the right hand margin of the text even; the left margin is ragged

right-click menu small pop-up menu that appears when you click on the right-hand button of a two-button mouse; often used to select formatting or the properties of an object. Windows 95 makes good use of the right-click menu. If you right-click over a blank part of the Desktop you can set the properties of the Desktop or create a new shortcut. If you right-click over a file or folder you can change its properties.

right-hand button button on the right-hand side of a two or three-button mouse. The left-hand button is used for most selection operations but the right-hand button is now being used more by Windows 95 to select the properties of a file or folder.

ring topology network architecture in which each node (computer or printer) is connected together in a loop; used in Token Ring network systems
compare with BUS TOPOLOGY

ringer equivalence number
see REN

RIP RASTER IMAGE PROCESSOR (printing) specialist computer or software application that converts a vector-based graphics image into a bit-map image. For example, to print an image or text page stored in the PostScript format, the file has to be converted to bit-map format using a RIP; in a PostScript printer, the RIP is part of the printer.

RIP ROUTING INFORMATION PROTOCOL (network) protocol that defines how routers exchange the information that describes the path the router should use to send data over the network (called the routing table). This protocol is now being replaced by the more efficient OSPF (open shortest path first) protocol.

RISC
see REDUCED INSTRUCTION SET COMPUTER

Rivest, Shamir, Adleman
see RSA

RJ-11 connector normally used in telephone sockets in the USA; if you travel to and from the USA and want to use your modem you will need a set of adapters to plug into the local telephone sockets

RJ-45 connector used in newer Ethernet local area networks that use twisted pair cabling and do not use coaxial cable
see also TWISTED PAIR

RLE RUN-LENGTH ENCODING data compression technique that stores any sequence of bits of data with the same value to a single vlaue

RLL RUN LENGTH LIMITED method of storing data onto the magnetic surface of a hard disk drive that is more efficient than MFM
see also MFM

robot or bot utility program that helps a user or other application carry out a particular task - for example a search robot will help a user search the Internet by submitting the query to several engines at once; a link robot will check that all the hyperlinks on a web site are correct

ROM cartridge software, data or font information stored in a ROM chip that is mounted in a cartridge which can easily be plugged into a computer or printer (often used to store extra font data)

ROM
see READ ONLY MEMORY

root or root directory topmost directory (in a file storage system on a disk) from which all other directories branch; in DOS and OS/2 and Unix this is represented as a single backslash character. For example, if you want to move to the root directory, you would issue the 'CD \' command in DOS. Confusingly, the root directory actually represents the top of the tree structure. As you move from the root directory to the subdirectories, you are moving into branches.

rot13 simple encoding that is used to scramble offensive messages posted in newsgroups; for example, offensive messages might be labeled 'rot13 reply' and this warns other users that the text has been encoded and that it is likely to be offensive. The encoding system is very simple: if A=1, B=2 and so on, add 13 to each number and display this text. Almost all newsreader applications can decode rot13 messages

route path that a data packet takes across a network from its source to its destination (if the data travels across the Internet, this route could cross many different server and networks before the data reaches its destination)

routed ROUTE-DAEMON software that manages the routes taken by traffic across a network, pronounced 'route-dee'
see also GATED

router device that connects one type of network to another; typically used to connect a local area network server or in-house Internet server to the Internet. A router is a device similar to a bridge but operating at a higher level within the OSI reference model. Routers detect protocols rather than the data they carry and use the destination address to work out the best route for the packet through a complex network. Typically used within an Internet or other wide area network, intelligent routers can select whether to use telephone links, LANs, or particular shortcuts through a network.

routine section of a computer program that carries out a particular function

routing information protocol (RIP) protocol used on the Internet to calculate the best route by which to transfer information over the Internet; RIP bases its selection on the distance that each route takes

row line of printed or displayed characters

RPC REMOTE PROCEDURE CALL method of defining a client-server system in which a user (the client) sends a request to the server that processes the request and returns the answer to the client

RS-232C standard that defines how to connect equipment together that communicates by sending data in a serial format (such as a modem to the serial port of a computer)

RS-422 newer version of the RS-232C standard that defines how serial devices are connected together; this new standard, approved by the EIA (Electronics Industries Association) supports higher rates of data transfer than the older RS-232C standard and allows simultaneous connections between more than two devices.
now mostly superseded by the USB

RS-485 standard that defines how serial devices are connected together for multipoint communications; this standard, approved by the EIA (Electronics Industries Association) supports higher rates of data transfer than the older RS-232C standard and allows more connections to one line than the RS-422 standard

RSA RIVEST, SHAMIR, ADLEMAN public-key cryptography system used to provide high-level of security
see PUBLIC-KEY

RSI
see REPETITIVE STRAIN INJURY

RTF
see RICH TEXT FORMAT

RTFM common abbreviation used in messages to mean 'read the manual'

RTP REAL-TIME TRANSPORT PROTOCOL (Internet) protocol used to transmit real time data, such as audio and video data and provides a basic technology with which to transmit streaming data (although extra software and protcols are required to manage streaming data)

RTS REQUEST TO SEND   signal used in an RS-232C serial port to control the flow of data from another device (such as a modem); when the computer is ready to receive more data, it sends a RTS signal to the modem that replies with a signal on the CTS pin of the RS-232C connector and then sends the next batch of data to to the computer
see also   HANDSHAKE, FLOW CONTROL, CLEAR TO SEND

ruler line   bar displayed on screen that indicates a unit of measurement; often used in design, DTP or word-processor software to help with layout or to set the tab stops.

rules   method of testing incoming electronic mail messages for certain conditions (such as the name of the sender or the contents) and acting upon them. For example, a rule could define that any mail from user 'boss' should be moved to the urgent folder
see also   FOLDER

run around   way in which a DTP or wordprocessing package can fit text around an image on a printed page. For example, if you insert a picture in a document and set its run around to 'nothing' the DTP package will assume the picture is not there and will overprint with text. If you set the run around to one point, the DTP package will leave a gap of one point around the border of the picture and will fit the text around the picture.

Run command   (in Windows) This command lets you type in the name of a program that you want to run or a DOS command your want to execute. To enter a command, select the File/Run menu command from the Program Manager of Windows 3.1x or the Start/Run menu option from Windows 95.

run-time   set of library routines required by an application when it is actually running. The program calls on the library of routines when it is running.

Ss

S-registers memory storage locations in a modem that contains the current configuration details for the way the modem operates
see also AT COMMAND SET

safe mode special operating mode of Windows that is automatically selected if Windows detects that there is a problem when starting. The safe mode does not let you do anything within Windows except to try and work out and fix the problem. When you first install Windows you should create a safe mode diskette that contains the initial configuration details for your PC. In case of problems, Windows will ask you to insert this diskette

sample measurement of a signal at a point in time, normally used to describe the action of a sound card that is converting a sound or noise into a form that can be stored on disk.

sample rate number of measurements of a signal that are recorded every second; a PC sound card normally supports one of the following three standard rates: 11,025, 22,050 and 44,100 samples per second (normally written as 11.025KHz, 22.05KHz and 44.1KHz)
see also ANALOG/DIGITAL CONVERSION, MPC, QUANTIZE

sample size size of the data word used to measure the level of the signal when it is sampled: normally either 8-bit or 16-bit words are used; an 8-bit word means that each sample can be one of 256 separate levels, a 16-bit word can have 65,536 levels and is more accurate at capturing the finer detail in the signal being sampled

save to store a document on a disk under a unique file name. Normally, Windows applications have a Ctrl-S shortcut for this function or you can choose the File/Save menu option.

save as menu option that allows you to save an open document to disk under a different name or in a different file format. For example, if you have written a message in Word and want to save it in plain text file format so that it can be sent as an electronic mail, you would select the File/SaveAs menu option and save it in a text file format.

scalable font font that can be displayed or printed in any size, without changing the shape of the font. Each character in a scalable font is described as a set of curves which can then be altered to print characters in just about any size without creating a jagged or ragged looking character.
see also OUTLINE FONT

scan (i) (optical) to convert a printed image or photograph into a digital bitmap form; (ii) (in a display) to move a picture beam across a screen, one line at a time, to refresh the image on the CRT; (iii) to convert an optical image (from a video camera) into a digital form by examining each pixel on one line of a frame, then moving down one line

ScanDisk utility supplied with MS-DOS (which is also part of Windows 95) that will check your hard disk for any problems and will try and correct problems that it finds. You should run ScanDisk once a month to keep your hard disk in shape.
see also DEFRAG

scanner device which uses photo-electric cells to convert an image or drawing or photograph or document into graphical data which can be manipulated by a computer; a scanner is connected and controlled by a computer which can then display or process the image data; a flat-bed scanner is a device with a flat sheet of glass on which the image or photograph or document is placed; the scan head moves below the glass and converts the image into data which can be manipulated by a computer; a hand-held scanner is a device that is held in your hand and contains a row of photo-electric cells which, when moved over an image, convert it into data which can be manipulated by a computer

Schedule+ software program that provides personal information management features, including a diary. The software is included as part of Microsoft Windows 95 but has been superseded by the Microsot Outlook software
see MICROSOFT OUTLOOK

scratchpad memory section of high-speed memory that is used to buffer data being transferred between a fast processor and a slower storage device (such as a disk drive)

screen (i) display device capable of showing a quantity of information, such as a CRT; (ii) grid of dots or lines placed between the camera and the artwork, which has the effect of dividing the picture up into small dots, creating an image which can be used for printing

screen angle angle at which a screen is set before the photograph is taken (different angles are used for the four process colours so as to avoid a moiré effect); the normal angles are black: 45 degrees; magenta: 75 degrees; yellow: 90 degrees; cyan: 105 degrees

screen attribute settings that define how each character will be displayed on screen. This includes the background and foreground colours and bold, italic or underline styles.

screen border margin around text displayed on a screen

screen buffer temporary storage area of memory chips - usually on a graphics adapter - that store the characters or graphics before they are displayed

screen burn   problem caused if a stationary image is displayed for too long on a monitor, burning the phosphor. This problem was the original reason why screen savers were developed. Now, screens are better made and the phosphor is more resilient. As a result, it is very difficult to cause screen burn...but the screen savers look good and are still used.

screen capture   to store the image currently displayed on screen in a file; it is useful when creating manuals about a software product; in Windows, you can capture the current screen to the Clipboard by pressing the PrintScreen key.
see also   PRINT SCREEN

screen dump   printed copy of what is displayed on the screen
see also   PRINT SCREEN

screen font   typeface and size of font used to display text on screen. Windows uses one font to display the names of all the files and folders and window titles. You can change this font setting from the Control Panel/Desktop settings.

screen grab   (i) digitizing a single frame from a display or television; (ii) see screen capture

screen saver   software that, after a pre-determined period of inactivity, replaces the existing image on screen and displays moving objects to protect against screen burn. This has now developed into an art form with screen savers often more complex than the applications running on the PC! Flying toasters are a favourite screen saver, although Windows includes a selection of less glamorous screen savers that can be setup and tested in the Control Panel/Desktop settings.
see also   SCREEN BURN

script   program that consists of a series of instructions that will be carried out by an application; a macro written to automate a feature of your wordprocessor is one type of script, a JavaScript program is a series of instructions included in a web page and executed by the web browser
see   JAVASCRIPT, JSCRIPT, MACRO, VBA

scroll   to move displayed text vertically up or down the screen, one line or pixel at a time

scroll arrows   arrows at the top and bottom of a scroll bar that, when clicked, move the contents of the window up or down or sideways

scroll bar   bar displayed along the side of a window with a marker which indicates how far you have scrolled through the document; by clicking on the scroll arrows at each end of the scoll bar a user can see different parts of the document. Some new mice have a small wheel between each button that, when it is turned, has the same effect as moving down the scroll bar

Scroll Lock key key that is rarely used but still included in the top right section of a keyboard; it changes how the cursor control keys operate and is sometimes used in laptops

SCSI SMALL COMPUTER SYSTEMS INTERFACE high-speed parallel interface used to connect computers to peripheral devices (such as disk drives and scanners). Fast-SCSI allows data to be transferred at a higher rate than with the original SCSI specification; SCSI-2 is a newer standard that provides a wider data bus and transfers data faster than the original SCSI specification; Wide-SCSI is a development that provides a wider data bus than the original SCSI specification, so can transfer more data at a time; SCSI is the current standard used to interface high-capacity, high-performance disk drives to computers; smaller disk drives are connected with an IDE interface, which is slower, but cheaper. SCSI replaced the older ESD' interface and allows several (normally eight) peripherals to be connected, in a daisy-chain, to one controller
see also IDE

search function that allows a user to find information, for example to find a word in a Word document, select the Edit/Find menu option. Windows 95/98 has a built-in function that will help you find information stored on your computer by looking in selected document files
see also FIND

search and replace function in a wordprocessor or database that lets you search for a word or phrase and replace it with something else. In some wordprocessors you can search and replace for formatting or text (for example, replacing all bold text with italic text).

search engine (on the Internet) software that carries out a search of a database when a user asks it to find information; on the Internet there are many search engines that list all the web sites and allow a user to find a web site by searching for particular information. Some of the most popular search engines on the Internet include Yahoo! (www.yahoo.com), AltaVista (www.altavista.com), and Excite (www.excite.com). Some search engines are selective (for example, Yahoo!) and use editors to check a site before it is added to the database. Other search engines (such as AltaVista) use specialist automated software tools (called spiders or robots) to try and find every new website on the Internet - an almost impossible task given the number of new sites that are launched every day. Each search engine has its own benefits and problems: for example, some specialise in a particular type of website (for example, sites about business or music). To help users there are metasearch sites, such as Google (www.google.com) and Ask (www.ask.com); these specialist websites will submit your search query to

dozens of search engines at once and compile the results to help you get the best from them all.
see also AGENT, GOPHER, METASEARCH

secondary memory permanent storage device in a computer that is used for storing files and data; in a computer, the primary or main memory is made from electronic memory components (RAM chips) that provide high-speed access to temporary data when the computer is working. However, main memory will not retain the information once the computer has been switched off and data that needs to be stored permanently has to be moved to a slower secondary memory device such as a hard disk drive, magnetic tape or optical disc.
compare with MAIN MEMORY, RAM

secondary service provider organisation that provide Internet access for a particular region of a country

sector smallest area on a magnetic disk which can be addressed by a computer; the disk is divided into concentric tracks, and each track is divided into sectors which, typically, can store 512 bytes of data

secure encryption payment protocol
see SEPP

secure electronic transactions
see SET

secure hypertext transfer protocol
see S-HTTP

secure/multipurpose internet mail extension (S/MIME) method of providing secure electronic mail messages; the system encrypts the main message using a standard cipher such as DES then sends the key in encrypted form using a second, public-key encryption system
see DES, PUBLIC-KEY

secure site *or* **website** website that includes features to ensure that any information transferred between the user and the site is encrypted and cannot be read by any hacker; normally used in a shopping site to allow a customer to type in their personal details (such as their credit-card number) without risk. Secure websites almost always use a system called SSL (secure sockets layer) that creates a secure channel when you visit the site; when you visit a secure site, the small padlock icon in the status bar at the bottom of your web browser is locked. If the padlock icon is open, this is not a secure site and you should not type in sensitive information, such as a credit card number.
see SSL

secure sockets layer
see SSL

security to ensure that your files or computer are protected against unauthorised access make sure that sensitive data or your PC is password protected. Some applications, such as Microsoft Excel, let you password-protect a file. Alternatively, you can configure Windows to require a user name and password before it starts

seek to move to a particular position in a file or on a disk

seek time time taken by a read/write head to find a particular track on a disk. Disk drives (and new computers) often state the access and seek times for the drive. The shorter the seek time, the faster the disk drive can move to the correct part of the disk and start reading information.

segment (i) length of cable in a network; (ii) amount of data that is used in a packet sent by a device using the TCP/IP protocol

select (i) to position a pointer over an object (such as a button or menu option) and click on the mouse-button; (ii) to find and retrieve specific information from a database

selection (in a paint program) to define an area of an image; often used to cut out an area of the image, or to limit a special effect to an area

selection handle small square displayed on the edge of an object or frame around a selected area that allows the user to change the shape of the area - this is particularly used in drawing and paint programs to let you adjust the shape or size of an object.

selection tool (in a paint or drawing program), the selection tool is an icon in a toolbar that allows a user to select an area of an image which can then be cut, copied or processed in some way

self extracting archive compressed file that has includes the software required to de-compress the contents; for example, if you download a demonstration program file from the Internet, sometimes it is compressed as a ZIP file - you need to use a separate de-compressing utility - or it is supplied as a program file that will automatically de-compress itself when you run it

Send To command menu command that is available from the File menu of Windows applications. It allows you to send the file or data currently open in the application to another application, such as an electronic mail system. If you choose the Send To menu option, you can send the document you are working on as an email to another user on the network or you can send it as a fax to a fax machine. The Send To command indicates that the application has been mail-enabled and can interact seamlessly with electronic mail programs.

sensitivity minimum strength or power of a received signal that is necessary for a microphone to distinguish the signal

SEPP SECURE ENCRYPTION PAYMENT PROTOCOL system developed to provide a secure link between a user's browser and a vendor's web site to allow the user to pay for goods over the Internet
see also PGP, S-HTTP, SSL, STT

sequencer (i) software that allows a user to compose tunes for MIDI instruments, record notes from instruments and mix together multiple tracks; (ii) hardware device that can record or playback a sequence of MIDI notes

serial line Internet protocol
see SLIP

serial port connector and circuit used to convert the data in a computer to and from a form in which each bit is transmitted one at a time over a single wire. Normally, data in a computer is transferred around the computer in parallel form that is eight or 16 bits wide. If you want to use a modem, you need to send the modem serial data that it can convert into sound signals that can be sent one at a time over a telephone line.

server dedicated computer which provides a function to a network, such as storing images, or printing data
see also NETWORK SERVER, WEB SERVER

server access logs
see ACCESS LOG

server side include (SSI) program that runs on a web server and is accessed from a web page to provide extra features such as a access counter, search engine or video delivery

service provider company that offers users a connection to the Internet; the service provider has a computer that acts as a domain name server and has a high-speed link to the Internet, it provides modem access to the Internet via point-of-presence telephone numbers. You connect to the Internet by setting up an account with the service provider then dialling into its point of presence telephone number with a modem.
see also ISP

session (i) one or more instances of an application; (ii) (in a PhotoCD) separate occasion when image data is recorded onto a disc

SET SECURE ELECTRONIC TRANSACTIONS secure method of paying for goods over the net; a more secure alternative to typing in your credit-card details - instead, your browser sends your unique identification code to the online shop, which it then passes on to a bank for confirmation; if you have money in your bank account, the bank confirms the transaction to the shop and transfers the cost of the goods to the shop's bank account.
see also SSL

setup program utility program that helps you configure your computer or a new software application

SGML STANDARD GENERALISED MARKUP LANGUAGE method of formatting and structuring the information in a document and includes commands to describe how information is related; normally used to produce multimedia titles or organise large quantities of information; HTML (used to describe web pages) was developed as a cut-down version of SGML and includes the simple formatting commands
see also HTML, WML, XML

shadow RAM method of improving the performance of a PC by copying the contents of a (slow) ROM chip to a faster RAM chip when the computer is first switched on

share-level access method used to set up network security to protect your local resources. This means that each resource (such as a printer, file or folder) that you want to share with other users on the network can be protected by a password. The alternative to share-level access is called user-level access. Windows for Workgroups and Windows 95 and later both let you setup share-level access for small networks of two or more PCs that have been connected together.

shared folder folder of files stored on your computer's local hard disk drive that can be used (or shared) by other users on the network. To share a folder, click once on the folder icon and then click on the right-hand mouse button. Select the Properties option from the pop-up menu and choose Sharing. Once you have set a folder as shareable, the icon for the folder changes so that it now appears with a cable running below the folder to remind you that other users have access to this folder.

shareware software which is available free to sample, but if kept the user is expected to pay a fee to the writer (often confused with public domain software which is provided completely free of charge)

sheet feed attachment device which can be attached to a printer to allow single sheets of paper to be fed in automatically

shell software which operates between the user and the operating system, often to try and make the operating system more friendly or easier to use; for example, COMMAND.COM is a basic shell that interprets commands typed in at the prompt; Windows 95 and later versions provide a complete, sophisticated shell with a GUI front-end that is operated by a mouse.

shell script scripting language (such as Perl) that is used to create programs that can enhance a web site, for example to search a site for a key word

shell out to temporarily exit from an application to the operating system whilst keeping the original application is still in memory; you can type in operating system commands and then return to the original application by typing the word EXIT.

shielded cable cable made up of a conductive core surrounded by an insulator, then a conductive layer to protect the transmitted signal against interference and a final outer plastic layer for protection

shielded twisted pair cable (STP) type of wiring, normally used in Token Ring networks

Shift key key on a keyboard that, when pressed with another character key will produce an alternative character; for example, the Shift key normally produces an uppercase character or the special character printed on the top part of the key

Shockwave system that allows web browsers to display complex multimedia effects, video clips and animation on a website; most web browsers include support for Shockwave, or you can download a plug-in from www.shockwave.com

shopping basket *or* **shopping cart** software that runs on a web server and provides an electronic version of a real shopping basket; the software allows a visitor to the web site to view items in the catalogue, add items to their shopping basket and then pay for the goods at an electronic checkout; some products (such a software) can then be downloaded from the web site and use immediately
see also REAL-TIME AUTHORIZATION, SECURE WEBSITE

shortcut feature of Windows that allows a user to define an icon that links to another file or application; for example, you could place shortcut icons on the Windows Desktop to allow you to start an application without using the menu commands. The shortcut has the same icon as the original file but has a tiny arrow in the bottom left-hand corner; the shortcut is not a duplicate of the original, rather it is a pointer to the original file.

short message service (SMS) system that allows short text messages to be sent between and to mobile telephones; the service depends upon the telephone company

shouting term of abuse that means you are typing a message or article in capital letters; if you submit an article to a newsgroup and the text is entirely in capitals, most other users will assume that you are a new user and do not know that this is disliked

S-HTTP SECURE HYPERTEXT TRANSFER PROTOCOL system developed to provide a secure link between a user's browser and a vendor's web site to allow the user to pay for goods over the Internet
see also PGP, SEPP, SET, SSL, STT

Shut Down (in Windows) command that will close down Windows and,

if you have a compatible PC, will switch off the computer. When you want
to switch off your PC, you should use the Shut Down command rather than
just switch off the computer since this ensures that all the files are closed
and that Windows sorts itself out internally before being switched off. To
exit Windows select the Start/Shut Down menu option. With some new
PCs, this will also automatically switch off the PC; with older PCs you need
to wait until the screen tells you it is safe to switch off the PC (which takes
around 20 seconds).

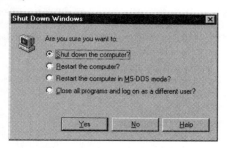

SIG SPECIAL INTEREST GROUP group of users who have a
particular interest and exchange email information or subscribe to a
newsgroup or mailing list

signal (i) generated analog or digital waveform used to carry
information; (ii) short message used to carry control codes

signature (i) special authentication code, such as a password, which a
user gives prior to accessing a system or prior to the execution of a task (to
prove his identity); (ii) a sentence or paragraph used to end email messages
and comments posted on the Internet. Normally a signature should be short -
no more than four lines - and might include a short advertisement for your
company and your email address. Most email programs can add a signature
automatically to the end of all email messages you send.

silicon chip small piece of silicon in and on the surface of which a
complete circuit or logic function has been produced (by depositing other
substances or by doping); silicon is used in the electronics industry as a base
material for integrated circuits. It is grown as a long crystal which is then
sliced into wafers before being etched or treated, producing several hundred
chips per wafer. Other materials, such as germanium or gallium arsenide,
are also used as a base for ICs

silicon disk or RAM disk area of RAM made to look and behave like
a high speed disk drive

SIMM SINGLE IN-LINE MEMORY MODULE small, compact circuit

board with an edge connector along one edge that carries densely-packed memory chips, and is used to expand a computer's main memory. If you want to upgrade your PC by increasing the amount of RAM it has, you can fit more memory by inserting SIMM cards. Make sure that you buy the correct SIMMs for your computer - you need to check the type of connector, the speed of the RAM and the capacity of the SIMM or they might not work in your PC. Generally, older PCs, especially 80286 and 80386 use SIMMs with 30-pins, whilst newer 80486 and Pentium-based computers use SIMMs with 72-pins. High-performance computers use modified SIMMs (called DIMMs) to provide faster data transfer
see also DIMM, EDO, PARITY, SYNCHRONOUS DRAM

simple device multimedia device that does not require a data file for playback, such as a CD drive used to play audio CDs

simple mail transfer protocol
see SMTP

simple network management protocol
see SNMP

simulation computer that is made to imitate a real life situation or a machine, and shows how something works or will work in the future

single in-line memory module
see SIMM

single speed speed at which a CD-ROM is spun by a drive - normally 230rpm
see also DOUBLE SPEED, QUAD SPEED

site
see WEBSITE

site licence licence between a software publisher and a user which allows any number of users in one site to use the software

sixteen-bit processor that handles data in sixteen bit words, providing much faster operation than older eight-bit processors. The Intel 80286 was a sixteen-bit processor that was been replaced by the faster 80386 that could operate on thirty-two bits of data; the 80486 and then the Pentium processor replaced followed - both are thirty-two bit processors
see also INTEL, PROCESSOR

slave one device that is controlled by another device

sleep computer that is conserving power while waiting for a user to do something. If you have installed power management on your PC you will find that the computer shuts down some sections of the computer to save electricity - such as the hard disk and monitor - after a period of inactivity; these devices will be supplied with full power as soon as you touch the

mouse or hit a key
see also ONNOW

SLIP SERIAL LINE INTERNET PROTOCOL communications
protocol that allows a computer to communicate with the Internet via a
serial connection (normally a modem and telephone line) rather than a direct
network connection; if you connecting to the Internet using a modem you
will need an account with an ISP or on-line provider - the communications
software will dial the access number and establish a SLIP session with the
remote computer
see also ISP, PPP, WINSOCK

slot
see EXPANSION SLOT

small computer systems interface
see SCSI

smiley face created with text characters, used to provide the real meaning
to an email message; for example, :-) means laughter or a joke, :-(means
sad, ;-) means joke and a wink. Look at this page sideways to see the face

S/MIME
see SECURE/MULTIPURPOSE INTERNET MAIL EXTENSION

SMS
see SHORT MESSAGE SERVICE

SMT
see SURFACE-MOUNT TECHNOLOGY

SMTP SIMPLE MAIL TRANSFER PROTOCOL standard used to
transfer electronic mail messages between computers, normally used to send
mail messages from your computer to an Internet mail server which can
then deliver the message to the correct mail server using SMTP; the
destination mail server stores the message until the user connects and reads
the message with email software that uses the POP3 or IMAP protocol
see also EMAIL, IMAP, POP3

snail mail slang term used to refer to the normal (slow) postal delivery
rather than (near instant) electronic mail delivery

snd (SouND) filename extension used to indicate a file that contains
digitized sound data
see also WAV

SNMP SIMPLE NETWORK MANAGEMENT PROTOCOL standard
set of commands that defines how computers, routers and other
communications equipment can be managed from a central location - often
used for intranets and large networks

snow Interference or a fault with a screen that appears as flickering white flecks on the monitor

soak to run a program or device continuously for a period of time to make sure it functions correctly

socket driver
see WINSOCK

SOCKS (network) protocol developed to support the transfer of TCP/IP (Internet) traffic through a proxy server. It is commonly used to provide a way for users on a local area network to access the Internet via a single shared connection - for example, users on an office network running web browser software to access the Internet via a shared Internet connection.

soft goods software that you purchase and pay for in an online shop, but you then download the software directly onto your computer instead of receiving a CD-ROM sent by post

software program or group of programs which instructs the hardware on how it should perform, including operating systems, word processors and applications programs

software flow control
see XON/OFF

software licence agreement between a user and a software house, giving details of the rights of the user to use or copy software

software life cycle period of time when a piece of software exists, from its initial design to the moment when it becomes out of date
see also VAPOURWARE

software modem modem that uses the main computer's processor to carry out all the signal processing required to modulate and demodulate data signals that can be sent to a dedicated serial port. External modems, in comparison, have their own processing components and transfer data to and from the computer, leaving the main computer's processor to carry on its other tasks. New PCs are often fitted with a software modem (often called a WinModem) that takes advantage of the powerful processors to provide a very cheap way of adding a modem function - and providing dial-up Internet access to a computer.

software-only video playback ability to display full-motion video standard that can be played back on any multimedia computer, that does not need special hardware - the decompression and display is carried out by software drivers; any software-only standard does not normally provide as sharp an image as a hardware compression system (such as MPEG) or full-screen playback

solid colour colour that can be displayed on a screen or printed on a colour printer without dithering *see also* DITHER

solid font printer printer that uses a whole character shape to print in one movement, such as a daisy wheel printer

solid modelling function in a graphics program that creates three-dimensional solid-looking objects by shading
see also RAY-TRACING

solid state disk mass storage device that uses electronic memory components with a backup battery to store data rather than a magnetic medium (such as a magnetic disk used in a hard disk drive)

sound bandwidth range of frequencies that a human ear can register, normally from 20Hz to 20KHz

Sound Blaster type of sound card for PC compatibles developed by Creative Labs that allows sounds to be recorded to disk (using a microphone) and played back; also includes an FM synthesizer and a MIDI port

sound card add-on device that plugs into an expansion slot inside your PC and generates analog sound signals. The sound card generates sound from digital data, using either a digital-to-analog converter or a FM synthesis chip; normally also provides functions to record sound in digital form (using an analog-to-digital converter) and control MIDI instruments. There are three major standards for PC sound cards: AdLib, SoundBlaster, and Windows- compatible; the MPC Level 1 specification states that a sound card should be able to record sound in 8-bits and sample at 11.025KHz and play back sounds at 11.025KHz and 22.05KHz; the MPC Level 2 specification states that the card should be able to record and play sound files: some sound cards provide built-in compression for wave files, but there are various methods used: the MPC recommends ADCPM. In addition, many PC sound cards include electronics to generate sounds from MIDI data on-board: there are two kinds of MIDI sound generation: FM synthesis simulates musical notes by modulating the frequency of a base carrier wave, whereas waveform synthesis uses digitized samples of the notes to produce a more realistic sound
see also ADPCM, MIDI, SAMPLE RATE, SAMPLE SIZE

sound file file stored on disk that contains sound data; this can either be a digitized analog sound signal or notes for a MIDI instrument

Sound Recorder utility included with Microsoft Windows that allows a user to playback digitized sound files (the .WAV standard) or record sound onto disk and carry out very basic editing once you have recorded the sound.

sound waves pressure waves produced by vibrations, which are transmitted through air (or a solid) and detected by the human ear or a microphone (in which they are converted to electrical signals)

source file   (in Windows) the file that contains the data referenced by an OLE object; for example, if you have an OLE object with a link to a spreadsheet, the spreadsheet file is the source file
see also OLE

source object   (in Windows) within a drag and drop operation the source object is the object that is first clicked on and then dragged

spam   slang term that refers to an article that has been posted to more than one newsgroup, so is likely to contain commercial messages; newsgroup users do not like spammed messages or spamming and will flame users that submit this type of article. If you plan to use contribute to a newsgroup or mailing list, make sure that you read its rules before you send a commercial message (newsgroups normally include the rules within a FAQ message, posted regularly in the group; mailing lists will usually send you their rules when you subscribe)

special interest group
see SIG

speech recognition   analysis of spoken words in such a way that a computer can recognize spoken words and commands

speech synthesis   to produce spoken words by a sound card or speech synthesizer
see also PHONEME

spellcheck   function of wordprocessors and DTP programs that can check the spelling of words in a document by comparing them with an exisitng dictionary file; the spellcheck function can sometimes include a thesaurus that will display similar words to the mis-spelt word or a sound-like function (called soundex) that displays words that sound the same but have different spellings.

spider   program that searches through the millions of pages that make up the world wide web for new information, changes or pages that have been deleted; these changes are then added to a search engine index to ensure that it is always up to date

spike   very short electrical pulse that can cause damage to electronic equipment

splash screen   initial screen that is displayed for a few seconds when you start a program. The splash screen normally displays the product logo and gives basic copyright information.

spool   to store documents in a queue before they are printed
see also PRINT QUEUE

split screen   to divide the display screen of an application into two or more sections that can then be viewed independently. For example, in many wordprocessors, you can view two different parts of the same document in separate areas of the screen at the same time

SPX SEQUENCED PACKET EXCHANGE protocol used by the Novell NetWare network operating system to guarantee that information transferred over a local area network arrives correctly; the SPX protocol uses the Novell IPX protocol to actually transfer the data, but ensures delivery
see also IPX, NETBIOS

SQL STRUCTURED QUERY LANGUAGE standard language used to maintain and search databases

SRAM
see STATIC RAM

SSI SERVER SIDE INCLUDE program that runs on a web server and is accessed from a web page to provide extra features such as a access counter, search engine or video delivery

SSL SECURE SOCKETS LAYER protocol designed by Netscape that provides secure communications over the Internet; normally used to protect a user when sending credit card or other payment details over the Internet. To provide a secure communications link, the user needs to have a web browser that can support SSL (such as the Netscape Navigator browser) and the company selling goods needs an Internet server that provides SSL feature. When the user connects to the secure web server, the browser automatically recognises that SSL is available and provides a secure link that encrypts any information before sending it over the telephone line. Your browser will indicate a secure SSL page by displaying a tiny closed padlock or key icon in the bottom line of the browser window: if the padlock icon is open or the key icon appears broken, you are not using a secure link, if the padlock is closed or the key icon is whole, then you are using a secure link. Web pages that implement SSL security generally use the prefix 'https:' rather than 'http:' within their address.
see also HTTPS, PGP, SECURE WEBSITE, SEPP, SET, S-HTTP, STT

ST-506 (old) interface standard for connecting a hard disk drive to a PC, now replaced by faster and more efficient interface standards such as SCSI and IDE
see also IDE, MFM, RLL

stack area of memory that is used to store data when a software program is being run; the stack is setup and managed automatically by the software

stack overflow error message that is sometimes displayed - if you see this error message when running an application it means that there is not enough free memory in your computer for the program's needs. Normally caused by poor programming; you should contact the software publisher

stand-alone something that works by itself and does not need another device. For example, a fax machine is a stand-alone device because it can work by itself.

standard memory first 1Mb of memory in a PC
see also EXPANDED MEMORY, UPPER MEMORY

standard mode (in an IBM PC) mode of operation of Microsoft Windows which uses extended memory but does not allow multitasking of DOS applications

star topology network configuration in which all nodes (computers or printers) are connected to a central device, called the hub, that ensures that data is correctly transferred from one node to another

start bit leading bit sent to indicate the start of a block of data that is normally used when sending data over an asynchronous serial link to indicate the start of each byte or character of data (such as between a computer and a modem)
see also FLOW CONTROL, PROTOCOL, STOP BIT

Start button button that is normally in the bottom left-hand corner of a Windows Desktop screen. The Start button provides a convenient route to the programs and files on your computer. Initially, the Start button has categories for Programs, Accessories, Settings and recently accessed documents. You can also add you own applications to the Start menu by moving the pointer over the Start button and clicking on the right-hand mouse button. A second tip, the Start button is at the very left of the taskbar in Windows. You can move the entire taskbar to any of the four sides of the screen by clicking on the bar and dragging it to another edge.

startup disk floppy disk which holds the operating system and system configuration files which can, in case of hard disk failure, be used to boot the computer

Startup folder (within Windows 95 and later) special folder that contains programs or shortcuts to programs that will be run automatically when you next start Windows. To run a program, such as a diary or calendar, each time you start Windows, move the program icon into the Startup folder or create a shortcut in the Startup folder

startup screen text or graphics displayed when an application or multimedia book is run; normally displays the product name, logo and copyright information and is only displayed for a few seconds before the main screen appears
see also SPLASH SCREEN

static electricity electrical charge that can build up in a person or electronic component; in a person, static electricity often builds up after walking on carpets and can seriously damage electronic components if you discharge the electricity by touching a computer

static RAM (SRAM) RAM that retains data for as long as the power supply is on, and does not require the data to be refreshed; static RAM requires less electrical power than dynamic RAM components and is normally faster, but costs more - it is often used for specialised functions where speed is important, such as in cache memory
see also RAM, REFRESH

status bar line at the top or bottom of a screen which gives information about the task currently being worked on (position of cursor, number of lines, filename, time, etc.)

stereo or stereophonic sound recorded onto two separate channels from two separate microphone elements and played back through a pair of headphones or two speakers; each channel is slightly different to give the impression that the sound is live rather than recorded, and has depth

stick model
see WIRE FRAME

stop bit information transmitted at the end of section of data to indicate to the receiver that this is the end of the data; normally used when sending data over an asynchronous serial link to indicate the end of each byte or character of data (such as between a computer and a modem)
see also FLOW CONTROL, PROTOCOL, START BIT

store-and-forward basic method of transferring mail by moving a copy of the message to another server on its way between the sender and the recipient
see also MHS

story board series of pictures or drawings that show how a video or animation progresses

STP
see SHIELDED TWISTED PAIR

stream mass of data transferred or managed as one continuous block

streaming audio digital audio data that is continuously transmitted (normally over the Internet) using a streaming protocol to provide stereo sound
see STREAMING DATA, REALAUDIO

streaming data or streaming protocol method of sending a continuous stream of data over the Internet to provide live video or sound transmission; older methods of sending continuous live data used a standard

web server (an HTTP server) to transmit the data - however, an HTTP
server is designed to send data when it is ready rather than sending a regular
stream of data that is required by multimedia. If you have ever tried to view
a video clip over the Internet, you will have encountered this
burst-transmission problem: when traffic or server load lightens, you can
watch 20 frames per second, when the server is busy, you can watch one
frame per minute. To provide a good multimedia server, the data delivery
must be regulated and ideally synchronised. There are many different
standards used to deliver sound and video over the Internet including
Progressive Network's RealAudio, Microsoft's NetShow server (that
supports both audio and video) and Netscape's MediaServer. Each of these
streaming data technologies allow the user or publisher to limit the delivery
of data to a maximum data rate. There are several standard formats used
including Microsoft's multimedia delivery format, ASF (active streaming
format) and other standards developed by Macromedia, VDOnet, Vivo, and
VXtreme.

streaming video video image data that is continuously transmitted
(normally over the Internet) using a streaming protocol to provide smooth
moving images
see STREAMING DATA, ASF, VIVO, VXTREME

string series of consecutive alphanumeric characters or words that are
manipulated and treated as a single unit by the computer

stroke (i) the width (in pixels) of the pen or brush used to draw
on-screen; (ii) the thickness of a printed character

STT SECURE TRANSACTION TECHNOLOGY system developed to
provide a secure link between a user's browser and a vendor's web site to
allow the user to pay for goods over the Internet
see also PGP, SEPP, SET, S-HTTP, SSL

style typeface, font, point size, colour, spacing and margins of text in a
formatted document

style sheet template which can be preformatted to automatically set the
style or layout of a document such as a manual, a book, a newsletter, etc.
The style sheet includes margins, fonts and type-styles used for different
paragraphs

subdirectory directory of disk or tape contents contained within another
directory

sub-domain second level of addressing on the Internet that normally
refers to a department name within a larger organisation

submenu secondary menu displayed as a choice from a menu; used if
there are too many choices to fit into one menu. A good example is the Start
button menu which has several submenus for the Program and Settings

menu option.

submit button button displayed on a web page that sends information entered by a user on a web form to a program running on a web server for processing (for example, the submit button could be used to start a search query)

subnet self-contained part of a large network (normally refers to one, independently-managed part of the Internet); a subnet is located using part of the IP address called the subnet address
see also IP ADDRESS

subnet address or subnet number part of an IP address that identifies a subnet that is connected to a larger network; the first part of the IP address identifies the network, the next part of the IP address identifies the subnet and the last part of the IP address identifies a single host server
see also IP ADDRESS

subnet mask filter that is used to select the portion of an IP address that contains the subnet address

subnotebook very small portable computer that is smaller and lighter than a standard full-size notebook or laptop computer; a subnotebook often has a smaller keyboard and display and often only includes a hard disk drive with any floppy disk drive or CD-ROM drive in a separate, external unit that can be plugged in when needed.

subscribe to add your name to a mailing list or listserv list so that you will receive any messages for the group; to subscribe to a list you normally send your name and email address to the manager of the list, but you should check beforehand. One of the best ways of finding out how to subscribe is to look at the www.liszt.com web site that lists every mailing list and tells you how to subscribe
see also LISTSERV, MAILING LIST, PUSH TECHNOLOGY

subscript small character which is printed below the line of other characters

sub-woofer large loudspeaker that can reproduce very low frequency sounds (normally with frequencies between 20 to 100Hz) that is used with normal loudspeakers to enhance the overall sound quality

Sun Microsystems company that developed the Java programming system used to extend web pages

supercomputer very powerful mainframe computer used for high speed mathematical or imaging tasks

superscript small character printed above the normal line of characters

super VGA
see SVGA

surf to explore a web site looking at the web pages in no particular order, but simply moving between pages using the links; normally used to mean exploring web pages for pleasure with no particular reason

surface-mount technology (SMT) method of manufacturing circuit boards in which the electronic components are bonded directly onto the surface of the board rather than being inserted into holes and soldered into place. Newer PCs and peripherals are now constructed with surface-mount technology which is cheaper and more reliable than the older method of using sockets. The only exception is memory (which is normally fitted in SIMM cards - themselves using surface-mount technology) and the processor which is normally fitted in a ZIF socket.

surge sudden increase in electrical power in a system, due to a fault or noise or component failure

surge protector electrical device (normally part of a power supply unit in a computer) that is used to protect electronic equipment against damage caused by a surge

suspend command that is used when running Windows on a battery-powered laptop computer to shut down almost all of the electronic components of the laptop, but to provide enough electrical power to the main memory so that it retains all the data and programs that you were running; after you have suspended the laptop you can switch the laptop on again and instantly resume work where you were. If you do not use the suspend mode and instead switch the laptop off, all power is cut off and, when you switch the laptop on again it will have to boot up and you will need to start the applications again
see also ONNOW

SVGA SUPER VGA enhancement to the standard VGA graphics display system which allows resolutions of up to 800x600pixels with 16million colours

swap to stop using one program, put it and its data into store temporarily, run another program, and when that is finished, return to the first one

swap file file stored on the hard disk used as a temporary storage area for data held in RAM, to provide virtual memory
see also PERMANENT SWAP FILE, VIRTUAL MEMORY

switch extra options that are added after the main command that is typed in at the command line; for example, if you type in DIR at the DOS prompt, you will see a list of the files stored on your computer; if you add the switch '/p' and type in 'DIR /P' the list of files will pause after each page

SX type of processor chip derived from the basic 80386 or 80486 processor that is slightly cheaper to manufacturer and buy; the 80386-SX does not have a floating point processor and only supports a 16-bit internal data path, the 80486-SX does not have a floating point processor

Symbol font TrueType font that is included with Windows and includes symbols and Greek characters
see also TRUETYPE

synchronous cache high-speed secondary cache system used in many computers that use the Pentium processor chip
see also SECONDARY CACHE

synchronous DRAM high-speed memory technology (used for the main memory of high-performance PCs) in which the memory components work from the same clock signal as the main processor, so are synchronized to the main processor and allowing data to be transferred quickly and efficiently without requiring extra timing or synchronizing signals
see also DIMM, SIMM

synchronous transmission data transmission at a fixed speed and in which the transmitter and receiver are synchronized so that no extra timing signal is required. Normally used by mainframe or high-speed computers to transfer data to another device
see also AUTOSYNC

SyQuest manufacturer of storage devices, including a range of removable hard disk drives and backup units
see also ZIP DISK

system general term that refers to a computer or to a computer and its associated peripherals or to the operating system software (such as Windows)

System 7 operating system software used on an Apple Macintosh computer

system administrator
see NETWORK ADMINISTRATOR

system backup copy of all the data stored on a computer, server or network. The system can be a single computer or could be a network of computers.

system board
see MOTHERBOARD

system clock electronic component that generates a regular signal that is used to synchronize all the components in the computer

system colours palette of 20 colours that are used by Windows for colouring window elements such as borders, captions, buttons

system disk disk which holds the system software that is used to boot up a computer and load the operating system ready for use. Most PCs have the operating system software stored on the internal hard disk.

System Monitor   utility provided with Windows 95 that allows you to view how the resources on your PC are performing and, if you have shared the device, who else on the network is using them.

system software   software which makes everything in your computer work correctly. The system software controls the hardware and manages programs. It looks after and controls all aspects of the computer; Windows is a form of system software, since it operates everything itself and does not rely on other software. This is different from Windows 3.1x which relied on MS-DOS to manage the hardware; in this latter case MS-DOS is the system software. In both cases, the useful software that a user would use - such as a wordprocessor - is called the application software.

system tray   (in Windows 95 and later versions) area of the taskbar normally in the bottom right-hand corner next to the clock; the system tray displays tiny icons that show which system software programs were run automatically when Windows started and are now running in the background. For example, the volume control, an anti-virus detector or power-management utility. To change the settings or close one of these system programs, right-click or double-click on the icon. User software applications (that a user can start by double-clicking on a program icon) are displayed in the main part of the taskbar.
see also   TASKBAR

system unit   main box of a personal computer that contains the motherboard and hard disk drive

Tt

T1 term that refers to a leased line connection that transfers data at 1.544Mbits per second in the US (in the UK and Europe, the transfer rate is 2.048Mbits per second) and can carry either data or 24 voice channels; if the link uses only part of this capacity, it is called a fractional T1 link. These links are normally used to connect ISPs together or to connect offices of a large organisation
see also ADSL, LEASED LINE

T3 high-speed communication link that is equivalent to 28 T1 lines and can transfer data at 44.736Mbits per second; sometimes called a 45Meg line

tab (i) to tabulate or to arrange text in columns with the cursor automatically running from one column to the next in keyboarding; (ii) in Windows, a method of moving from one button or field to another without using the mouse, but by pressing the tab key to move the focus

tabbing order order in which the focus moves from one button or field to the next as the user presses the tab key

tab key key on a keyboard, normally positioned on the far left, beside the 'Q' key, with two arrows pointing in opposite horizontal directions, used to insert a tab character into text and so align the text at a preset tab stop

table HTML command that allows a web page designer to display text or other information within a series of columns and rows on a web page; tables are often used to create a basic layout for a web page as well as to display information in a tabular format (such as a price list or catalogue)
see APPENDIX

tab rack graduated scale, displayed along the top of the screen, showing the position of tabulation columns

tab settings or tab stops preset points where the cursor will stop each time the tab key is pressed

table of contents (i) (in a CD) data at the start of the disc that describes how many tracks are on the CD, their position and length; (ii) (in a multimedia title) page with a list of the headings of all the other main pages in the title and links so that a user can move to them

tag word or letters within HTML that carries out a function; for example, the tag <b> will format the text as bold, the tag r will display a horizontal line. *See also the Appendix.*

tag image file format
see TIFF

tape backup high-capacity storage device that uses a tape cartridge or
tape cassette to hold a large amount of data; normally used to create a
backup copy of the information stored on a hard disk

TAPI TELEPHONY APPLICATION PROGRAM INTERFACE
standard set of system software commands and functions that can be used
by a Windows application to control a telephone, telephone exchange or
other telephony system

tar TAPE ARCHIVE file compression system used on a computer
running the Unix operating system

task one program that being run and managed by the operating system;
each time a user starts a program, the operating system assigns it a task
number and provides it with system resources such as an area of memory
and disk space. One application can be run many times at once, each time
being assigned a new task number. In some advanced operating systems one
complex program might be split into several smaller tasks (that might then
be managed by different processors within the computer) in a process called
multithreading
see also MULTITHREADING, SYSTEM TRAY, TASKBAR

taskbar bar that normally runs along the bottom of the screen in
Windows 95 and displays the Start button and a list of other programs or
windows that are currently active. You can move the entire taskbar to any of
the four sides of the screen by clicking on the bar and dragging it to another
edge. In the Windows operating system, the programs that a user starts are
shown as wide buttons in the taskbar normally displayed at the bottom of
the screen; programs started automatically by Windows itself are displayed
as icons in the System Tray section of the taskbar.

TCP TRANSMISSION CONTROL PROTOCOL (network) protocol
that is used to set up and maintain a connection between two computers
linked to a network to allow data to be transferred; TCP is the main part of
the TCP/IP protocol used on the Internet and many local area networks. The
IP (internet protocol) protocol only manages the individual packets of data.

TCP/IP TRANSMISSION CONTROL PROTOCOL / INTERNET
PROTOCOL
set of communications protocols developed by the US Department of
Defense (DOD), originally for use in military applications. TCP/IP bundles
and unbundles sent and received data into packets, manages packet
transmission and checks for errors across networks. Originally found
binding Unix networks together, its flexibility and portability are making it
a de facto standard for any LAN and WAN and it is used to establish all
communications on the public Internet. The TCP part of the protocol

manages the connection between two computers to allow data to be transferred and the IP part manages the individual packets of data being transferred.

technical support person who provides technical advice to a user to explain how to use software or hardware or explain why it might not work

telecommuting practice of working on a computer in one place (normally from home) that is linked by modem to the company's central office allowing messages and data to be transferred

teleconferencing to link video, audio and computer signals from different locations so that distant people can talk and see each other, as if in a conference room

telephony series of standards that define the way in which computers can work with a telephone system to provide voice-mail, telephone answering, and fax services

telephony application program interface (TAPI) standard set of system software commands and functions that can be used by a Windows application to control a telephone, telephone exchange or other telephony system

telnet software that allows you to connect to and control via the Internet a remote computer as if you were there and type in commands as if you were sitting in front of the computer. In practice, Telnet is normally used when you are setting up your web site to create directories, set up security and move files.

template (in a wordprocessor) file containing standard section of text (such as a memo or invoice) into which specific details (company address or prices or quantities) can be added
see also STYLE SHEET

10Base-T cabling and connection standard used to carry Ethernet signals. 10BaseT is the offspring of the generic Ethernet specification which defines data transmission of 10Mbits per second using 802.3 data packets over twisted pair cable with telephone-style RJ-45 connectors. Unlike Thin-Wire Ethernet, 10Base-T has a physical star topology that makes it more robust and more secure than its predecessor, however, it needs a central hub
see also ETHERNET, TWISTED-PAIR

Terminal simple communications program that is supplied with Windows 3.1x (Windows 95 includes the similar HyperTerminal program) and can be used to connect to bulletin boards but cannot connect directly to the Internet.

terminal adapter device that connects a computer to a digital communications line; for example, to link a PC to an ISDN line. A terminal adapter transfers digital signals from the computer to the line, wheras a modem is used to connect a computer to an analogue communications line, such as a telephone line, and needs to convert digital signals to and from an analogue form.

terminal emulation software software program that is used to allow a computer to interpret the special display codes used to control a specialist workstation; normally used with a modem to allow you to connect to a remote mainframe computer system

terminate and stay resident (TSR) program program which loads itself into main memory and carries out a function when activated, normally by a special key sequence or an instruction; used for utilities and for drivers (such as a CD-ROM driver)

terminator small connector that includes a resistor that fits onto the last SCSI device in your computer. SCSI devices, such as CD-ROM drives or scanners, are connected in a one after another (in daisy-chain fashion) and the terminator is fitted to the last SCSI device to create a complete electrical circuit

tessellate to transform an object in an image into simple geometric shapes (triangles, squares and other polygons) that are easier to manipulate mathematically - for example, to add shading or to rotate the image.

text file file stored on disk that contains text rather than graphics or data; the text is not formatted or laid out in any way and the file contains no font or typeface information; to edit a text file you can the EDIT utility from the MS-DOS prompt, or the NotePad utility in Windows; alternatively, you can use any wordprocessor that can save to an ASCII or text file format

text mode operating mode of a computer or display screen that will only display pre-defined characters and will not allow graphic images to be displayed; Windows operates in a graphics mode, MS-DOS normally operates in a text mode

texture mapping (i) special computer graphics effect using algorithms to produce an image that looks like the surface of something (such as marble, brick, stone or water); (ii) to cover one image with another to give the first a texture; for example, if you have an image of a house, you could cover it with an image of a brick and the result is a house filled with a brick pattern

TFT screen THIN FILM TRANSISTOR SCREEN method of creating a high-quality colour LCD display used in laptop computers. A TFT screen can display very clear, bright and sharp images with tens of thousands of different colours but are more expensive to manufacture and require more electrical power.

TFTP TRIVIAL FILE TRANSFER PROTOCOL simple form of the

standard FTP (file transfer protocol) system; commonly used to load the operating system software onto a diskless workstation from a server when the workstation boots up when it is switched on.
see also FTP

thesaurus file that contains synonyms that are displayed as alternatives to a misspelt word during a spellcheck

thin film transistor screen
see TFT SCREEN

third generation (3G) latest specification for mobile communication systems (including mobile telephones); the third generation includes very fast data transfer rates of between 128Kbps and 2Mbps (depending on whether the person is walking, in a car or at their base station). This will allow high-speed Internet access, even live video links, to a portable telephone. Previous generations included: the first generation of mobile telephone were analogue cellular telephones, digital PCS were the second generation.

thirty-two bit system (32-bit) processor that can manipulate data thirty-two bits at a time; the original PC processor could manipulate 8-bits at a time, current Pentium processors can manipulate 32-bits at a time and so are more powerful and faster
see PROCESSOR

thrashing (i) excessive disk activity; (ii) configuration or program fault in a virtual memory system, that results in a CPU wasting time moving pages of data between main memory and disk or backing store

thread series of related messages or replies to an original message within a discussion group or newsgroup; most newsreader programs will organise threads of messages so that you can read them together

3G
see THIRD GENERATION

3D *or* **three dimensions** image that has the appearance of depth as well as height and width to provide a scene that looks like real life

threshold preset level which causes an action if a signal exceeds or drops below it; for example, if using a microphone in a noisy environment you might set the threshold high so that only loud noises are recorded

throughput amount of data transferred or processed in a period of time; for example, the throughput of a modem refers to the amount of data it can transmit, and this can be increased by data compression and by a faster modem

thumbnail miniature graphical representation of an image; used as a quick and convenient method of viewing the contents of graphics or DTP

files before they are retrieved

TIFF TAG IMAGE FILE FORMAT file format used to store graphic images (developed by Aldus and Microsoft) that can handle monochrome, grey-scale, 8-bit or 24-bit colour images; there have been many different versions of TIFF that include several different compression algorithms

time out (i) connection closed because a response has not been received within the time expected; (ii) feature of communications software that will cut the modem connection if you do not type anything for a period of time

tile to arrange a group of windows so that they are displayed side by side without overlapping

title bar horizontal bar at the top of a window which displays the title of the window or application

token special code used in some network systems (particularly the Token Ring network system) that are used to control which computer can transmit information onto the network

Token Ring network network system developed by IBM; the nodes of the network (computers and printers) are connected together in a loop *compare with* ETHERNET

tone dialing method of dialing a telephone number using sounds to represent the digits of the number; this method of dialing is the current standard method of dialing numbers and has generally replaced the older pulse dialing system; a Hayes-compatible modem can dial the number '123' using tone dialing with the AT command 'ATDT123' or using pulse dialing with the AT command 'ATDP123'
see also AT COMMAND SET, PULSE DIALING

toner finely powdered ink (usually black) that is used in laser printers; the toner is transferred onto the paper by electrical charge, then fixed permanently to the paper by heating. As a tip, if you spill toner onto your clothes or hands when changing a toner cartridge, wash off with cold water. If you wash the toner with hot water, this will fix it permanently to your hands or clothes!

toner cartridge plastic container that holds powdered toner for use in a laser printer

toolbar window that contains a range of icons that access tools; for example, paint programs normally have a toolbar that includes icons for colour, brush, circle, and eraser tools; a floating toolbar is a moveable window that can be positioned anywhere on screen

ToolTips feature of applications that work under Windows that display a line of descriptive text under an icon when you move the pointer over the icon.

topology arrangement of connections within a network; for example, a ring topology means that all the nodes of the network are connected to form a closed loop; in a star topology each node is connected to a central hub and in a bus topology each node is connected to a long cable that has a terminator at each end

touch pad flat device which can sense where on its surface and when it is touched, used to control the cursor position. Touch pads are now fitted to some laptops instead of a trackball or mouse as a way of controlling Windows.

touch screen computer display which has a grid of infrared transmitters and receivers, positioned on either side of the screen, used to control a cursor position (when a user wants to make a selection or move the cursor, he points to the screen, breaking two of the beams, which gives the position of his finger)

traceroute software utility that finds and displays the route taken for data travelling between your computer and a distant server on the Internet. The display shows the different servers that your data travels through, together with the time taken to travel between each server (called a hop). Traceroute works by sending out a time-to-live (TTL) query data packet to the distant server; it starts by sending out packets with a very low time-to-live, then gradually increasing the length of time that the packet can survive until one is returned by the host - this then provides the lowest time it will take to reach the host. If you are trying to view a website you can use traceroute to check which section of the link to the website's server is the slowest. Windows includes a traceroute utility: 'tracert'. Click the Start button and select the Run option then type in 'tracert' followed by the domain name of the distant web server. For example 'tracert www.petercollin.com'.

tracing function of a graphics program that takes a bitmap image and processes it to find the edges of the shapes and so convert these into a vector line image that can be more easily manipulated

track (i) (in a music CD) a song; (ii) (in a MIDI file) method of separating the notes within a tune either by channel or by part or instrument; (iii) (in multimedia authoring software) series of instructions that define how an object moves with time

trackball device used to move a cursor on-screen, which is controlled by turning a ball contained in a case with the palm of your hand; rather similar to a mechanical mouse turned up-side down

tracking
see MOUSE TRACKING

traffic data that is being transmitted over a network or communications link

transaction one complete action (normally on a database) that is performed fully and correctly

Transmission Control Protocol / Internet Protocol
see TCP/IP

transparent GIF graphic image stored in the GIF file format with one colour (from the palette) assigned as the transparent colour - when the image is displayed, any part of the image in this colour will be transparent to allow any image beneath to show through (this feature is used a lot in web pages to place images on a patterned background)
see also GIF

transputer single, large, very powerful processor that can be connected in parallel to other similar processors and which effectively multiplies the processing power.

tree of folders view of all the folders stored on your disk arranged to show folders and sub-folders.

TrueType outline font technology introduced by Apple and Microsoft as a means of printing exactly what is displayed on screen and providing fonts that can be scaled to any point size whilst still being smooth
see also OUTLINE FONT

TSR
see TERMINATE AND STAY RESIDENT (PROGRAM)

tunnelling method of enclosing a packet of data from one type of network within another packet so that it can be sent over a different, incompatible, network

TWAIN standard software interface that allows image or paint software to control a scanner

tweening
see MORPHING

twisted pair network cable that is made by twisting together two thin insulated wires, this type of cable is much cheaper and easier to handle than coaxial cable and the twisting helps to cut down interference from other electrical equipment; twisted pair cable is normally used with 10Base-T networking equipment
compare with COAXIAL

type size size of a font, measured in points

type style weight and angle of a font, such as bold or italic

typeface set of characters in a particular design and particular weight

Uu

UART UNIVERSAL ASYNCHRONOUS RECEIVER/
TRANSMITTER
circuit that converts between the parallel data used by PCs and the serial
data used by modems. Serial ports have a UART, while internal modems
supply their own. For high DTE rates on systems with a heavy processing
load (typically those that use Windows), a 16550A UART provides better,
more reliable performance.

UDP
see USER DATAGRAM PROTOCOL

Ultra ATA version of the AT Attachment (ATA) hard disk drive interface
standard that can support a data transfer rate of up to 33MBps; to manage
this high-speed data transfer from the hard disk interface to the rest of your
PC, it needs to have a high-speed version of DMA.

UMTS UNIVERSAL MOBILE TELECOMMUNICATIONS SYSTEM
Third Generation (3G) mobile communication system that will support
voice, data, and video signals to the handset; due to launch during 2001.
see also THIRD GENERATION

undelete function of Windows and DOS that lets you restore deleted
information or a deleted file; in DOS you can type Undelete and DOS will
attempt to recover your file. If you have mistakenly deleted a file, do not
save any other files onto the disk, but run the undelete command
immediately. In Windows, you can retrieve the file from the Recycle Bin:
double-click on the Recycle bin icon on the Desktop to see a list of files that
can be undeleted.

underline or underscore (i) line drawn or printed under a piece of
text; (ii) to draw a line under a piece of text

undo function of some wordprocessors and other applications that will let
you undo the command youive just carried out - for example it can undo a
paste or a delete operation. Microsoft applications have now standardised on
Ctrl-Z as the keyboard shortcut to undo the last action

uniform resource locator
see URL

uninterruptable power supply
see UPS

universal serial bus
see USB

Unix multiuser, multitasking operating system developed by AT&T Bell Laboratories to run on almost any computer, from a PC to minicomputers and large mainframes; there are a number of graphical user interfaces, such as Open Look, that hide the Unix command-line; Unix is the operating system that is normally used to run web server software, such as Apache

Unix-to-Unix Copy (UUCP) (historically) software utility that allowed one computer running Unix to send files to another computer running Unix over a telephone line using modems; the term is now generally used to describe the way electronic mail messages are transferred between server computers on a network or the Internet

unmoderated list mailing list that sends any material submitted to the listserv on to all the subscribers without a person reading or checking the content
see also MAILING LIST, LISTSERV

unsolicited mail an advertising email message that has not been requested. Often called 'spam' email. Don't send out unsolicited mail to unknown email addresses unless you want to annoy the recipients and damage your company's reputation.
compare with OPT-IN MAILING LIST

upgrade to improve the performance or specification of your computer by adding more RAM, a bigger hard disk or some other improvement.

upload to send a file from your computer to the hard disk of another computer, particularly used to refer to sending files over the Internet to another server
compare DOWNLOAD

upper memory (in an IBM PC) 384Kb of memory located between the 640Kb and 1Mb limits; upper memory is located after the 640Kb conventional memory, before the high memory areas above the 1Mb range

UPS UNINTERRUPTABLE POWER SUPPLY electrical device that will supply electrical power to a computer if the mains power is cut off; a UPS normally works from a battery and gives the user a few extra minutes in which to save data files and shutdown the computer

URL UNIFORM RESOURCE LOCATOR Uniform resource locator. The correct name for the full address of a web page. For example, 'petercollin.com' is a domain name, 'www.petercollin.com' is the website address for Peter Collin Publishing and 'www.petercollin.com/index.html' is the URL to the site's home page.
see also DNS

usability measure of the ease with which hardware or software can be used

USB UNIVESAL SERIAL BUS standard that defines a high-speed serial interface that transfers data at up to 12Mbps and allows up to 127 compatible peripherals to be connected to a computer; this bus is now available on many new computers and allows all the peripherals to be linked to the computer using via this one port; the USB port is likely to eventually replace the separate connectors required for a keyboard, mouse, modem, and printer
see also FIREWIRE

Usenet section of the Internet that provides forums (called newsgroups) in which any user can add a message or comment on any other message; often the busiest part of the Internet
see also NEWSGROUPS

user datagram protocol (UDP) Internet communication protocol standard that provides added reliability to the TCP/IP protocol

user-friendly software that is easy to use and interact with

user group group of users who share a common interest in a particular aspect of computing; some user groups are split into sections, each covering a particular specialist area of interest (called Special Interest Groups, SIG), some user groups only meet online

user interface part of the software that a user sees and works with; often refers to the operating system features that make the operating system more friendly or easier to use; for example, MS-DOS is a basic shell that interprets commands typed in at the prompt; the Microsoft Windows is a graphical user interface that is easier to use
see also GUI

UUCP
see UNIX-TO-UNIX COPY

Uuencoding method of converting documents and files to a pseudo-text format that allows you to transmit them as an electronic mail message. This gets around the Internet is inability to transfer messages that are not text. Now been largely replaced by MIME
see also MIME

Vv

V series CCITT standards (listed above) used to define data transmission methods using a modem
see also KFLEX, X2

V.21 (old) full duplex communications at 300baud (in the USA, the Bell 103 standard was used instead)

V.22 half-duplex communication at 1,200bps (in the USA, the Bell 212A standard was more commonly used)

V.22bis full-duplex modem communication transferring data at up to 2,400bps

V.29 half-duplex modem communication transferring data at up to 9,600bps (this standard is generally used by fax modems)

V.32 full-duplex modem communication standard that can transfer data at up to 9,600bps but can also automatically adjust its speed based on the quality of the telephone line - to avoid errors

V.32bis   similar to the V.32 protocol, but able to transfer data at rates up to 14,400 bps.

V.34 full-duplex modem communication standard that can transfer data at up to 28,800 bps. Like V.32, the V.34 standard allows the modem to automatically adjust its speed based on the quality of the telephone line to avoid errors.

V.42 error-detection system that can be used to reduce errors due to poor telephone line quality (see also the competing MNP standard)

V.42bis   data compression system that increases the data transfer rate up to 34,000 bps.

V.90 full-duplex modem data communication at up to 56,600 bps.

vapourware products which exist in name only

VB VISUAL BASIC programming tool developed by Microsoft, that allows users to create Windows applications very easily. Visual Basic is a rapid application development (RAD) tool that allows users with little programming knowledge to create a complex Windows application - although the finished applications are not usually as fast as programs written in a low-level compiled language such as C

VBA VISUAL BASIC FOR APPLICATIONS complex macro language developed by Microsoft from its Visual Basic programming tool. Now, almost all Microsoft applications, including Word, Excel and Access can use macros written in the VBA language providing a very powerful macro language

VBScript set of programming commands that can be included within a normal web page (that is written using HTML commands); the VBScript commands carry out a function to enhance the web page - such as providing the time of day, animation or form processing. An ActiveX applet is a self-contained program file that is downloaded separately from the web page and run on the user's computer; a VBScript program is a series of commands included within a web page HTML file and executed by the web browser. To write VBScript you need to learn the script commands and then use an editor to add them into your web page file; to create an ActiveX application you need a program compiler and programming skills
see also ACTIVEX APPLET, JAVA, JAVASCRIPT

VBX VISUAL BASIC EXTENSION Windows custom software module that adds functionality to another application, similar to the OCX control; originally developed as a way of adding extra programming features to the Microsoft Visual Basic programming language, it is now a standard that can be used by many Windows programming tools; a VBX can be used in 16-bit or 32-bit Windows (versions 3.x or 95) wheras an OCX control will only work with 32-bit Windows (version 95 and later)

vector font shape of characters within a font that are drawn using curves and lines (vector graphics) allowing the characters to be scaled to almost any size without changing the quality
compare with BIT-MAPPED FONT

vector graphics or vector image or vector scan system of drawing objects using curves and lines. The images are described by line length and direction from an origin to plot lines and so build up an image rather than a description of each pixel, as in a bitmap; a vector image can be easily and accurately re-sized with no loss of detail
compare with BITMAP IMAGE

vendor-independent messaging
see VIM

Veronica tool that works with Gopher to help a user find information or files on the WWW
see also GOPHER

vertical portal (VORTAL) portal website that contains information for just one particular industry or interest group; general-interest portals, such as AOL, Yahoo! and Excite provide a whole range of general-interest information for users, including news, weather, sports, and financial information. Vertical portals such as Buzzsaw (www.buzzsaw.com) provide news and resources for the construction industry.

vertical application program that has been designed for a specific use, rather than for general use. For example, a wordprocessor is a general use program whereas software to run a betting shop is a vertical application

vertical justification adjustment of the spacing between lines of text to fit a section of text into the height of a page

VESA local bus (VL-bus) VIDEO ELECTRONICS STANDARDS ASSOCIATION
standard defined by VESA that provides a high-speed local bus that runs at 40 or 60MHz and transfers parallel data 32-bits or 64-bits at a time. The system is most often used in Pentium-based personal computers for network or graphics adapters. This high-speed connection on the motherboard of your PC can be used by components that need to exchange large amounts of information at high speed without interrupting the main processor, so improving performance
compare with PCI

vestigial side band
see VSB

VFW
see VIDEO FOR WINDOWS

VGA VIDEO GRAPHICS ARRAY (in an IBM PC) standard of video adapter developed by IBM that can support a display with a resolution up to 640x480 pixels in up to 256 colours; superseded by SVGA which is an enhancement to the standard VGA graphics display system that allows resolutions of up to 800x600pixels with 16 million colours

VGA feature connector 26-pin edge connector or port (normally at the top edge) of a VGA display adapter that allows another device to access its palette information and clock signals; often used to provide overlays; for example, a board that displays TV images in a window on screen needs to be synchronized with the VGA adapter

video adapter or board or controller board that plugs into an expansion socket inside your PC and converts data into electrical signals to drive a monitor and display text and graphics

video capture board board that plugs into an expansion socket inside your PC and lets you capture a TV picture and store it in memory so that it can then be processed by a computer

video conference to link two or more computers that can capture and display video and audio in real time so that distant people can talk and see each other, as if in a conference room

video digitizer high speed digital sampling circuit which stores a TV picture in memory so that it can then be processed by a computer

videodisc read-only optical disc that can store up to two hours of video data; normally used either to store a complete film (as a rival to video cassette) or to use in an interactive system with text, video and still images - for interactive use, a videodisc can store 54,000 frames of information. NOTE: if the videodisc contains a complete film, the data is recorded using a constant linear velocity format; if used to store interactive data, it is stored in a constant angular velocity format

Video Electronics Standards Association
see VESA

Video for Windows (VFW) set of software drivers and utilities for Microsoft Windows 3.1, developed by Microsoft, that allows AVI-format video files to be played back in a window; Video for Windows supports several different compression methods including Microsoft Video 1, Microsoft RLE and Intel's Indeo. Once the Video for Windows driver is installed, Video clips can be played back using the Windows Media Player utility; sequences can be edited using the supplied VidEdit utility and video recorded with the VidCap utility; the quality of the video playback depends on the performance of the PC hardware, and the size of the playback window. With a window size of 160x120 pixels, any 486 or higher processor can display flicker-free video; for full-screen video playback at 640x480 pixels only a Pentium-based PC can display smooth motion

video game game played on a computer that can be either an adventure game where you have to explore an electronic world or an arcade game in which you have to outwit electronic enemies

video graphics array
see VGA

video graphics card or overlay card expansion card that fits into an expansion slot inside your PC and that allows a computer to display both generated text and graphics and moving video images from an external camera or VCR

video memory or video RAM (VRAM) section of memory fitted on a video adapter that is used as a temporary store for image data sent from the computer's main memory or to store an image as it is built up and before it is displayed on the screen

VIM VENDOR-INDEPENDENT MESSAGING set of standards developed by IBM, Borland, Novell and Apple, that provides a way of sending electronic mail messages between applications
compare with MAPI

virtual   something that does not actually exist, except in an imaginary form in a computer

virtual address   address that refers to a location in virtual memory

virtual desktop or screen   area that is bigger than the physical limits of the monitor, and which can contain text, images, windows, etc; the monitor acts as a window onto this area and a user can scroll around to view a different parts of the virtual screen; often used to help organise a window that has lots of icons

virtual image   complete image stored in memory rather than the part of it that is displayed

virtual machine (VM)   software that allows a Java application to run on a computer; when a developer writes a program in Java, it is compiled to a file format called bytecode (or pseudocode), this file can then be run using another application (the virtual machine) that is specific to the particular computer platform - there are virtual machine applications for PC, Macintosh and Sun and each can run the same Java bytecode file making Java a platform-independent language
see also   JAVA, BYTECODE

virtual memory   large, imaginary, main memory made available to an operating system by storing unused parts of the virtual memory on disk and then transferring these pages into available main memory as and when they are required

virtual reality (VR)   simulation of a real-life scene or environment by a computer with which you can interact and explore

virtual reality modeling language
see   VRML

virus   software that is designed to corrupt your data files and copy itself automatically from one computer to another, usually by attaching itself to a normal application file; if you download a lot of programs from the Internet, you should carry out a regular check with a virus checker that your computer has not been infected by a virus

virus checker   software that is used to try and detect and remove unwanted virus programs from the hard disk of your computer

Visual Basic   programming tool developed by Microsoft, that allows users to create Windows applications very easily. Visual Basic is a rapid application development (RAD) tool that allows users with little programming knowledge to create a complex Windows application - although the finished applications are not usually as fast as programs written in a low-level compiled language such as C

Visual Basic Script
see VBSCRIPT

Visual Basic for Applications (VBA)
see VBA

VL-bus or VL local bus
see VESA

VM
see VIRTUAL MACHINE

VME bus VERSAMODULE EUROCARD BUS   expansion bus standard that supports 32-bit data transfer; this bus is mostly used in industrial and test equipment.

voice (i) (in MIDI) another name for a note or sound effect (such as a whistle); instruments that are multi-voice can play several notes at the same time; (ii) sound of a person speaking

voice mail sophisticated telephone answering machine normally used in large companies, but also a feature of some new modems

volatile electronic memory component that does not retain information when the electrical power is switched off

volume convenient name used to identify a particular hard disk, CD-ROM drive or tape unit within a computer; if you are using a very large hard disk you can split it into several volumes to help organise your files

volume label name given to a hard disk using the VOL command from MS-DOS or by selecting the Properties page of the disk within Windows

VORTAL
see VERTICAL PORTAL

VR
see VIRTUAL REALITY

VRAM
see VIDEO RAM

VRML VIRTUAL REALITY MODELING LANGUAGE   system that allows developers to create three-dimensional worlds within a web page; a user can move through the three-dimensional world to see shops, products, and shapes in shaded three-dimensions. This system provides a way of allowing the user to explore a web site by moving through the landscape rather than viewing fixed, two-dimensional images. In order to view a web site that uses VRML you will need a web browser with a VRML 3-D plug-in extension. Netscape currently use a VRML system called Live3D, Microsoft use ActiveVRML
see also PLUG-IN

VSB VESTIGIAL SIDE BAND method of transferring data over coaxial cable, used to modulate and transmit digital television signals

VxD VIRTUAL DEVICE DRIVER device driver used to control one part of the Windows operating system or to link a peripheral to the Windows operating system

Ww

W3 WORLD WIDE WEB
see WWW

W3C WORLD WIDE WEB CONSORTIUM   group of international
industry members that work together to develop common standards for the
world wide web; visit the www.w3.org website for new standards and
developments

wake-on-LAN   technology that allows a personal computer or
workstation to be switched on automatically by sending it a signal over a
local area network connection; the system is built into the network interface
card fitted to the computer and allows a network manager or network server
software to manage the computers linked to the network.

WAIS   WIDE AREA INFORMATION SERVER   system that allows a
user to search for information stored on the Internet, based on a large search
index of documents, files and sites
see also   ARCHIE, GOPHER, SEARCH INDEX

wait state   delay that is introduced to allow a fast central processor to
store or retrieve data from slower memory components

wallpaper   (in Microsoft Windows) image or pattern used as a
background in a window. You can change the background colour or image
displayed by Windows from within the Control Panel/Desktop icon settings.

WAN   WIDE AREA NETWORK   many small, linked local area networks
or a network with multiple servers linked together using public telephone
circuits, leased lines or high-speed bridges.

WAP   WIRELESS APPLICATION PROTOCOL   system that allows a
user to access information on an Internet server using a wireless handheld
device, such as a mobile telephone. WAP can be used over almost all of the
current wireless networks, including the popular GSM mobile telephone
standard, and can run on almost any operating system or hardware device. A
device that supports WAP provides a very simple browser that can display
basic graphics and text-based pages of information on a small,
monochrome, 6-10 line display, similar to a tiny, simple web page. The user
can navigate between pages using two or three buttons on the handheld
device or mobile telephone. The arrival of WAP allows users to access
email and news-based websites from a mobile telephone, but users have
been put off by the very slow speed (no more than 9600bps) at which data

can be transferred over current wireless telephone systems.

WAP Browser simple web browser that works on a handheld WAP device; a WAP browser supports the HTML and XML web page markup standards, but also supports its own markup system, WML (WAP markup language) that allows designers to create simple pages that can be transferred efficiently over the often slow wireless link (normally at a maximum of 9600bps) and navigated using two or three buttons on the handheld device or mobile telephone.

WAP markup language (WML) web page formatting language that is similar to a very simple version of the standard HTML web page coding system, but does not include many of the extra features that cannot be displayed on the small screen of a WAP handheld device or navigated with two or three buttons

WAP markup language script (WMLScript) scripting language similar to a very simple version of JavaScript that allows WML web pages to include scripting functions

warm boot reset operation that will load the operating system, but does not clear all of the computer's memory; if your computer stops working correctly you might have to carry out a warm boot by pressing the Ctrl-Alt-Del keys together
see also RESET

WAV file
see WAVE

WAVE *or* WAV file standard method of storing an analog signal in digital form under Microsoft Windows (files have the .WAV extension)

wavetable memory in a sound card that contains a recording of a real musical instrument that is played back; this method of producing sounds is different from an FM synthesis sound card that generates the sound using mathematical equations

web *or* www *or* world wide web collection of the millions of web sites and web pages that together form the part of the Internet that is most often seen by users (although the Internet also includes electronic mail, Usenet and newsgroups); each web site is a collection of web pages; each web page contains text, graphics and links to other web sites. Each page is created using the HTML language and is viewed by a user with a web browser. To navigate between web pages and web sites is called surfing; this requires a computer with a link to the Internet (normally using a modem) and a web browser to view the web pages stored on the remote web servers.

web application software program that works behind the scenes at a web site, runs on a web server and uses the HTTP protocol to deliver information to a user; an example is a database of information that can be searched from a web page or a method of ordering and paying for a product using a web page

web browser
see BROWSER

web cam   video camera linked to a web site that allows visitors to see live video images of a scene - these devices have become very popular and have been used to display inside an office, the view over a city, an office coffee machine, inside a bedroom and many other scenes

web crawler   software that moves over every new web page on the Internet and produces an index based on the content of the web pages - normally used by search engines to ensure that they are up to date

web page   single file stored on a web server that contains formatted text, graphics and hypertext links to other pages on the Internet. A web page is created using HTML codes and is viewed with a browser
see BROWSER, HTML, APPENDIX A

web page design software   software that provides features that make it easier for a user to create web pages; new design software is similar to desktop publishing software and allows you to drag text and images onto a page, create tables and change the style of text from menu options, without having to edit complex HTML commands

web portal   website that provides a wide range of information and resources that tries to include everything a particular user might want from the Internet, on one site; the biggest web portals include AOL, MSN, Yahoo! and Excite that offer a wide range of general services including news, sports, email, weather, shopping and a search engine
see also VERTICAL PORTAL

web server   computer that stores the collection of web pages that make up a web site. Normally, web servers store hundreds of separate websites, but in the case of vast sites such as BBC (www.bbc.co.uk) or CNN (www.cnn.com), the website is big enough to deserve its own web server.

website   collection of web pages that have been produced by one company or individual and are linked together by hyperlinks; although the individual web pages within a web site can be accessed separately, the initial, opening page of a website is viewed if you enter the domain name of the website - for example, the Peter Collin Publishing website contains pages that describe each of our specialist dictionaries; you can see the main introduction page by entering the domain name 'www.petercollin.com' in your web browser

WebTV   television that also lets you view web pages; some TVs include a computer and modem, other systems use an external box that links to the

TV and a telephone socket; some interactive television and cable television installations do not use a telephone socket but instead download and display web pages via the television cable.

webBot software utility program used in Microsoft FrontPage Internet software that helps a user create a particular function in a web page; for example, a webBot can create a catalogue request form or can create a table for information. Instead of using complex HTML commands, you can enter the information into the webBot and it will create the elements. If you want to use webBots in your web page, your web server must support the webBot extensions
see also BOT, SSI

webmaster person in charge of a web site; if you have a problem or complaint about a web you could send an email message to 'webmaster@xxx.xxx'

what you see is what you get (WYSIWYG) wordprocessing or DTP program where what you see on the screen is exactly the same as the image or text that will be printed, including graphics and special fonts

white pages database of users and their email address stored on the Internet to help other users find an email address; normally you have to add your own email address to the database

whois (Internet) utility that displays information about the owner of a particular domain name

wide area information server
see WAIS

wide area network
see WAN

wild card character symbol used when searching for files or data which represents all files; in DOS, UNIX and PC operating systems, the wild card character '?' will match any single character in this position; the wild card character 'or' means match any number of any characters
see also QUESTION MARK

window (i) reserved section of screen used to display special information, that can be selected and looked at any time and which overwrites information already on the screen; (ii) part of a document currently displayed on a screen; (iii) area of memory or access to a storage device

Windows multitasking graphical user interface for the IBM PC developed by Microsoft Corporation that is designed to be easy to use; Windows uses icons to represent files and devices and can be controlled using a mouse, unlike MS-DOS where commands are typed in

Windows 3.1 first of the new generation of Windows which provided features including OLE and drag and drop.

Windows 3.11
see WINDOWS FOR WORKGROUPS

Windows 3.1x refers to any version of Windows after version 3, including 3.1 and 3.11

Windows 95 version of Microsoft's Windows that provides support for long filenames, an interface that is easier to use and better support for networks and the Internet. It does, however, require a faster processor and more memory to get good results - an absolute minimum of 8Mb and a fast 80486 processor are required.

Windows 98 new version of Microsoft Windows that provides closer integration with the Internet, information sources and networks

Windows 2000 latest version of Microsoft Windows operating system that improves on the speed and features of Windows 98 closer integration with the Internet, information sources and networks and better support for plug-and-play and error-detection and prevention

Windows CE software operating system developed by Microsoft and designed to run on small PDA or palmtop or palm computers that use either a pen input or a keyboard instead of a mouse; this version looks like and can run similar applications to Windows 95

Windows Explorer software utility included with Windows 95 that lets you view the folders and files on your hard disk, floppy disk, CD-ROM and any shared network drives.

Windows for Workgroups version of Microsoft Windows that includes the functions that let you connect several computers together to form a network and share files, printers and exchange data. It also includes software for email, fax and scheduler utilities

Windows NT high-performance operating system derived from Microsoft Windows that provides a robust, fast operating system for network workstations or for the central server in a network

Windows sockets or winsock utility software that is required to control the modem when connecting to the Internet under MS-DOS or Windows 3 and allows the computer to communicate using the TCP/IP protocol. Windows 95 has its own version of this utility built in - Windows 95 configures this protocol automatically when you install Internet software
see also TCP/IP

WINS WINDOWS INTERNET NAMING SERVICE system that works with a network of computers running Microsoft Windows and provides a database of the IP addresses of each computer on the network; this is more

difficult than it sounds, since a computer is usually given a different IP address every time it is switched on. The WINS service provides 'name resolution' for Windows networks, DNS provides a similar service for networks with fixed IP addresses, including the public Internet.
see also DNS, IP ADDRESS, NAME RESOLUTION

Winsock software that lets your computer communicate with the Internet via a standard dial-up connection; Windows includes a Winsock utility and it's configured automatically - you shouldn't need to do anything!

wire frame model (in graphics and CAD) objects displayed using lines and arcs rather than filled areas or having the appearance of being solid

Wireless Application Protocol (WAP) system that allows a user to access information on an Internet server using a wireless handheld device, such as a mobile telephone. WAP can be used over almost all of the current wireless networks, including the popular GSM mobile telephone standard, and can run on almost any operating system or hardware device. A device that supports WAP provides a very simple browser that can display basic graphics and text-based pages of information on a small, monochrome, 6-10 line display, similar to a tiny, simple web page. The user can navigate between pages using two or three buttons on the handheld device or mobile telephone. The arrival of WAP allows users to access email and news-based websites from a mobile telephone, but users have been put off by the very slow speed (no more than 9600bps) at which data can be transferred over current wireless telephone systems.
see also WAP BROWSER, WML

wireless modem modem that can be used with a wireless mobile telephone system (a wireless modem normally includes the telephone hardware and an aerial, so does not need to be plugged into a separate mobile telephone)

wizard software utility that helps you create something; for example, if you want to design a new database using Microsoft Access, there is a wizard that will ask you various questions about the new database and then will create it for you

WML WAP MARKUP LANGUAGE web page formatting language that is similar to a very simple version of the standard HTML web page coding system, but does not include many of the extra features that cannot be displayed on the small screen of a WAP handheld device or navigated with two or three buttons
see also HTML, SGML, WAP, XML

WMLScript WAP MARKUP LANGUAGE SCRIPT scripting language similar to a very simple version of JavaScript that allows WML web pages to include scripting functions
see also JAVASCRIPT, WAP

word two bytes of data, equivalent to sixteen bits of data

WordPad software utility included with Windows 95 that provides the basic functions of Microsoft Word 6. It can read and save Word 6 files and lets you format text and write complex documents.

word wrap or wraparound system in an editing or word processing application in which the operator does not have to indicate the line endings, but can keyboard continuously, leaving the program to insert word breaks and to continue the text on the next line

workgroup general term that refers to a collection of computers connected by a network. The workgroup would normally refer to a group of PCs that are doing similar things or within a section of a company. For example, in a magazine there might be a workgroup for the editorial journalists, another for the production department and a third for the sales department.

world wide web
see WWW

worlds three-dimensional scene that is displayed on a web site and allows a user to move around the scene exploring the objects visible; the entire scene is often called a 'world' and is created using a special plug-in extension to the web browser - often VRML
see VRML

worm small program that automatically travels across the Internet and replicates itself as many times as it can; unlike a virus, a worm is not harmful but is intended as a research or programming challenge - unfortunately, some successful worms can replicate themselves so efficiently that they can slow down or halt the entire Internet

WORM WRITE ONCE READ MANY TIMES MEMORY optical disc storage system that allows the user to write data to the disc once, but the user can then read the data from the disc many times

wrapper special software that is used to provide a single, convenient file that can be distributed over the Internet; wrapper software often includes security features, to prevent unauthorised copying, and compression to reduce the size of the files. A user double-clicks the file and it automatically installs the software enclosed in the wrapper on their computer

write-back cache temporary cache memory that will only save the information to disk or main memory when the computer instructs it to do so; this can be dangerous, since you might think that you have saved a document but it is actually stored in the write-back cache and has not been saved

write head
see RECORD HEAD

write protect   to prevent data from being saved to a floppy disk; 3.5-inch disks have a sliding switch in the top right hand corner: if the switch is pushed down and you cannot see through the hole, then you can save data to the floppy disk, if the switch is pushed up and you can see through the hole, you cannot save data to the disk

WWW   WORLD WIDE WEB   collection of the millions of web sites and web pages that together form the part of the Internet that is most often seen by users (although the Internet also includes electronic mail, Usenet and newsgroups); each web site is a collection of web pages; each web page contains text, graphics and links to other web sites. Each page is created using the HTML language and is viewed by a user with a web browser. To navigate between web pages and web sites is called surfing; this requires a computer with a link to the Internet (normally using a modem) and a web browser to view the web pages stored on the remote web servers.
see also BROWSER, CERN, HTML, INTERNET, WEB PAGE

WYSIWYG
see WHAT YOU SEE IS WHAT YOU GET

Xx

X2 communications standard developed by US Robotics for its range of high-speed modems that can transfer data at 56,000 bits per second
see also V SERIES

X.400 CCITT standard that defines the way in which electronic mail can be transferred between different systems in a network

X.500 CCITT standard that defines a global directory service in which all objects (computers, servers, people) linked to a network or Internet have a unique address and can be easily found, located and used
see also DIRECTORY SERVICE

XA
see CD-ROM XA

XHTML EXTENSIBLE HYPERTEXT MARKUP LANGUAGE
combination of the HTML and XML web page markup languages; XHTML is actually written using the XML language and provides a simpler way of creating web pages that will be displayed in the same way over a wide range of web browser platforms

XML EXTENSIBLE MARKUP LANGUAGE web page markup language that is a simplifed version of the SGML system and allows a designer to create their own customised markup tags to improve flexibility

Xmodem method of transferring files over a communications link that provides error detection features (normally using a modem over a telephone line); this method is not as fast as Zmodem because it sends smaller packets of data

XON/XOFF method of controlling the transfer of data between two devices (for example, between a computer and modem) under the control of the communications software; there are two types of flow control - hardware flow control (also called CTS/RTS) uses the electronic hardware to manage the transfer; software flow control (also called XON/XOFF) requires the software to generate and decode special messages sent with the data, it is slower than the hardware system
see also CTS/RTS, FLOW CONTROL

XT original version of the first IBM PC, developed by IBM, that used an 8088 processor and included a hard disk

XT keyboard type of keyboard used with the IBM PC which had ten function keys running in two columns along the left-hand side of the keyboard. The current standard is called the AT or Windows keyboard that includes 12 function keys and, in the case of a Windows keyboard, a special button that is equivalent to pressing the Start button on-screen.

Yy

year 2000 *or* **Y2K problem**   problem that, it was predicted, would affect millions of computers and businesses around the world on the 1st of January 2000; original PCs and other types of computer system were often designed with the assumption that the year would start 19xx and so only supported the last two numbers for each year (no one thought of this problem in 1983 when PCs were first developed) this works in the 20th Century but does not work in the year 2000; as a result, many older computer systems and software applications will fail to correctly recognise the new date on January 1, 2000. New computers provide millennium compliance and new software should provide support for the year 2000. In the event, there was little disruption - the banks, telephone companies, and air-traffic systems were modified before the end of the last millenium and few businesses suffered the catostrophic chaos the was predicted.
see also   MILLENNIUM COMPLIANCE

Ymodem   method of transferring files over a communications link that takes into account the reliability of modem technology and modifies the Xmodem standard to transmit larger data packets and batches of files

Zz

zero insertion force (ZIF) socket   socket on a motherboard in a computer that has movable connection terminals, allowing the chip to be inserted without using any force; a small lever is turned to grip the legs of the chip. ZIF sockets are used to hold processor chips inside your computer making it easier to replace or upgrade the processor.

zero wait state   electronic device (normally a processor or memory chip) that is fast enough to run at the same speed as the other components in a computer, so does not have to be artificially slowed down by inserting wait states

ZIF
see ZERO INSERTION FORCE SOCKET

ZIP   filename extension given to files that contain compressed data, normally generated by the PKZIP shareware utility program
see also COMPRESS, SELF EXTRACTING ARCHIVE

Zip disk   proprietary type of removable storage device, similar to a removable hard disk drive, manufactured by Iomega Corp. to provide a convenient backup and storage medium with 100Mb or 1Gb disk capacity
see also IOMEGA

Zmodem   method of transferring files over a modem link that provides error detection and adjusts the size of each packet of data sent according to the reliability of the telephone line; if the telephone line is clear without noise, then Zmodem will send large packets of data

zoom   to enlarge an area of text or graphics (to make it easier to see or work on)

ZV Port   ZOOMED VIDEO PORT   interface port that allows data to be transferred from a PC Card directly to the computer's video controller without passing through the computer's central processor; used to allow a laptop computer to display live images from a video camera plugged into the computer's PC Card socket

Appendix - Internet resources

General Search Engines

AllTheWeb	www.alltheweb.com
AltaVista	www.altavista.com
Euroseek	www.euroseek.net
Excite	www.excite.com
GOD	www.god.co.uk
HotBot	www.hotbot.com
InfoSeek	www.infoseek.com
Lycos	www.lycos.com
MSN	www.msn.co.uk
NorthernLight	www.northernlight.com
WebCrawler	www.webcrawler.com
Yahoo!	www.yahoo.com
Yahoo! UK	www.yahoo.co.uk

General Directories and Portals

About	www.about.com
LookSmart	www.looksmart.co.uk
Scoot	www.scoot.co.uk
UK Plus	www.ukplus.com
Yell	www.yell.co.uk

Business-oriented search engines

BigBook	www.bigbook.com
BizWeb	www.bizweb.com
Magellan	www.mckinley.com
Yell	www.yell.co.uk

Metasearch sites

Sites that submit your search term to top search engines, then filter the results - saves time and effort

All-in-One	www.allonesearch.com
AskJeeves	www.askjeeves.com
DogPile	www.dogpile.com
Google	www.google.com
Inference Fine	www.infind.com
Metacrawler	www.metacrawler.com
SavvySearch	www.savvysearch.com
Taxi	www.taxi.com

Searching Newsgroups

The main general search engines also index newsgroups

Deja	www.deja.com
Remarq	www.remarq.com
TileNet News	www.tilenet.news.com

Finding mailing lists

Liszt	www.liszt.com

Finding email addresses

Four11	www.four11.com
Yahoo!	www.yahoo.com
WhoWhere	www.whowhere.com

Appendix - basic HTML tags

<a> .. </a>
creates a hyperlink target or source. For example,
```
<a href="www.pcp.co.uk">link to PCP</a>
```
will create a hyperlink to the PCP web page.

<address> .. </address>
enclosed text is formatted in smaller typeface as an address

<applet> .. </applet>
defines an applet within the document

<area>
defines the area of a graphic image that will respond to a mouse click using a client-side image map

<b> .. </b>
formats enclosed text in a bold typeface

<base>
defines the URL address that is added in front of all relative URLs used within the document

<basefont>
defines the point size of the font used to format for the following text

<bgsound>
defines the audio file that is played as a background sound to the document (used in MS-IE 2 and later)

<big> .. </big>
formats enclosed text in a bigger typeface

<blockquote> .. </blockquote>
formats the enclosed text as a quotation

<body> .. </body>
defines the start and finish of this document is body text; also used to define a graphic image used as a background, and to set the default colour of the text, hyperlinks and margins for the document

**
**
inserts a line break in the text, the <p> code also inserts a carriage return

<caption> .. </caption>
defines the caption for a table

<center> .. </center>
formats enclosed text to be centered across the line

<cite> .. </cite>
formats enclosed text as a citation

<code> .. </code>
formats enclosed text as program code, normally using the Courier typeface

<col>
defines the properties for a column that has been defined using <colgroup>; available in MS-IE 2 and above

<colgroup>
defines a column; available in MS-IE 2 and above

<comment> .. </comment>
defines the enclosed text to be a comment; only works in MS IE 2, with any other browser you should use the <!> comment <> tag format

<dd> .. </dd>
defines one element of a definition list

<dfn> .. </dfn>
formats enclosed text as a definition

<dir> .. </dir>
creates a directory list using the <li> to create entries

<div> .. </div>
divides the text within a document and formats each division

<dl> .. </dl>
creates a definition list using the <dd> and <dt> tags to create entries

<dt> .. </dt>
defines the definition part of an entry within a definition list

<em> .. </em>
formats enclosed text with emphasis (often the same as a bold typeface)

<embed> .. </embed>
points to an object to embed in a document

<font> .. </font>
defines the size, colour and typeface of the font to use for the enclosed text

<form> .. </form>
defines the following tags to be treated as one form; also defines how to process the form and where to send the encoded information

<frame> .. </frame>
defines a frame, including its border, colour, name and text

<frameset> .. </frameset>
defines a collection of frames

<h> .. </h>

defines a pre-set font size, such as <h1> for a large headings, <h4> for small headings

<hr>

breaks the current line of text and inserts a horizontal rule across the page

<html> .. </html>

defines the start and end of the entire html document

<i>.. </i>

formats enclosed text using an italic typeface

<iframe> .. </iframe>

defines a floating frame, used only in MS-IE 3

<img>

includes an image within a document, also defines a border for the image, size, alternative caption text and whether the image is a video clip

<input type=checkbox>

defines a checkbox button within a form

<input type=file>

defines a file-selection list within a form

<input type=image>

defines an image input element within a form

<input type=password>

defines a text input that displays an asterisk when text is entered

<input type=radio>

defines a radio button within a form

<input type=reset>

defines a button to reset the formis contents

<input type=submit>

defines a button to submit the formis contents to the named process

<input type=text>

defines a text input element to allow users to enter a line of text

<isindex>

defines the html document to be searchable by a defined search engine

<kbd> .. </kbd>

formats enclosed text as a keyboard input

<li> .. </li>

defines an item in a list; the list can be ordered using <ol> or unordered using <ul>

<link>

defines a link within a document header

\<listing\> .. \</listing\>
old tag that is the same as a the \<pre\> tag

\<map\> .. \</map\>
defines an image map that contains hotspots

\<marquee\> .. \</marquee\>
creates an animated scrolling text line, used in MS-IE 2 and after

\<menu\> .. \</menu\>
defines a menu that has items created using the \<li\> tag

\<meta\>
allows the programmer to include extra information about the document

\<multicol\> .. \</multicol\>
defines multiple columns within the document, used in Netscape Navigator 3 only

\<nextid\>
used by automated html document generators as a reference point within a file

\<nobr\> .. \</nobr\>
prevents the browser adding breaks within the enclosed text

\<noframes\> .. \</noframes\>
defines content that should be displayed if the browser does not support frames

\<noscript\> .. \</noscript\>
defines content that should be used if the browser does not support Java; only for Netscape Navigator 3 and after

\<object\> .. \</object\>
defines an object, applet or OLE object to be inserted into the document; used for MS-IE 3 and after

\<ol\> .. \</ol\>
defines the start and end of a numbered list; items are inserted using the \<li\> tag

\<option\> .. \</option\>
defines one option within a \<select\> tag

\<p\> .. \</p\>
defines the start and end of a paragraph

\<param\> .. \</param\>
defines the paramaters to be passed to an enclosed applet or object

\<plaintext\>
formats the rest of the document as plain text with spaces and breaks

\<pre\> .. \</pre\>
formats the enclosed text as plain text with spaces and breaks

<s> .. </s>
formats enclosed text with a strikethrough, horizontal line

<samp> .. </samp>
defines enclosed text as a sample

<script> .. </script>
defines the start and end of a script written in a supported language, such as JavaScript or VBScript

<select> .. </select>
defines a list of options within a form, each created using the <option> tag

<small> .. </small>
formats enclosed text in a small typesize

<spacer>
inserts a character space within a line of text; only used in Netscape Navigator 3

<span> .. </span>
define a style sheet that formats text over several tags; only used in MS-IE 3

<strike> .. </strike>
formats enclosed text with a strikethrough line

<strong> .. </strong>
formats enclosed text with emphasis, similar to bold

<style> .. </style>
defines a collection of text formatting commands that can be referred to with this style command; used for MS-IE 3 only

<sub> .. </sub>
formats enclosed text as subscript

<sup> .. </sup>
formats enclosed text as superscript

<table> .. </table>
defines a table including border, colour, size and width; columns are added with <td> and rows with <tr>

<tbody>
group of rows within a table; used in MS-IE 2

<td> .. </td>
defines a cell within a table, effectively adds a column to the table

<textarea> .. </textarea>
defines a multiple line text input element for a form

<tfoot>
defines rows within a table that are formatted as a footer to the table; used in Microsoft-IE 2

<th> .. </th>
defines the header to each column in a table

<thead>
defines rows within a table that are formatted as a header to the table; used in Microsoft-IE 2

<title> .. </title>
defines the title to this html document

<tr> .. </tr>
defines a row of cells within a table

<tt> .. </tt>
formats enclosed text in a monospaced typewrite-style font

<ul> .. </ul>
defines the start and end of a bulleted list of elements, each element is add using <li>

<var> .. </var>
enclosed text is the name of a variable

<wbr>
defines a possible point for a word break within a <nobr> line

<xmp> .. </xmp>
old tag that formats enclosed text, similar to <pre>